PREY NO LO[

A Step-by-Step Guide for Survivors of Sexual Abuse

SHARI L. KARNEY, ESQ.

FIRST EDITION PUBLISHED 2012

VOICE PUBLICATIONS

Los Angeles

Table of Contents

Preface...i

Dedication..iv

Introduction..viii
   What Can I Expect to Get Out of This Book...................................viii
   How to Determine if You Were Sexually Abused............................x
   The Law and Sexual Abuse..xii
   Sexual Abuse is Addressed by Both Civil Law and Criminal Law.........xiii
   About the Stories and Cases Used in This Book............................xvi
   A Prey No Longer Journal..xix
   This Book Will be User Friendly...xxvi

CHAPTER ONE: You Can Heal - You Are Not Alone.........................1

   You Are Not Alone..1
   The Good News - You Can Heal...3
   A Word About Feeling Anger - The Lonely Tiger..........................4
   A Word About Feeling Shame..5
   Survivors are Amazing and Uniquely Gifted.................................6
   The Law Is Changing Giving Survivors More Rights to Sue.........10
   The Public Is Beginning To Wake Up...11
   Recognizing & Understanding Your Damages................................12
   Honoring What You Did To Survive..14

CHAPTER TWO: Getting Ready to Take Action..............................16

   Am I Ready – The Emotional Issues..16
   What Suing Can Do..17
   What Suing Can't Do..21
   Getting Support..28
   Supporting Yourself...32
   Gathering Evidence – A Key Part of Being Ready.........................33
   Your Testimony - The Best Evidence...34
   Witnesses..36
   Lay Witnesses...36
   Expert Witnesses..37
   Medical Records 38
   Other Evidence...39

The Status Check 41

CHAPTER THREE: Can I Sue After All This Time................................46

Time, Memory, & the Law...46
Why People Forget Abuse..47
When People Remember...50
What Happens When Adults Tell...54
Legal Basics of Time & The Law..57
Statutes of Limitations - A Critical Issue!.......................................58
Why Having a SOL for Childhood Sexual Abuse is Unfair..............................59
Tolling of the Statute Until You Reach Your 18th Birthday.........................59
Three Legal Methods for Defeating the Statute of Limitations......................60
Delayed Discovery...60
Fraudulent Concealment..61
Window of Opportunity - "Window Legislation".....................................63
State By State Statutes of Limitations Reference Chart............................64

CHAPTER FOUR: Holding Your Perpetrator Responsible................................75

Who Can I Sue?..75
Where Should I Sue?...78
The Handprint of Abuse - Organizing Your Damages.................................82
Physical Damages (Your Body)...83
Emotional Damages (Self-Esteem)..85
Sexual Damages (Sexuality)...90
Relationship Damages (Capacity for Intimacy).....................................94
Damages to Education, Work, Career (Ability to Work).............................95

CHAPTER FIVE: How Do I Start My Case...98

How Do I Find an Attorney..98
So how do you find the right lawyer? 100
Be Open & Honest With Potential Attorneys - Attorney Client Privilege.......101
How to Make the Calls..102
37 Questions You Can Ask Potential Attorneys.....................................104
How Much Will My Case Cost?..110
Assessing the Perpetrator's Assets..112

CHAPTER SIX: The Art Of War..115

Knowing What Makes Your Abuser Tick..115

Who Commits Child Sexual Abuse?..116
The Typical Incest Perpetrator..118
The Situational Abuser 120
The Sociopath 122
The Hardcore Pedophile..122
How to Spot a Perpetrator...123

CHAPTER SEVEN: The Lawsuit Walkthrough...126

What To Expect - One Step At A Time..126
The Demand Letter..127
Filing the Complaint...129
Service of Process...130
How Your Abuser Can Respond..131
They Can Respond With a Motion...131
They Can Respond With an Answer..132
The Discovery Process..133
Interrogatories..134
Requests for Admission...135
Requests for Production of Documents and Other Evidence..............................136
Depositions..137
Your Deposition..140
Your Abuser's Deposition (and the Depositions of Other Parties)......................143
The Physical/Psychological Exam..144
The Settlement Process...147
Alternatives to Trial - Mediation...149
Trial—General Considerations...150
Experts – Finding Them...152
Your Performance and Behavior at Trial...154
Testifying...156
Win, Lose, Heal – From Victim to Victor..166
How to Collect a Verdict...167

CHAPTER EIGHT: It Can Stop Today...170

How to Deal with Ongoing Abuse..170
If You are a Teenager Living in an Abusive Home.....................................171
Other Than School, Where Else Can I Turn..171
Getting Out Of The Abusive Situation Permanently....................................172
If Your Friend or Sibling is Being Abused...174
If Your Child is Being Abused...175

CHAPTER NINE: It's A Crime – Can I Send My Abuser To Jail......................179

Child Sexual Abuse Is Also A Crime..................................179
Pre-Trial Stages..181
Preliminary Hearing..183
"Criminal Discovery"...184
Pre-Trial Conferences - Plea Bargaining..........................185
Criminal Trial...186
Use The State's Power - Other Options For Stopping Your Abuser...187

AFTERWORD...189

How We Changed The Law...189
I Wish You The Best In Your Journey..............................195
Contact Shari..196

RESOURCES...197

Attorney Listing (Alphabetical by State).....................198

Alabama..198
Alaska...202
Arizona..203
Arkansas...206
California...207
Colorado...211
Connecticut..215
Delaware...219
Florida..221
Georgia..225
Hawaii...229
Idaho..231
Illinois...233
Indiana..237
Iowa...241
Kansas...244
Kentucky...247
Louisiana..251
Maine..254
Maryland...257
Massachusetts..261
Michigan...264

Minnesota...267
Mississippi...270
Missouri..273
Montana..276
Nebraska...278
Nevada...281
New Hampshire...285
New Jersey..287
New Mexico...291
New York..293
North Carolina..297
North Dakota..301
Ohio..302
Oklahoma...306
Oregon...309
Pennsylvania..311
Rhode Island..315
South Carolina..317
South Dakota..321
Tennessee..323
Texas...327
Utah..331
Vermont...334
Virginia..335
Washington..339
West Virginia...342
Wisconsin...344
Wyoming..347
Washington D.C..349

Support Groups and Organizations...................................352

Index of Journal Exercises

Journal Exercise – What are my Goals? 28
Journal Exercise – My Sanity Plan 33
Journal Exercise – Storyteller 36
Journal Exercise – Be Your Own Private Detective..............................41
Journal Exercise – I'm Not Helpless Anymore: Growing Up 42
Journal Exercise – I'm Not Helpless Anymore: Today 42
Journal Exercise – Emotional Readiness & Support 43
Journal Exercise – What I Really Want 45
Journal Exercise – Spot the Nonsense 57
Journal Exercise – Where You Can Sue 79
Journal Exercise – Physical Damages 85
Journal Exercise – The Handprint of Sexual Abuse 97

You are more powerful than you know; you are beautiful just as you are.

– Melissa Etheridge

It took me quite a long time to develop a voice, and now that I have it, I am not going to be silent.

– Madeleine Albright

The most common way people give up their power is thinking they don't have any.

– Alice Walker

You become courageous by doing courageous acts...Courage is a habit.

– Mary Daly

Wherever we put our attention is where we put our power.

– PMH Atwater

Preface

The first incest case I took got me arrested and nearly disbarred. It altered my life forever. It forced me to finally see my own childhood and brought me face-to-face with my own sexual abuse. The last incest case I took, *Mary Doe v. John Doe*, went all the way to the California Supreme Court and changed not only the law, but my life and career forever.

Mary Doe was a 26-year woman who was referred to us by her therapist. She wanted to sue her father so she could pay for her therapy. She was sick of being a victim and was ready to take her life back. Her story: From infancy to age 5 she was sexually molested, sodomized, and repeatedly raped by her father. Because of her young age, he was able to exploit her relationship of dependency and trust in him to sexually abuse her in secret for years.

Here's what she told us:

I stood on a rock and looked down into the river.
I wanted to jump off the rock into the river and die.
I just wanted to drown and float away.
I was three years old and I wanted to die.

I remember the moment she told me those words - it was like getting hit with a thunderbolt. It was a life defining moment, and it was one of many moments in my life that has led me here to you. Mary Doe's case came at the crescendo of my career as a litigator, fighting shoulder-to-shoulder along side victims of sexual abuse who were trying to take their lives back. Her story and her words planted a seed in my mind, that someday I should gather the lessons I have learned in my journey, and turn them into a tool-box that survivors can use to shine light on their abuse and bring justice down upon their abusers.

That is what this book is. It is hundreds of stories of trauma, triumph, healing, and holding accountable. It is the life lessons, methods, secrets, tactics, and techniques used by the lawyers, investigators, judges, therapists, and successful former victims I have encountered over the years. It can help you understand your perpetrator in order to overcome him, and it can help you understand yourself in order to overcome your fears.

We are connected through the bonds of shared experience, and I want us to speak as loudly as possible. This book is for you to use to find a voice for yourself, and then take that strength and courage and knowledge and spread it beyond you, to the next person that needs healing or the next child that needs protecting.

I know the dark places that abuse can send you, but I also have felt the sunlight of feeling healthy and whole and listened to, free of the chains of shame and silence. If you had asked me twenty-nine years ago who I was, "incest survivor" would have been at the top of my list. If you asked me that question today, I would reply, "I am engaged to be married to the man of my dreams, a business owner (BARWINNERS), an author, attorney, speaker, teacher, spiritual searcher, friend, sister, and political activist." It's not my past that has changed; my relationship to it has. And that slow transformation occurred not because I ignored my abuse or hoped it would go away, but because I made an unwavering commitment to each and every step of the recovery process, and then, as part of my recovery, I took action. I wasn't able to use the law to sue my own abusers, but I changed the law so that survivors in California had that choice.

These days, as a child sexual abuse advocate I no longer focus on the trauma, but instead I think about holding predators accountable and seeing that justice be done. I think about all the kids that are protected when an abuser is brought to justice or even just exposed to the daylight of truth. I think of this as an opportunity to be part of changing history for the better. When I close my eyes, I see victims who take their power back, find their voice, speak up, step up, and stand up, and it is awe inspiring. I feel privileged to be trusted by this beautiful community and it always makes me proud that survivors feel safe in telling me their most personal stories.

I want us all to be part of the Child Protection Movement, and that's just the beginning. We need a Children's Bill of Rights here at home so that all children are protected, and then we need to take those legal and constitutional rights worldwide. I want to live in a world where no child has to suffer sexual abuse.

Our road is not an easy one, but we have truth, love, and each other. We walk together on this road. Truth has the power to bring about change, even in the face of terrible pain. We share sorrow, but we also share strength. I welcome you to share this sacred journey with us, other survivors, supporters, friends, and allies. You are not alone.

-Shari Karney, 2012

Dedication

I dedicate this book to the millions of survivors of childhood sexual abuse who deserve their day in court.

There's an old saying: "it takes a village to raise a child." It also takes a village to heal a sexual abuse survivor. Luckily for me, my "village" has been filled with wonderfully supportive and loving people. My village has been filled with *warriors*, fighting by my side, saving my life, and pulling me from the brink.

I'd like to thank and dedicate this book to some of my warriors:

First and foremost, to the love of my life, my fiancée, Leonard Ludovico: Leonard you are my first warrior, gifted man-extraordinaire, you believed in me and saw my gift from the moment we met. When the African Shaman called you the "Prophet," he spoke the truth. You are the wind beneath my wings, my spiritual guide, angel, mentor, healer, teacher, lover, soul mate, and the love of my life. You inspired me to write this book, and when I stalled and cried and threw a tantrum, you looked at me with those piercing sapphire-blue eyes, and told me I better get busy, and that I had a lot of work to do. I adore and love you. You complete me. Without you, I cannot breathe.

To my brilliant and beautiful sister, Dr. Rona Karney, who has always encouraged me to write and who has been there for me through more than any sister should have to be. I love you Rona and I always will. You saved me.

And to my sisters-of-the-heart, Rosemary McDermott-Formanack, Dean Jean Boylan, Diane Olson, La La, and Anne Mosbergen. I feel such overwhelming gratitude for your love, support, friendship, encouragement, and boots-on-the ground help. You carried the flag, held me throughout, and helped me achieve. Your love and support keeps me afloat. Without you five women, I would not be where I am today. Thank you doesn't even begin to describe my profound and humble appreciation and love.

To my BFF Donnie Weiss, xxoo forever, from your Karnucuss. You inspire me and I will always love you, my Bette Davis Eyes.

To five of my incredible teachers and mentors who believed in me and got me started, thank you for loving me and guiding me through the darkest times and days of my life: Dr. Arlene Drake, Ph.D., Rev. Gabrielle Michel, Dr. Shevy Healey, Ph.D., Rochelle Schreiber, MFT, and Dr. Alba Vasquez, DDS.

To Dell Wolfensparger, my savant, computer and technological genius, futurist, game creator, long-time friend, light years ahead of the rest of us, who loved me enough and had the patience to push me forward into the next millennium, walking me step-by-Skype, over Facetime, Linked-In, Facebook, Google+, Twitter and e-mail through the brave new world of technology and what is now possible. Thank you for all the pushing, shoving, and dragging me to (and through) the next step, level, challenge, and/or lesson. Yet you've always refused to take any credit and instead insisted that you were simply the messenger. Thank you Delly.

A special thank you to Natalie Nelson for her boundless energy and "we can do it" attitude. You kept me going. Rose Robles, for her countless hours spent compiling, researching and working on the Attorney listing and Survivor's Resources Guide.

Shari Karney

Thank you hardly covers what you have given to this project. Gail Hine Cover Art and Design, she is a talented artist with the patience of Job and a world-renowned "sailing maven." A special shout-out to Aaron Simpson for his midnight hour rescue of the manuscript thorough his super-sonic learning of the intricacies of eBook publishing.

Lisya McGuire, thank you for your outstanding work on the state-by-state statute of limitation guide and for caring so much about survivors.

Loyola Law School. Thank you for everything. I would not be where I am today without you.

And lastly to David Angeloff, Esq.. Thanks for your hard work, editorial aplomb, collaboration, writing talent, kindness and patience with my middle of the night e-mail ideas and edits. You were a gift from God and I bless you. What a bright and successful future you have. You are a beautiful man.

Without you all I could never have triumphed over the trauma. Thank you for being my "village."

WARNING—DISCLAIMER

This book was written solely to provide information about the subject matter covered. It is sold with the explicit understanding that the publisher and the author are not engaged in rendering legal or other professional advice or services. If you believe you need legal or other professional services, the services of a competent professional should be sought. <u>This book is absolutely NOT a substitute for working with a competent attorney to pursue your case.</u>

This book does not contain all the information available to the publisher and the authors. It is written merely to give a basic understanding about the topic. You are urged to research other materials for additional information that may be helpful or necessary for your individual circumstances. Be aware that the law often changes and may have changed since this version was printed.

As stated throughout the book, if you are a survivor it is imperative that you contact an attorney as soon as possible if you are considering filing a civil suit. Statutes of limitations impose serious deadlines covering when you can and *cannot* bring forth a civil suit and vary by state. <u>Do not assume that your time periods for filing such a suit have expired, even if after reading this book it appears that your time periods may have expired</u>. Individual courts and judges construe statutes of limitations very differently. A competent professional should be consulted to review your particular facts.

The only purpose of this book is to give general information to help survivors and their supporters in assessing whether legal means will aid them in healing from childhood sexual abuse. No attorney client relationship of any kind will be formed and this is not legal advice. The author and the publisher shall not assume any liability or responsibility for any actions taken or not taken based on the information in this book.

If you do not wish to be bound by this disclaimer, you may return the book to the author for a full refund.

Introduction

What Can I Expect to Get Out of This Book

First and foremost, this book is intended to reach out to all survivors from all over the world to let you know that you are not alone in this struggle.

This book is a hands-on legal guide for adult survivors of sexual abuse who want to sue their perpetrator(s) for money damages or try to get them criminally prosecuted. It is a handbook for maneuvering through our legal system. It will answer many of the questions I have been asked over the years by thousands of survivors. Survivors want to know:

- Can I sue my father (or my abuser, the Catholic Church, or my coach) for what he did to me as a child?

- What is the law in my state? I can't seem to find out if I still have any legal rights.

- How do I find an attorney who is willing to take my case?

- What can I expect during my case, what should I be prepared for?

- What can I do to strengthen my case? How can I prove what happened to me?

- How can I get my abuser arrested and prosecuted for what he did?

- Will my story be made public?

- I'm a teenager who still lives at home. How can I protect myself?

- What can I do to protect my brothers and sisters (or others) who are still living in the same household with my abuser?

- My stepfather, who sexually abused me, has now remarried a woman who has young children. Is there anything I can do to protect them?

I want to empower you by providing you with the answers to these questions, and give you hands on know-how if you choose to take action. Knowledge is power. Our written laws take this crime very seriously on the books but not always in practice. Often far too little is done to vindicate victims and punish predators, but it doesn't have to be that way. Once you understand the legal system and how it works, you can decide what your best next step is. You need to know what your options are. Knowledge gives you control and gives you choice in how to proceed. As children, too often our choices were taken away from us. This book is about giving you the information you need to have the power to decide how you want to go forward.

How to Determine if You Were Sexually Abused

If you, as a child or a teenager, were:

- Fondled, molested, touched, kissed, or held for an adult's (or older child or siblings') sexual gratification?

- Forced to sexually touch, kiss, or hold an adult for their sexual gratification?

- Forced to perform oral sex?

- Raped or anally penetrated?

- Fondled, molested, touched genitally or inappropriately while being dressed or bathed?

- Subjected to unnecessary medical treatments that satisfied an adult's sexual needs?

- Made to watch or participate in sexual acts?

- Exposed to adult nudity and other inappropriate sexual behaviors for an adult's or older child/sibling's sexual gratification?

- Subjected to excessive talk about sex?

- Shown sexual movies or other pornography?

- Made to pose for sexual photographs or used in pornography?

- Forced into child prostitution or pornography?

- Treated as an adult's mate, or sexual partner for their sexual gratification, with or without being sexually touched?

It can be very hard to acknowledge that you were, in fact, sexually abused. But it is the first step in healing, and it is necessary if you want to hold your abuser(s) legally responsible for what they did to you as a child or teenager.

The Law and Sexual Abuse

The law defines and classifies sexual abuse somewhat differently than how survivors and lay people commonly would. You will find that legal definitions are very specific, very carefully worded, and generally more complicated than how we define things normally in society. Try to get comfortable with the legal definitions you come across, because these definitions are an important part of identifying (and proving) what happened to you.

For example, as a layperson, I would call what my father did to me *incest*. However, under the law, since my father did not have sexual intercourse with me, it would not be classified as incest, but rather, *child molestation*. That difference is important because in both civil suits and criminal prosecutions, different laws and rules apply for different acts.

Sexual Abuse is Addressed by Both Civil Law and Criminal Law

Civil Law

For our purposes, we are talking mostly about the way the civil law governs *torts*. A tort is basically a *wrong,* it is a breach of a *civil duty* that one person in society owes to another. In a civil lawsuit, you, the survivor, institute an action by filing in a court. Your goal is to prove your case and have a jury award you money damages. In civil court you and your attorney get to make all the decisions about how to proceed but you also carry *all* the responsibility. Ultimately you and your attorney are responsible for satisfying the *burden of proof,* which means you have to prove your case to either a jury or a judge to a level that has been defined by the law.

In civil court, MONEY is the ONLY thing that a jury can award you. The judge and/or jury CANNOT order your abuser into therapy or require your abuser to apologize to you. The judge or jury cannot mandate supervision or order your abuser to stay away from sisters, brothers, or other children. However, the money damages you are awarded represents *victory.* When you are awarded money damages you have been vindicated in the eyes of the law. You will have officially held your perpetrator accountable for what he or she did to you.

Let's face it - the only thing abusers hate more than giving up *control* is giving up their *money*. In my experience, which is over 10 years of litigating sexual abuse cases, almost nothing makes abusers angrier than having to give up their money. One perpetrator was so obsessed with hiding his money that he buried it in the backyard of his house. We hired a cash-sniffing dog to sniff out where the money was hidden and then proceeded to dig up his entire backyard. We found it! Score one for justice!

Criminal Law

In criminal law, the State, not you, institutes an action through a state prosecutor (like on Law and Order, often called a "District Attorney") and if your abuser is found guilty of breaking the law, he or she can be sent to jail or prison. Because punishment by imprisonment means depriving a person of their liberty the laws for prosecuting an abuser criminally are much narrower and stricter than they are in a civil action.

You have neither the same control nor the same responsibility as you would in a civil case. The state may or may not choose to prosecute your abuser, because the District Attorney has "prosecutorial discretion" to decide which cases will be filed in court. Generally, these decisions are made based on likelihood of conviction, severity of the crime, strength of proof, and community interest, but it changes from prosecutor to prosecutor. You can help the state, but you are not in control and are not the "plaintiff," you are merely a victim of the crime. You might be called to testify as a witness for the state or to fill out a victim impact statement, but you don't have to pay anyone or file anything for the case to go forward if the District Attorney chooses to prosecute. Remember - in a criminal case the defendant's *constitutional rights* come into play, and this means certain strict procedures will have to be followed during the investigation and trial. Your abuser cannot be made to testify against himself or made to admit what he's done and his guilt must be proven *beyond a reasonable doubt* by the prosecutor.

If your abuser is convicted, the Judge can impose a sentence that includes jail time, prison time, restitution to you (for medical expenses and other expenses you can prove), probation after your abuser is released from jail, mandatory therapy, and in some states, mandatory registration as a sex offender.

More on Civil and Criminal Law

It's critical to get a grasp on these two very important branches of the law. Some things are crimes but not torts, like gambling. Other things are torts but not crimes, like if someone slips on a negligently maintained stairway. Many things can be both, like the classic example of murder in the O.J. Simpson case; he was acquitted of murder in his criminal prosecution, but was then sued civilly by Ron Goldman's family and was found liable for wrongful death and battery. They are related, but exist and work totally separately and can even reach different results.

Both areas of the law (civil and criminal) deal with the crimes of child sexual abuse and incest, just in different ways. In criminal cases, the state can force your perpetrator to pay some "restitution" (money) to you but it is not the purpose of the criminal action. The following is an oversimplification, but it illustrates the point: The purpose of a criminal action is for the state to PUNISH wrongdoers, as in if they find your abuser guilty, they will send them to jail or put them on probation (or something of the like). The sole purpose of a civil action is COMPENSATION, as in making wrongdoers financially responsible for their actions.

Often with sex cases, conviction or acquittal in a criminal case will be admissible in a subsequent civil trial and vice versa. That fact will be an important strategic consideration in deciding how and when to sue. Also, both civil and criminal convictions can be useful and relevant in taking other actions, such as getting a restraining order or protecting others in the abuser's household.

The differing uses of the two systems will become clearer as we move further into this book. In the later chapters I will explain the specific steps you can take to attempt to use the civil and/or criminal systems to vindicate yourself and bring your perpetrator to justice.

About the Stories and Cases Used in This Book

Over the course of my career, I have spoken with thousands of survivors of child sexual abuse. Survivors from all over the country called me after seeing the NBC television movie, *Shattered Trust: The Shari Karney Story*. When I appeared on Oprah my mailbox was flooded with letters from survivors who wanted to heal and find justice. Every time I appeared on TV or the radio or posted a blog, survivors would contact me. Some reached out for help, some reached out TO help, and some just needed someone to reach out to.

This has been one of the greatest gifts of my life. Hundreds of survivors and their loved ones have shared their stories with me. I have heard from people from coast to coast and around the world by phone, over email, Skype, and through social media. This has allowed me to see the justice system *through the eyes of survivors across the country*, and to get a sense of how the courts handle survivor cases across the United States.

Throughout the text, you will see unidentified quotes as well as longer stories about the process of healing and taking legal action. Sometimes I share parts of my own personal story. At those times, I simply use "I" to identify my own experiences.

You will also hear the stories of other survivors from all economic backgrounds, ages, races, religions, and sexual orientations. You will read about survivors who are at different stages of healing and at different stages of taking action. You will hear about survivors who have taken their cases as high as their State's Supreme Court and who have changed the law and the Constitution in their own state. You will hear from survivors who have sent their abusers to jail, who have exposed them in the national press, and who have held their abusers accountable in their communities, schools, churches, and families. Finally, you will read about survivors who did the hardest thing -- they stood up and confronted their perpetrator.

I also often use only a male pronoun such as "he" or "his" when talking about abusers. Both men and women can sexually abuse children, but male abusers are far more common and this book was written primarily from a male-abuser standpoint. If your abuser was female, please know all the information still applies.

Confidentiality

In this book, I have included the stories of some of my clients who filed suit against their abusers. All names and other identifying information has been changed to protect their privacy and to fulfill the duties of confidentiality I hold as their former attorney. I have included stories from other survivors represented by other attorneys as well, and those names have also been changed. Even when a survivor wanted to use his or her real name or identity, there were often court orders and settlement agreements which prevented us from doing so. I wanted to respect the privacy of the survivors as well as honor the legal agreements and court orders they were bound by, and so all the names in this book have been changed.

Most of all I wanted to honor and protect the privacy and trust of those who have shared with me over the years. The stories in this book are your stories. This is our voice, these are our memories, and these shall be our victories.

A Prey No Longer Journal

The Importance of Creating and Writing in Your Journal

For survivors, writing can be both sacred and scary. It is the place where we reveal our true selves. Where we can't take it back once we write it down. Writing makes our experiences real. When I started incest group therapy, my therapist gave written homework assignments weekly. At first I hated it. I would have quit if the therapy hadn't been court-ordered. The writing assignments put me into a panic. It made my memories and my experiences concrete. There was something about putting the words on paper that made me stop denying, trivializing, and running from the truth. It opened up realms of my memory I couldn't reach with my conscious mind. That is why I want you to *take the time to write and do the journal work*, with your whole attention and your whole heart. It can help you build your case, reveal hidden facts, and organize data that can be enormously helpful to you in whatever action you may want to take against your abuser. <u>There are important steps you must take to legally protect the confidentiality of your journal, should you decide to sue, please read this entire section carefully.</u>

The Basic Method

Try to forget everything anyone has ever told you about writing – re-boot your brain. This is a different breed of writing. This isn't for your professor or your boss, you're not trying to be published, and no one will ever grade you on this work. What you're going to be doing is stream-of-consciousness writing. You're going to let yourself write down anything that comes to mind. Don't worry about spelling, punctuation, grammar, or anything else that can distract you. Just let it flow, from your heart, through the pen, to the paper. The important thing is to get your feelings and thoughts down - to unlock and unblock what's inside of you - to get past the conscious critical mind. Give yourself at least an uninterrupted half hour to do the journal work. I have broken the journal work into sections of about 10 minutes each. It may take you longer, and that's okay, the important thing is to set aside the time.

Sit somewhere quiet and private. Choose a time and place in which you won't be interrupted. It may take a little negotiating, but you deserve to do this work in privacy and in peace. Don't try to do more than you can handle or are reasonably comfortable with. Be strong, and know that you may be rising to the challenge of writing about difficult subjects. Give yourself a little time after you've finished to breathe, think, and rest.

The Purpose of the Journal Work

The journal exercises are designed to be the building blocks of your case. They are designed to save you time, money, and emotional pain when you see an attorney. If done in order, they will prepare the groundwork for a successful civil case, and/or ready you to assist the police and prosecutors in a criminal case. An attorney will be much more likely to take your case if you are well prepared and ready to proceed. If you are prepared to create a well kept journal, an attorney will also be able to better see the merits of your claim and will have better evidence and documentation to go forward. Remember, I recommend that you do not start your journal until you have spoken to an attorney in your state because I want you to be absolutely sure your journal will never be "discoverable" by the other side. I know that holding off on preparing until you have an attorney creates a bit of a "Catch-22," but this is just one more way the law can work against survivors, and I want you to be protected.

Some of the journal work is designed to be torn/cut directly out of the book and brought to your attorney, prosecutor, school board, church meeting, or legal hearing. Some of the journal work is private and for yourself only. (Please use the form I have below to protect the contents of your journal – **We recommend only starting the journal once you have consulted an attorney and spoken with them specifically about protecting your journal work.)**

Even if you feel resistance about doing some of them, or don't know what good they will do, do them anyway. I will never ask you to do something unless it's going to get you somewhere.

For those readers who cannot sue or choose not to sue, I urge you to do the journal work anyway. It can and will help with your recovery and it can help you in your healing process. Doing the journal work can help you see the big-picture of the legal option, and you may find yourself thinking differently when you read your journal later.

Being Heard

One of the main problems survivors have is that we don't feel *heard.* And the truth is, often we aren't heard. A therapist friend of mine always says "listen to the whispers so you don't have to hear the screams." We need to listen to our own whispers. We need to respect and listen to *ourselves*. After all, who else should listen to us if even we don't!? When you read what you have written in your journal, you are *listening* to yourself and making your experiences concrete. No matter what path your journey of healing takes you down, these exercises will help to shed daylight on your injuries and what happened to you.

The journal exercises in the Damages Section are the most important ones in this book. They are extremely powerful in proving one of the most difficult parts of a sexual abuse case, assessing the damages in monetary terms. They can help an attorney assess whether you have a case and can help your attorney litigate your case more effectively. Finally, it can potentially increase the amount you can sue for, whether the case settles, and for how much.

Start your *"Prey No Longer"* journal in a special notebook you'll use only for the journal work. You can also write your own thoughts and notes of course, but no reminders or shopping lists, make it exclusively a personal journal. You might want to use a special pen, maybe with your favorite color ink. As simple as this may seem, it brings respect to your work here. You may also want to do your journal work on your computer. That's okay, as long as you take precaution because digital files are so easily copied and accessed. Maybe store the files only on a portable flash drive, or only in a special folder on your private computer protected by a secret password.

No matter what kind of journal you keep, date each journal entry at the top. Also, label each entry to match the journal exercise you are working on. This will help you recall the main points and will make it easier for you to refer back to it later.

Imagine

Imagine if each of us filled a journal with our memories and then we bound them all together in a book. Imagine how legislators, families, churches, schools, and communities could be moved and laws could be changed if survivors' words were in volumes and volumes of books, traveling from city to city like a survivors' AIDS quilt. This journal is your patch of fabric, your story, your badge of honor. Write in it and wear it with pride, when you write you write for all of us.

When You Can Refer to Your Journal

The journal work is set up so you can use it as a helpful resource at every stage:

- Considering Suing Your Abuser
- Preparing to Sue
- Interviewing Attorneys to Take Your Case
- Preparing for Deposition or Trial
- Going to the Police
- Proceeding with a Criminal Action or Investigation
- Preparing to Testify or Be Interviewed by the Police
- To Help You Heal and Assist With Therapy and Recovery

A WORD ABOUT LEGALLY PROTECTING YOUR JOURNAL WORK

In civil cases, part of the pre-trial process is an exchange of evidence and information called "Discovery," we will discuss it more later along the way. I want to show you right at the start how you can protect your journal and keep it out of that process. **If you are considering taking legal action against your perpetrator(s) or are currently involved in legal action against your abuser you must read the following page carefully in order to protect your journal work from potentially being seen or used by the other side in your case.**

DO NOT BEGIN YOUR JOURNAL UNTIL YOU HAVE CONFERRED WITH YOUR ATTORNEY ABOUT KEEPING IT CONFIDENTIAL AND PROTECTED BY THE ATTORNEY CLIENT PRIVILEGE

On the first page of your journal, write the following:

THIS JOURNAL IS BEING PREPARED IN ANTICIPATION OF LITIGATION. IT IS FOR MY ATTORNEY'S USE ONLY AND IS INTENDED TO BE A CONFIDENTIAL AND PRIVILEGED COMMUNICATION.

I (your name), intend for this communication to be privileged. I am the holder of this privilege, this communication is intended to be confidential, and I do not waive the privilege. I intend for this privileged and confidential, communication to be part of my attorney/client relationship.

SIGN: _____

DATE: _____

Shari Karney

This Book Will be User Friendly

Finally, I will do everything I can to make this book user-friendly for you. One of the things that drives me crazy about the legal profession is the language. Legal language is incredibly complex and it can often seem like a jumble of legalese. The law is so focused on *precedent*, is so traditional, and is so slow to change that we still use many terms that come from very old English law.

Think of legal language as a foreign language, a very *precise* language. When speaking and writing in legal terms, if you change even one word, you can change the whole meaning of a legal phrase. There is beauty in that precision, it makes our law very efficient and functional, but the down side is that sometimes it feels like you had to go to law school to understand certain sentences (sometimes when it gets really tough, we lawyers feel like not even law school helps!). My goal is to present the law for you in a way that is clear and correct, but still easy to use and understand. I believe this material should be available to everyone, regardless of education. Sometimes, however, in order to simplify a legal idea, it may get generalized in a way that could compromise the strict legal interpretation of a particular law or statute. That is why this book is neither intended nor should be used as a replacement for an attorney or for legal advice. If legal or professional assistance is required, the services of a competent professional should be sought. Basically, I'm going to make it as clear as I can, but this book is still no substitute for a lawyer who knows you and knows your case.

CHAPTER ONE: **You Can Heal - You Are Not Alone**
Triumph Over Trauma

Trauma [**trou**-m*uh*]

> noun

> emotional shock, bodily injury

Triumph [**trahy**-*uh*mf]

> noun

> to win or achieve success, to prevail, to obtain victory

"I learned that courage was not the absence of fear, but the triumph over it. The brave man is not he who does not feel afraid, but he who conquers that fear."

- Nelson Mandela

You Are Not Alone

I am here, and so is a world full of other survivors and people who care. One out of every three to four girls and one out of every four to five boys are sexually abused in some way by the time they reach the age of eighteen. Sexual abuse happens to children of every class, race, culture, religion, sexual orientation, and gender worldwide. Fathers, stepfathers, brothers, sisters, mothers, aunts, uncles, grandparents, neighbors, family friends, babysitters, teachers, doctors, clergy, and strangers can abuse children.

Marci Hamilton, a Professor of Law at Benjamin N. Cardozo School of Law, Yeshiva University, tells us that "child sex abuse is a massive problem; at least 25% of girls and 20% of boys are sexually abused." It is not only a massive regional problem, it's a *global* problem. According to a U.N. report on sexual violence "*150 million girls and 73 million boys under 18* experienced forced sexual abuse, intercourse, and other forms of sexual violence in 2002." The World Health Organization's Division of Family and Reproductive Health released a report titled "Sexual Violence: A Hidden Epidemic" that shed staggering light on the prevalence of sexual abuse. The report found that, globally, somewhere between 7% and 36% of girls and 3% and 29% of boys have suffered from some form of sexual abuse. What compounds the problem, and what makes individual sufferers feel so alone, is that this act goes unreported and *unspoken* so often that survivors can sometimes feel like the universe inflicted this act of shame and violence upon *them alone.* In 2005, the very prestigious journal SCIENCE ran an article titled The Science of Child Sexual Abuse, in that article the author, Jennifer Freyd, who is a psychologist and expert on trauma and disassociation, cited World Health Organization data in saying "Surveys likely underestimate prevalence because of under reporting and memory failure… [C]lose to 90 percent of sexual abuse cases are never reported to authorities." These numbers are jaw dropping to most survivors.

"We feel profoundly alone and profoundly silenced for so much of our lives, to find out that so many others suffered along with us is both heartbreaking and empowering."

- Delaney, Survivor

And the statistics don't stop with me. Get online, hit the local library, join a local support network, and come see how big your community of brothers and sisters really is. You are not alone.

The Good News - You Can Heal

"Although the world is full of suffering, it is full also of overcoming it."

-Helen Keller

You can heal from it, I promise you. You can be de-victimized *because you are just like me*. I was victimized but I am no longer a victim, and there can come a day where you can say that too. Sexual abuse will always be a part of who and what we are but we don't have to let it control our lives forever. Even if you didn't have control in the past, *you* are in control of your future. If you are currently in a situation of ongoing abuse, we need to address that immediately. There can be no healing in that dark place. If you are an adult, it is never too late to leave and get help, you may *feel* powerless to leave, but you are not. I urge you to find a local shelter or go to the police, there are resources out there that can help you, keep you safe, and get your life on track. If you are a minor or other dependent, living in a household with your abuser, there are ways even you can be free. See Part Eight for more details.

Some survivors don't believe it at first but it is possible to thrive and triumph over the trauma. You *can* remove the handprint of sexual abuse. Thriving means more than just numbing the symptoms and barely functioning. It is more than just living under the radar, avoiding conflict, hoping to get by to survive another day. Triumph means being free of the victimization of sexual abuse. It means living a life that is whole and full, with friends and loving relationships. It means reclaiming and owning your body and your sexuality. It means satisfaction in your life and work and genuine love and trust in your relationships. It means having a voice, speaking up, standing up for yourself, and understanding who you are *now*.

No victim has control over their perpetrators. You can't undo the forces that made them who and what they are. We can't make them apologize, can't make them be good people, and can't make them go back in time and take it back. All we can do is the best we can, and that means processing the feelings that have been thrust upon us; the anger, sorrow, betrayal, rage, anxiety, all the emotions, and ultimately come back to who we deserve to be. Part of that process can be using the law to seek justice.

"I had no idea how much power to heal myself that I had. Once everything started happening I felt like the only thing stopping me and keeping me scared all those years was not knowing."

- Maria, Survivor

A Word About Feeling Anger - The Lonely Tiger

Staying a victim, living in anger, living in fear, living *debilitated*, only means your abusers have won. You suffer - they don't. I was angry so much of the time after my memories surfaced that it almost *became* me. My anger motivated me 24/7 to fight tooth and nail and kick ass and change the law (The sign on my law office desk read, *"The Fuck Stops Here"*). The problem was, my anger was isolating me. I was living in kick-box mode all the time. It was poisonous. It didn't allow me to trust or get close to people. I was a lonely tiger.

> *"Some days my anger toward you is unbearable. But you laugh when my pain is so deep, and I will NEVER give you that satisfaction again. NEVER will you have that power over me. It's my life, and you can't ruin what's mine!"*

> - Anonymous, Survivor

Suing your abuser doesn't necessarily have to be about anger or revenge (although it can be and that's okay too). It's about *justice*. If someone runs you down in a crosswalk and hurts you, you can sue him or her to recover for your injuries. Why should childhood sexual abuse be any different? Just because many of the injuries from child sexual abuse are emotional and/or psychological doesn't make them any less valid than if the injuries were a broken arm, or leg, or lasting paralysis or harm. *Connect* with that sense of justice so you don't become a lonely tiger. Remember that living well is the best revenge.

A Word About Feeling Shame

Shame is a truth suppressant. Too many times in my career I have seen survivors hold back when talking to lawyers or investigators or to the police because they were ashamed. Many of us grow up and feel ashamed of what has been done to us, as if we have done something we should feel guilty about. I will always remember a powerful phrase that I heard from another survivor:

> *"It's not my shame, it's his."*

Remember those words. It is much easier said than done but we have to connect with the fact that these were not our choices, not our acts, and not our decisions to be ashamed of. Your abuser should be ashamed, not you, and taking legal action can shift who has to bear that burden.

Sometimes a dangerous cycle takes place between victims and abusers. Sometimes sexual abuse victims are so ashamed or embarrassed about what has happened that they go out of their way to hide the truth and protect their abuser. Through this vicious cycle, shame protects abusers while victims continue to suffer. **Don't ever let any shame you may feel be a shield for your abuser - don't let your suffering protect the one who caused your suffering.** When you are writing in your journal, speaking to your attorney, or talking to the police or an investigator, never let fear or shame or embarrassment hold you back from the truth. At the end of the day, it is truth that will banish that shame. The courage to tell the truth can be the difference between success and defeat in a lawsuit, and can be the difference between healing and just-getting-by.

Survivors are Amazing and Uniquely Gifted

Sexual abuse survivors are some of the most beautiful, soulful, intelligent, deeply spiritual, clever, funny, persevering, hard working, caring, compassionate, intuitive, driven, no-excuses warriors and fighters, and inspirational and unstoppable heroes that I have ever had the honor to meet and know.

Sexual abuse survivors have accomplished more, personally and professionally, and impacted other's lives more than any other human beings that I have ever met. We rock! You do! And so do I! We are the survivors, the movers, the shakers, the tough-as-nails, no-excuses, no-holds-barred warriors in life. You are all my heroes.

Our survival through the worst of childhoods made us deeper and more caring individuals. Think about it; would you have all the same qualities if not for the abuse you suffered as a child? Would you be the same unique, aware, loveable, heroic person you are today? Abuse is a trauma, and I would never ask you to celebrate it, but I do want you to remember that your strength was forged through adversity.

Survivors have had to see human nature at its worst. Ours is a difficult human experience. Life is not simple for us, nor easy. We have had to fight our way through everything, even our own feelings and emotions, just to function, work, have careers, get educated, raise families, have intimate relationships, love others, and to give to our community. We have had a unique human experience. We can allow it to destroy us, along with our faith, health, and our ability to love, *or* we can see it as something we survived and overcame that taught us lessons we can appreciate and honor. In appreciating and honoring those lessons you can learn to appreciate, love, and honor yourself. Thus, hidden in your greatest trauma…is also a gift, a great lesson about strength, perseverance, and survival. There is a silver lining to this very dark cloud. It is said that the higher the soul, the harder the lessons. If so, we survivors must be very high souls, because our lessons have been so hard. We just need to make sure the lessons were *well learned.*

If you ever doubt that you can live a normal life after abuse, take a look at some of the people you may not know you have something in common with:

Many prominent, successful females are survivors:

- *Oprah* (media megastar) – Raped by her cousin and later sexually abused by an uncle and a family friend.
- *Terri Hatcher* (actress) – Sexually abused repeatedly by her uncle. She went to the police and assisted in his prosecution 30 years later after finding out another girl he had molested had killed herself.
- *Roseanne Arnold* (comedian/feminist) – Was abused by her mother from infancy through age 6. She revealed her abuse in a *People Magazine* cover story.
- *Maya Angelou* (poet) – Sexually abused and raped by her mother's boyfriend, she stopped speaking completely for several years.
- *Ashley Judd* (actress) – Sexually abused by at least one family friend.
- *Mary J. Blige* (singer) – Sexually abused by a family friend at age 5.
- *Anne Heche* (actress) – Sexually abused and raped by her father, a choir-teacher at a Baptist church.
- *Queen Latifah* (musician/model) – Sexually abused by a teenage male babysitter.

I believe this next list is very important to read for male survivors. Some of the toughest, smartest, most quintessentially masculine men in the public eye were victimized as kids and overcame it. These men are living proof that it can happen to anybody:

- *Henry Rollins* (rock star) Sexually abused by his mother's boyfriend.
- *Sugar Ray Leonard* (world champion boxer) – Sexually abused by an Olympic boxing coach as a teenager.
- *Carlos Santana* (musician) – Was molested at age 11 by a stranger and repressed the memories for years until they came out in therapy.
- *Johannes Brahms* (composer) Sexually abused while working in a bar/brothel at a young age.
- *Laverneus Coles* (NFL all-star wide receiver) – Sexually abused at a very young age by his future stepfather.
- *Tyler Perry* (actor/screenwriter) – Sexually abused by his stepfather at gunpoint from ages 10 to 13.
- *Tom Arnold* (actor/comedian) - From age four to seven was sexually abused by a 19-year-old male babysitter. The sexual abuse occurred several times a week. Years later as an adult Arnold confronted his abuser.
- *James Dean* (actor) – Molested by his minister as a young boy.
- *Richard Pryor* (comedian) – Raped at age 6 by a teen neighbor and later molested by a Catholic priest.

See! You are far from alone. There are many others out there who have faced this horror and come away victorious and successful. They fought, they struggled, and they suffered just like you, but all of them had the courage to heal and to be open about their story. Some of them repressed their memories, some lived in silence, some self-medicated with drugs and alcohol for years. In they end, they honored the journey and became who they deserved to be.

Throughout this book, especially while doing the journal exercises and learning about your potential legal rights, you will uncover who and what *you* are. You will uncover your gift – this I promise you. You will learn how to break the silence, speak up, stand up, step up, but hopefully most of all you will learn to stand up *for yourself* – because you are worth standing up for.

The Law Is Changing Giving Survivors More Rights to Sue

In 1984, when I first began to represent children being sexually abused, the law in California mandated that adult survivors sue by their 19th birthday or forever be barred from suing. After a six-year fight, waged and funded by me and my law partner, we were able to change the law in California so that adult survivors have a right to sue their abusers up until they reach the age of 26. If they are older than 26, they have three years from the date they discover (like me) or reasonably should have discovered the *psychological injury or illness* caused by their sexual abuse.

This is just one example of how the landscape has changed for the better for adult survivors since the old days. After the statute of limitations in California was extended, 40 other states enacted legislation giving adult survivors more rights. All across the country, attitudes are changing, doors are opening, and light is shining in on these cases. This is not to say that the road will be easy or that our justice system is anywhere near perfect, it is only to say that now we are more likely than ever before to get our day in court.

The Public Is Beginning To Wake Up

Not only is the law changing, but judicial and legal attitudes are slowly evolving as well. In the 1980s, it was nearly impossible for survivors to even find a lawyer that would consider representing a sexual abuse victim. The taboo was so powerful and made people so uncomfortable that it drove them away. Just to let you know how bad it was for survivors of incest in 1984, take the example of my first TV appearance. It was a live interview on the *Home Show* with Gary Collins. I was supposed to be on the show to tell my story and be interviewed. It was one of the first times that the word "incest" was even mentioned on national television. The interview was to be aired nationally and I was more than a little nervous heading into it!

After I answered Gary's questions, they brought on a psychiatrist to talk about incest and to share his expertise. The psychiatrist looked straight into the camera and said that incest happens to only one-in-one million girls in the United States and to only one-in-three million Jewish girls. I was crushed. Now I believed, that not only did my parents abandon me, but so did God. If God picked me out of three million women to suffer sexual assault, he must hate me. I was spiritually devastated. That never should have happened! We know now that those statistics are ludicrously off-base.

Nowadays, the statistics are more accurate. Instead of making us feel even more alone, they remind us that we are **not** alone. "Sexual abuse" and "incest" are no longer dirty words that shouldn't be said in public. Because of the battles fought for women's and children's and survivor's rights, the public is beginning to wake up to the fact that sexual abuse can and does happen. There is more acceptance, there are

11

more support groups, more resources, more online communities to help survivors get the information they need to heal and get free and fight back.

The tide of battle is turning, slowly but surely. I believe there is a coming civil rights movement for children that will be similar to the African American civil rights movement in the 1960's and the gay/lesbian civil rights movement happening now. As survivors, we need to lead the fight and have our voices heard. In the courts the roads to justice continue to open as old laws are repealed or updated. In attorney's offices and judge's chambers attitudes are changing. In communities across the country the stigma is lifting. Your fight will not be easy, but I want you to know that you stand on strong footing, and I want you to remember how far we've come and be encouraged.

Recognizing & Understanding Your Damages

It is vital that you recognize and understand your damages. We will talk about it in great detail in Chapter 4, where we go through building your case step by step, but for now you need a basic understanding to lay the foundation for what's to come.

The sexual abuse you suffered was damaging, and the trauma didn't/doesn't end when the abuse ends. If you were sexually abused as a child, you are probably suffering long-term effects that interfere with your daily functioning. You may be specifically aware of these effects, semi-aware of them, or not be able to see them at all. It is the invisible handprint. These long-term effects can be so pervasive that it's sometimes hard, even with therapy, to pinpoint exactly how the abuse affected you. The abuse I suffered affected the way I dressed, felt about my body, felt about sex, and gave me anxiety attacks for years, and I didn't even realize it. Human beings are complicated creatures. We are the ultimate survivors, and sometimes what we do to survive manifests itself in unique and complicated ways.

How the sexual abuse damaged you is an important issue, not only for the quality of your life, but also in your lawsuit against your abuser. Your damages will help you determine if you have a case and it will determine how much you can recover from your abuser. We will go into this issue in great detail in Chapter Four. The long term effects of abuse generally fall into five basic categories:

Emotional Damages (Self Esteem)

Physical Damages (Your Body)

Sexual Damages (Sexuality)

Relationship Damages (Capacity for Intimacy)

Work, Career (Ability to Work)

If you feel overwhelmed just thinking about the long term damaging effects of abuse, remember that you have already lived through the worst part—the abuse itself. You have survived against all odds. One thing all survivors have is inner strength. That inner strength will not only ultimately lead you to survival and healing, but it will support you through your legal action. Remember, the sign on my law office desk said, "The Fuck Stops Here" It stops here, for all of us, for all survivors.

Honoring What You Did To Survive

Surviving what you went through, and being who you are today, is a miracle.

YOU ARE A MIRACLE.

As a young child or a teen, you survived one of the worst things that one human being can do to another. Sexual abuse is a form of torture. Just because it was done by someone you know, or someone you love, or who you were related to, or a neighbor, or someone from of your church, synagogue, mosque, temple, or who was a teacher, doctor, or family friend, doesn't change the fact that you were *tortured*. It is a war crime. The problem is, it is a secret war that goes on behind closed doors. But even in war, the war eventually ends, and prisoners of war are returned home. The problem with sexual abuse survivors is that we *are* home. The war never ends; we are never released from our prison until we are able to release ourselves through therapy, spirituality, love, and sometimes vindication.

Honor what you did to survive. Whatever it is you had to do, you did it to cope. Everyone deals with trauma differently. As a young survivor, you may have turned to alcohol or drugs. You might have become an over-achiever, excelling in school and become a caretaker of everyone at home. You might have blocked out or blacked out huge parts of your childhood—where there are huge gaps that you simply cannot remember. You might have used food, sex, drugs, or shopping to numb your feelings. You might have withdrawn into yourself, or cut off all emotion. You may have developed medical problems, internalizing and using your body to absorb the memories and trauma. You might have externalized your anger and frustration, and bullied others or fought or stolen. You might have sought the "control" of an eating disorder or had body issues. You may have buried yourself in work, or spent all your time involved in other people's traumas and dramas. As a child, given whatever limited psychological resources you had at the time, you coped using whatever means were available to you.

Most survivors feel ashamed of what they did to cope with what happened. None of us are perfect. As a child in a terrible situation, you did the best that you could do—and you continue to do so, even today. Working through those issues and imperfections is called life, and it's never too late to begin to be who you want to be. If we've done bad things or developed bad habits, all we can do is try to make it right.

When I was fighting to get the laws changed for survivors of sexual abuse in California, I was standing in a pit, testifying in front of the Senate Judiciary Committee. The Committee members were perched above me on massive black swivel chairs like riders of the Apocalypse. With my heart pounding and my throat so dry I could barely speak, I kept telling myself, that I had survived my childhood, what could these people do to me that was worse than that! It got me through the experience and made me even tougher and more fearless. You have already survived the worst, and you did it when you were only a kid. Think of all the things that you are capable of today.

CHAPTER TWO: **Getting Ready to Take Action**
The Next Steps

Ready [**red**-ee]
    adjective
    prepared mentally or physically for some experience or action

"Before everything else, getting ready is the secret of success."

- Henry Ford

Am I Ready – The Emotional Issues

Before we move forward you need to have a thorough, clear-eyed understanding of what will be involved in making the decision to sue your abuser and then following through on that decision. This means being aware of the emotional, logistical, legal, financial, and social issues that will arise and having the *self-awareness* to reflect, organize, and prepare accordingly. We will discuss what suing your abuser can and cannot achieve and also go through the general pros and cons of using legal means to get justice.

Suing isn't for everybody, but I think it's critical that you know everything about this option, so you can make the choice responsibly. I believe victims should have the right to sue whether or not they choose to exercise those rights. It is empowering even just to know that you can take action if you choose to. A victim remains quiet because they have been silenced by an outside force. Someone in command of their own life makes an intelligent decision not to take action when they could if they wanted to. I want you to be in the latter category.

Whether or not you were a victim of child sexual abuse and, if you were, whether or not you choose to sue your perpetrator I urge you to read the next three chapters as if you were going to take action. See what it does for your sense of personal empowerment to put yourself in the shoes of someone who is considering this step. Even if you are not a victim of abuse yourself but are a supporter of someone who is, you will be better equipped to empathize with a survivor in this position if you have imagined being in their shoes and facing the decisions they face. If we as a community are to understand and prevent this crime from happening to other children and our own children, then we must all be willing to look at how it from a new perspective, the perspective of a *survivor*.

What Suing Can Do

"You get to know who you really are in a crisis."

- Oprah Winfrey, CSA Survivor

There can be many benefits to suing. There are emotional and psychological benefits that can come from just the act of *considering* a suit. First and foremost, suing your abuser civilly may be the best way for you to vindicate yourself and to hold your abuser accountable in a public, official, serious forum. That has the obvious benefits of justice, compensation, finality, and putting the truth on record.

It can also be transformative and symbolic. You were abused as a child, but (if you choose to) you will sue as an empowered adult who no longer needs to be afraid. Taking a big, symbolic step like going forward with a lawsuit represents that you are in control of your life, and you are no longer that child. It also brings crystal clarity to the fact that a wrong was committed upon you.

> *"When a rapist is a stranger who wears a ski mask and uses*
> *a knife, everyone accepts and understands how wrong it is.*
> *Why is a family member any different?"*

- Shari Karney, Survivor

Society freely accepts that acts of sexual coercion and violence committed by strangers are wrongs of the highest order. But because child sexual abuse usually takes place within a family or community, the issue can get blurry, especially for conflicted young victims. When someone is abused by a family member who provides for them, and who is a person that they love, it creates a terrible and lasting confusion. After all, for some of us, these were the people that gave us life, fed us, sheltered us, and brought us up. This confusion and guilt retreats when the legal system validates a victim and draws stark contrast between right and wrong. Legal action will remind you that you deserved a healthy, happy home as a child and *no one* ever had any right to hurt you.

Suing requires that you pick a side: your own. You get to be on your own team, with members of your choosing. When you do this, even when you consider doing this, you can and will see that there is love and support and understanding for you out there, after all, it's *your team*. It might be friends, supporters, loving family members, or professionals like your attorney and your therapist, but you will have a team.

Many who come into the legal process feeling vulnerable and weak develop a sense of mission, purpose, and personal strength during the process. It becomes a reminder that they are not victims anymore. The process itself can be healing and can help you to de-victimize. There is a journalist named Kelly Gust who wrote a beautiful series of articles in the Oakland Tribune about abuse. She wrote about survivors who had used the law to pursue their abusers. One was a teenage girl who, after being in therapy for two years, finally decided to file a personal injury suit against her step-father, she said:

> *"I was dealing with a lot of guilt... Now I feel like I am right. Now finally maybe someone else will say it. Filing suit has made me a heck of a lot stronger person. Now I know I've done everything I can do."*

Another survivor said of his legal fight:

> *"I had misgivings about doing it, it sounds like you're doing it for the money but I knew that wasn't it... Since I was 10 years old I was told 'you don't talk about it.' It was bad, it was embarrassing... It was always 'John, just forget about it. It happened a long time ago'... I wanted my perpetrator to know it's been 20 years but I haven't forgotten that I suffered for what he did."*

Mary Doe wanted there to be no question about what had happened to her:

"What happened to me was rape. I hope I'll give other incest survivors the courage to assert their rights as rape victims."

Finally, a prominent trial attorney in the CSA field shared this message he was sent by one of his clients about the burden we carry and how powerful this process can be:

"The night you called to talk to me about authority to settle the case, I was sitting on my bed with a loaded gun. My wife and the girls were visiting California. I had rationalized the details of how I was gonna do it. I was gonna wrap a towel around my head, and do it in the shower so my wife wouldn't have to clean it up.

Then you called. You saved my life. I was beaten by my step-father and handed over to [redacted]. I spent 4 years in [redacted]'s bed. It wasn't because of money, but because of hope. I'm going to be able to provide for my family, be able to be a man. I've dreamed of a having a house my 3 daughters can grow up in, since yesterday I've even been looking at a home. We are all going to begin therapy. I now have a future where [redacted] doesn't control me anymore. Since I was a small child I've been trying to rediscover what that would have been like. Thank you for saving my life and making the world listen to me."

That is the true power of taking action. It can be life saving! All of these survivors found their power and their voice through taking action. You can too. Now, *you* have the power.

What Suing Can't Do

"Do what you feel in your heart to be right - for you'll be criticized anyway. You'll be damned if you do, and damned if you don't."

- Eleanor Roosevelt

Always remember that legal action is only one tool, one part among many, in the journey towards health and happiness. I want to dispel the illusion that suing is a magic bullet that can make everything right in one shot. It is important and it can be a *massive* step in the healing process, but it has limits.

A lot of people call me and want to sue, and the first thing they say after telling me their story, with both rage and grief in their voice, is that they want to sue to alleviate those feelings. I have to be honest and tell them that suing will *not do this*. Suing can never make up for not having parents who loved and protected you the way you deserved to be loved and protected as a child. It can't bring back your innocence. The goal is legal "compensation" but it can never truly *compensate* you for the physical and psychological damage that child sexual abuse leaves behind. Ray Boucher, who is a nationally recognized plaintiff's trial lawyer who has handled many high profile sexual abuse cases says this about the downside of the litigation process:

"Survivors need to understand that litigation is a very long, drawn out, painful, and ultimately unsatisfying process. You can't bring vengeance or revenge, the system doesn't allow that. It can't get back the life that was lost, and it can't take away that pain."

Shari Karney

Most survivors who want to sue have a noble fantasy: they hope that once the perpetrator is confronted in public and the courts hear the case, that the perpetrator will *admit what they did, take responsibility* and *make amends*. They hope that once their family knows all the facts that they will rally behind them and support them. They'll see how badly you were hurt, will see what a terrible effect it had on your life, will understand the failures in your life, empathize with the difficulties you've had in relationships, in holding a job, in getting good grades, in focusing on a career, maybe even sympathize with drug and alcohol problems.

In essence, the fantasy is that you will be seen and understood by them for the first time, and the blame and rage and disappointment will be finally focused *not at you* for the mess your life may have been, but on your perpetrator. They'll give you the love and support you've always needed. They'll be the family you dreamed of and not the family you actually had. **Let's be clear - suing is not going to give you the family you've always wanted - it can't**.

> *"All I wanted was for my brother to believe me and love me again. I thought about it all the time. No one mattered more than him to me, and he was the only one I needed on my side, I didn't care about my parents. When he stuck with them, I cried and I cried and I cried. I thought that when all the proof came out in court, he would join me. But even after I WON my case, he still wouldn't talk to me. It took me years to realize that he just couldn't be who I wanted him to be, and nothing could change that."*

– Margarita, Sibling Abuse Survivor

22

Some people think that if they sue, it will bring the family back together, and this is one of the most dangerous misconceptions. It is *possible* that through this dramatic act, some family healing can occur. It is far more likely, however, that suing will have a polarizing effect, be it in your family or church or community, and you need to understand that. Suing can, and very well might, bring out some of the worst anger and denial you have seen yet from your abuser and those in his or her circle.

Consider the story of Chantelle, who was abused by her minister father from when she was just an 18-month-old baby until she was 5. She not only sued her father, but she and her husband crusaded in their home state and got the laws changed so that others could do the same. She recounts how her sister was initially supportive, but then everything changed:

> *"At first we would talk and I felt she understood. But then she wrote me a nasty letter saying my counseling was witchcraft... I attributed that to my mom and dad - the family line... She won't even contact me now. Now that everything is settled I've gotten used to being without my family."*

I did *not* include this quote to scare you away from pursuing your legal rights, I included it because it is critical that you are realistic from the beginning about this process. You need to know ahead of time that this process can really bring out the crazy in certain people! And let's be honest – most of us come from "crazy" dysfunctional families, and our abuse thrived in the chaos.

But there is good news as well! Some of my clients have been shown incredible support from their families during a lawsuit. I have seen cases where the family rallied behind the victim in support. Take, for example, my former client, we'll call her Lindsay. Lindsay was sexually abused by her father.

"When I was a kid my father raped me and would pee on me and my little brother and sister. My father would dress up my brother like a girl when he misbehaved and make him go outside. He would touch me under the covers while the whole family was watching TV. He even had sex with me while my mom was in the same bed. My mother later claimed she thought he was just tickling me."

Worried about her younger sister and brother, at 16 Lindsay finally confronted her mother with what had been going on since Lindsay was 4 years old. The mother finally opened her eyes to the abuse, confronted her husband, and then reported it to the police. Unfortunately, no further action was taken by the authorities at the time. Soon afterwards Lindsay's mother left her husband and began to have memories of her own sexual abuse as a child. She went into therapy. She began to look at not only what she had experienced herself but what she had allowed to be done to her own children. After Lindsay had finished incest therapy she decided she wanted to sue her father.

Throughout the process, Lindsay's mother completely supported her emotionally and financially. What was wonderful about having her mother's support was that she was also able to provide corroboration to prove the sexual abuse. Her mother was willing to testify on Lindsay's behalf. She took responsibility for her inaction and silence and apologized. She also provided documents like old medical reports, showing broken bones and bruises. With the mother's support we were able to present overwhelming evidence of the abuse; Lindsay's father had no choice but to settle. This process took about a year and a half. For Lindsay, taking this action with the support of her mother was a critical step toward healing. She said to me:

"When I looked at my father in court for the first time I felt good. He was never going to treat me bad again. And he just looked down and couldn't look at me in the eye and it made me feel like what I'd done by telling was right."

Lindsay also gained more than the monetary award. She got her mother's protection and support. She also got a sense of her own ability to be an adult and not to a child victim anymore. She used the money to go to a community college and to seek medical attention for the lasting injury her father's abuse had caused her reproductive system. She began to build a new life for herself and she told me she was surprised at how good she felt about the whole process.

Lindsay was lucky. The act of suing her father brought part of her family closer together, but she is the exception, not the rule. Typically, if brothers and sisters knew about the abuse, they feel guilty and ashamed. If they didn't know what was going on, they can feel like their memories of the family are being threatened when they learn about it. Denial is powerful. Not only siblings, but mothers, aunts, cousins, and grandmothers can also desperately cling to how they *want* things to be, even when the truth is in their face. They can stand by the *illusion* of who they want to believe their husband/son/boyfriend is even when that person is a predator. Listen to this dose of reality from a Florida sexual abuse attorney:

"It doesn't change the things you might hope would change. You get money, and the money is important, but it's not everything on the emotional level. ...It's a big decision to sue your family. That's the end of a family relationship no matter how false it has been."

In cases where the survivor has no relationship (or virtually no relationship) with the family or where the relationship couldn't get any worse, this is not a problem. I believe that what survivors want most is the support of their mothers, and unfortunately they seldom find it. Even if the mother is no longer with the perpetrator she may still be playing the role of keeper of the secret and frequently won't believe you or will pretend not to believe you. Pain and trauma have different effects on different people, and sometimes the people we want to love the most are unable to be who we need them to be or want them to be.

Another hope many survivors hold is that the perpetrator will be sorry for his actions and apologize. Unfortunately, suing is not going to make your perpetrator say he's sorry. It can *make him sorry*, by exposing him to the world and garnishing his wages, but it can't make him admit it. Take it from me:

*"You can hold your abuser **responsible**, but you can't make him **say he's sorry**."*

- Jerry, Priest Abuse Survivor

For an abuser to say he's "sorry" means not only is he going to have to admit he is what society considers a monster but that what he or she did hurt you terribly.

26

Often this is an admission that he deeply wounded his own flesh and blood or someone he should have protected instead. In my experience as a survivor, litigator, and a fighter for the rights of the abused, overwhelmingly the men that commit these acts have no ability to empathize with their victims.

Nicolas Groh, the director of a sex offender rehabilitation program says that in his 12 years of practice he has *never* seen a self-referral for help from a child molester. He finds that "genuine remorse or shame is *uncharacteristic*" of most of the men that are ordered to take his classes.

It is important to understand what you are going to be dealing with. This is a topic we will explore more later, but these men view their victims as objects and not people. This explains the perpetrator's surprise and shock when the non-entity (child) holds them to task for their behavior. To expect that this person who abused you for his own gratification is suddenly going to be a caring parent or adult, sorry for his acts, and wanting to make amends when confronted with a lawsuit, is not realistic or very likely to happen.

No matter what, remember this quote by Children's Defense Fund president and lifelong activist Marian Wright Edelman:

"You're not obligated to win. You're obligated to keep trying to do the best you can every day."

Journal Exercise – What are my Goals?

- **This is a simple exercise. Write down your goals and everything you would hope to accomplish by suing.**
- **Now use what you have just learned to identify goals that are not realistic, circle those and draw a line through them.**
- **Look at your remaining goals, those are what you can accomplish.**

Getting Support

I want you to be equipped with every source of support you can have. This means 3 things: Contacting a survivors support group for some community, help, and advice, finding a therapist if you do not already have one, and being committed to *supporting yourself.*

Finding Support Groups

Here are the names and contact information for some groups and/or websites that might be helpful for you to contact as part of this process. This is not a specific endorsement of any group, because they are all different, and it is up to you to find the one that will serve you best. Be aware that this list is only current as of the publishing date of this book, so be on the lookout for new groups as well.

- Adult Survivors of Sexual Abuse
  www.ascasupport.org
  ASCA is an international group with many local subsidiaries focusing on a 21 step recovery program for adult survivors. It was founded and created by the Morris Center, which is a non profit organization dedicated to helping victims of sexual abuse. Their website has a wealth of survivor information available for download

- After Silence
  www.aftersilence.org

After Silence is an online community of rape and sexual abuse survivors. It provides safely moderated, anonymous online support groups, message boards, and chat rooms

- Survivors of Incest Anonymous
  www.siawso.org
  This is an online incest support group with local chapters. It is a welcoming group - they define incest very broadly. They provide community, support, and information for survivors. This organization is faith based, similar to Alcoholics Anonymous

- Darkness to Light
  www.d2l.org
  Darkness to Light focuses on the fight to end child sexual abuse. It provides online information for individuals and groups about prevention techniques and has a region-by-region guide for reporting sexual abuse

- Master the Past
  www.masterthepast.com
  This website is run by life-coach and alternative therapist Leonard Ludovico. His organization offers individual counseling in person, over the phone, and via Skype.

- SNAP - Survivors Network of those Abused by Priests
  www.snapnetwork.org
  SNAP is non-profit that specializes in providing support and resources for those abused by religious authority figures. They are large and well organized, with many chapters across the globe.

- MaleSurvivor
  www.malesurvivor.org
  MaleSurvivor is dedicated to tackling the specific issues that male survivors face. It provides a wealth of information and resources online and can put you in connection with both professional help and local survivor groups

This list is not even close to exhaustive! There are countless groups out there that help survivors and make a difference every day, it's just up to you to find the right one. We have included a more expansive list of support groups and professionals for you in the resource section in the back of the book.

Finding the Right Therapist

"If a victim doesn't totally reclaim and have the "pink slip" to themselves, they can never really go out in the world and just be who they are. A part of them always belongs to the aggressor. My job – a therapist's job – is to reclaim that whole person. So they belong to themselves 100%."

- Dr. Arlene Drake, Ph.D.

In my experience, therapy is a critical part of the healing process and it is important not only to have a therapist, but also to make sure you have the *right* therapist. On the legal side, you should know that there are some states where you cannot bring a suit for child sexual abuse without having first seen a therapist. Every therapist is different, and one thing I want to tell you based on my years of experience as a litigator, is that some therapists will be more supportive than others when it comes to suing your abuser. If your goal is to sue, you should know that many therapists who understand how to help you heal may not necessarily be the best people to help you in your lawsuit. Some therapists don't believe that suing is an appropriate step to take for survivors of incest and child sexual abuse. You need a therapist who's on board, and who understands the process of suing and will support you. One of my mentors (and a truly compassionate, brilliant advocate) is sexual abuse therapist Arlene Drake. Here is her take:

"I think the therapist needs to know the workings of the legal system because the legal system is appalling. It's not about justice... I think

that they should know something about the workings of the legal system or they'll be thrown off track."

The right therapist can be an enormous source of strength and support. For example, about halfway through Mary Doe's case, just before her deposition (getting questioned by the opposing attorney under oath) was scheduled, she had a sudden change of heart and wanted to drop the case. She lost focus as to why she was suing and she wanted to abandon the lawsuit. Her therapist, who had worked very closely with her and knew her very well, realized what was going on: She was panicking from the thought of facing her father. She was feeling overwhelmed, powerless, helpless, and afraid.

Her therapist, understanding what a deposition is, was able to work with her, explain the situation, and calm her down. She did exercises with Mary in her therapy group that helped her prepare to be deposed. Mary found her center, found her inner strength, and put her fear behind her. She not only did beautifully in her deposition, but she was also able to conquer a huge amount of the fear she had of her father. After the deposition, she was *so* glad she didn't give in to her fear. In Mary's case, the right therapist mattered, which is something you should know when selecting one for yourself.

Here are some things I recommend you look for in a therapist:

1) They make you feel comfortable in talking to them and they make you feel safe.
2) They support speaking out and taking a strong stand.
3) They understand and have helped other clients through the legal process or

are interested in learning.

4) They believe in empowering you and healing you so you can move on.

5) They understand and are open to a confrontation with your perpetrator and/or others who may have allowed the perpetration to go on.

6) They are going to be there for you, above and beyond the sessions, during your suit.

7) Finally, they have a manner, personality, and education you believe can help you accomplish your goals.

Supporting Yourself

It's very important if you are going to face the rigors of a lawsuit that you nurture and take care of *yourself* throughout the process. Treat yourself the way you would treat and love a child who you knew was currently being sexually abused. It is a way of nurturing the child within you that went through it. Be nurturing, be gentle, be sympathetic. Be *forgiving* when you aren't perfect, allow yourself to feel, to heal, and to grieve. Be accepting no matter what happens.

Always remember to connect with positive things so you can relax and get grounded and be comfortable with yourself. Go to the movies, play sports, get into your hobbies, take vacations, hang out and laugh with your loved ones, do special things for your significant other, smile, eat good healthy food, and enjoy life when it gives you the opportunity, even if its only for a couple minutes at a time. This process will be tough, don't make it tougher by putting your life on hold while you are going through it.

Journal Exercise – My Sanity Plan

- **This exercise will make sure you take some time for YOURSELF during this process.**

- **Write a list of 10 simple things you can do that always make you feel better and feel like yourself.**

- **Next, write down a short plan of how you will do at least 3 of these things a week whenever you are working on your case.**

Gathering Evidence – A Key Part of Being Ready

Prepare yourself for some difficult sections to come, this is where we start getting real about preparing to make your case. If it helps, think of yourself as a private detective on the hunt for evidence.

How to prove what happened to you and prove how much it damaged you is a topic we will revisit many times in this book. Sexual abuse that happened in the past can be incredibly difficult to prove. With the exception of permanent or lasting injuries, most physical evidence of abuse disappears within 12 to 24 hours. People are reluctant to testify. Very rarely is it ever documented, abusers usually do not keep records of their crimes. This can be a difficult hurdle because if you can't prove your case, you simply cannot win.

I am going to try to give you a familiarity with the most common ways sexual abuse is proved in civil court so that you can prepare yourself and gather the best evidence and the most useful tools available to you. The way I think of it, and the way you should try to think of it is: What does the court want to see? What does your lawyer want to present? What does your abuser ***not*** want to see in court? And what would convince a jury member/stranger that you should be compensated?

Your Testimony - The Best Evidence

In the vast majority of sexual abuse cases the testimony of the abuse victim is the centerpiece that the case is built on. Some victims have triumphed in court *when the only piece of evidence they had was their testimony.* It's that important. In many ways, trying a civil case comes down to telling a story: the story of a wrongdoer hurting a victim. The acts and the people in the story have to be *real* to the jury. You know the story of your abuse better than anyone else, you know how much it hurt you, you know how much it affected the quality of your life. No one else is equipped to tell that story the way you are.

You need to do some things to make sure that your testimony will be as strong and as believable as possible. You need to sit down and focus and make sure that you have clear, accurate memories of your abuse, especially if there has ever been any repression of these memories. You need to work with your therapist to have a clear understanding of how the abuse damaged you. Many victims don't see the ways they have been damaged by their abuse, and some are in denial. Leonard Ludovico, a transpersonal hypnotherapist who specializes in helping survivors remove the trauma of sexual abuse says:

> *"Victims, and in my experience especially male victims, don't always make the connection between their life and their abuse. You'll have guys that say 'I have problems with sex. I'm anxious all the time. I*

never trust anyone. I'm depressed.' And then later when you're talking
he'll say 'It happened when I was a kid. I'm fine now, It wasn't a big
deal.' They have to learn to see it for what it is."

- Leonard Ludovico, Transpersonal Trauma Therapist

Leonard believes if you're able to say it, then you will be able to hear it; if you are able to hear it, then you will learn from it. If you are able to learn from it, then you are able to grow from it and the handprint of the abuse will be removed.

You also have to be strong enough to tell your story, get through it, and be articulate, clear, and genuine. If when you're talking to your therapist you can't make it through recounting a memory of abuse without breaking down, you probably have more healing and more work to do before you will be ready to testify.

Do the journal work below to test yourself, and make sure you can tell a clear story of your abuse. If you can do that, your attorney should be able to build the case, starting with your testimony. Your attorney should *never* be telling you exactly what to say, they can coach you, encourage you, give you advice, and guide you, but if they are "scripting" you it is unethical and can badly damage your case if the other side finds out.

Journal Exercise – Storyteller

- Start on a fresh blank page, and write in your journal as if you are telling a friend exactly what happened to you. Go through a single instance, and tell it from the first person, something like this, but your own story:

- "I am in my bed, my room is totally dark, I remember seeing the light in the hallway turn on under my door. I am terrified and I hold my breath. Then my door opens and I see him…"

- Be real, be honest, be unembarrassed, and be accurate. When you are done, read it quietly to yourself as if you were the jury member.

Witnesses

Witnesses are critical to establishing proof of the events and establishing damages. In the courtroom setting, there are 2 types of witnesses you need to know about *lay witnesses* and *expert witnesses*.

Lay Witnesses

Lay witnesses are people who actually saw or experienced something relevant that they can tell the court (testify) about from memory. It could be a sister who saw your abuse, or who was also raped. It could be your mother or your aunt who saw some injuries to your body. It could be a school counselor that you told about your abuse. All of those are relevant to a jury who is trying to determine if you were abused.

Expert Witnesses

Expert witnesses are not the same as lay witnesses, they didn't see the abuse, they are there because they have examined other evidence and can give a professional opinion about it. In other civil cases, they are the experts that speculate how fast a car was going or the engineers that testify that the brakes were defective. In sexual abuse cases, these witnesses will often be your therapist or psychologist, who can testify that the source of your current psychological and emotional problems was your abuse. Or, it can be a doctor who testifies that, for example, the permanent damage to your uterus or anus came from being raped as a very young child.

You are the person who knows the most about what lay witnesses can be found for your case. Remember, you have to find people with information who can help you, who are also *willing to testify*. In sexual abuse cases, often times witnesses who should testify do not, because they are embarrassed or in denial or do not want to "hurt the family" or for countless other excuses. Be prepared for this. Your job is to find the people who know something who will be on your side and will testify on your behalf.

Your attorney will be far better equipped than you are for finding expert witnesses for your case. He or she will know whether to call your therapist, get an independent psychologist, etc. A good attorney will know what doctors to send you to and/or what doctors to have testify when the time comes.

Medical Records

Medical records can play an important role in proving that your young body was abused. Your task is to try to remember in as much detail as possible each time you went to the doctor as a kid for injuries related to your abuse, because medical records are almost always kept for very long periods of time. Did you see a doctor for rashes or irritation? Urinary tract infections? Soreness, redness, etc.? Did you ever have any dramatic procedures like surgery or an abortion? Don't try to filter out what was relevant and not relevant yourself, only a doctor is qualified to decide what is and is not medical evidence of abuse.

Evidence of anxiety, depression, and mental problems as a child or teenager is also evidence you want. Just try to remember the doctors' names and the best recollection you have of the date you saw them. If you can't remember that, try to remember the hospital or clinic or city or neighborhood you lived in when you saw the doctor. Try to prepare as much detail as possible for your attorney, and he or she can try to find the records. At some point, your attorney should ask you to sign a *medical release*, which is your authorization for doctor's offices and hospitals to release your medical records to your attorney. This is fine, and this is a good thing, because it allows your attorney to try to obtain your old medical records through requests and searches.

> *"We eventually found a little clinic in my hometown that had records from when I went there as a kid. At first I was disappointed because nothing seemed like it proved what happened, then we realized that one record showed I had bruises on my wrist and neck that backed up what I said my brother was doing to me at that time."*

- Margarita, Survivor

Other Evidence

Other documentation is rare, but it does exist. Maybe your abuser took photos or videos of the things he did. Maybe you kept a journal. Maybe the school counselor made a record when you told them you were being abused. You need to begin to think what kinds of other documents exist that can prove your case. You'd be surprised at what you can uncover when you start poking through old paperwork, boxes, files, family photos and memorabilia in attics and garages.

You can ask your grandmother, aunt, or other family members for their permission to look though items in their possession, such as family photo albums, family records, or boxes in their attic, basement, or storage unit. It's a lot easier to snoop around now to get records and information that you may need for your lawsuit then to wait until the lawsuit is filed. Once your lawsuit has been filed and your perpetrator(s) have been served, it's less likely that anyone in your family (or otherwise), will willingly provide you with information to help you pursue your case.

"Once I served my grandfather with the court papers, my whole family clammed up. I wasn't invited to my sisters wedding and not even my grandma would talk to me."

- Brittany, Incest Survivor

Many of these, like old records or things in the custody of other people will need to be reached through a *subpoena*, which is a court order to produce evidence, and is used as part of the discovery process which we will discuss much more later. What your attorney will need first, though, is a list of things you believe may exist so he or she can try to secure them.

Don't forget the internet! The web is an incredible source of information that should not be discounted. My clients have found invaluable things on websites, Facebook, and by doing online background checks. You may find things that you didn't even know existed.

In some states it is legal to record in-person conversations without consent (in many states it is not – so watch out). It is a hugely complicated but potentially possible to confront your abuser and get them on tape admitting what they did! Consult with your lawyer about whether this tactic is legal in your jurisdiction and whether the tape would be admissible in court. Be aware that many therapists, with the best of intentions, arrange confrontations with abuser parents/family members that may waste this opportunity. You should consider the possibility of taping or recording your abuser, but always keep your safety, your healing process, and staying on the right side of the law as higher priorities.

There are a few extra things in this category that you can find to help your attorney. First of all, find pictures of yourself as a kid. Find the cutest most innocent pictures of yourself that you can find as a child. Your attorney can use this to show the jury that it was an innocent, sweet child that was brutalized, and make it real for them. Maybe you can find a picture of yourself as a kid where you clearly look sad and distant. Basically, you need some pictures of the child who was abused, to show the jury what a monster your abuser was. Even old home movies can help your case.

Pictures speak a thousand words. These pictures and movies can show a jury just how young and vulnerable you were when the abuse was going on. They can also paint a vivid picture of your abuser.

Certain other records are helpful too, if you have been self paying for any therapy, medical treatment, counseling, or anything else to help deal with your issues, make sure you save the receipts and invoices. These may count as damages.

Journal Exercise – Be Your Own Private Detective

This is an exercise that will organize the evidence you have found so far

- **Draw a magnifying glass, then write "Evidence"**

- **Then, make a list of every piece of evidence YOU WISH YOU COULD FIND about what happened to you – YOU DON'T NEED TO ACTUALLY HAVE IT.**

- **This list of "perfect" evidence will be a good starting point for working with your attorney to find evidence you can use.**

The Status Check

Now it's time to begin the actual process of evaluating your capability and readiness to undertake a lawsuit. You are going to self-gauge a number of different aspects that will help you make that evaluation. Let's take them one by one.

Emotional Readiness

Your first and most basic status check is going to be a "gut" check. You are going to look inside yourself and see if, at this present moment, you have enough strength to carry this process out, or if you have more healing to do before you use the law. Ask yourself some questions: Can I articulately describe what happened to me? Do I panic or have anxiety attacks when I have to talk or think about my abuse? Do I have access to enough relevant memories of my abuse, or are part or most of them repressed? What is my day-to-day level of emotional stability? What is my commitment level to suing my abuser? All of these questions lead up to the big question: Am I stable, capable, and strong enough to go through a very important but *difficult* process? If not, your immediate priority needs to be seeking the help, support, and therapy that can get you to that point. Doing a "where I am today check" can help you if you have lingering fear of your abuser:

Journal Exercise – I'm Not Helpless Anymore: Growing Up

This is an exercise that will put in perspective how much has changed, and alleviate the feeling of powerlessness survivors feel

- **Divide a page of your journal in half. On one side put the name you had for your abuser then, and on the other side put the name you know him by now, for me it was "Daddy" and "Mort."**

- **Then make a list from the child's point of view of who the perpetrator was when you saw him or her as a child: how big the perpetrator was, how large his hands were, how much taller than you he was, what power they had in the household, etc.**

Journal Exercise – I'm Not Helpless Anymore: Today

- **Use the other half of the page to list how things are now. Mort is an old man who is not that much bigger than me. He no longer feeds or clothes me, I am no longer under his control. When you take the time to complete this list, you will be surprised how much has changed. You are not that helpless child anymore.**

Support Structure

This is a question about the people and things in your life that you can draw strength and support from. Make a mental inventory of your allies in this fight. Who has your back, any day of the week, no matter what? Who are your friends and confidants? What family members do you love and trust get along with? Who are the non-family members that love you and make you happy? Are you seeing a therapist that can help you heal and guide you through this process? A support network can be incredibly helpful, people to talk to, people to have different perspectives, and people you can just hang out with and goof around with to blow off steam. People are important, but other parts of our lives can be critical too. Take inventory of healthy things that you draw strength and stability from: your job, your pets, your routine, your hobbies, etc. We all need to have outlets, especially in times of stress, the *infrastructure* of your life can be great to take comfort in when times are hard.

Journal Exercise – Emotional Readiness & Support

- **Sit down with your journal and open it to 2 blank pages. On the first page, write a paragraph about your Emotional Readiness, do some stream of consciousness about how capable and strong you feel.**

- **Underneath that, write "Support Structure" and make a list of the people and things you can rely on and draw strength from.**

Financial Awareness

There are two issues financially that I think are worth mentioning. First, a lawsuit may be demanding of your time and energy in a way that could potentially conflict with your work or employment situation. This effect is not dramatic, but you may need to arrange a free weekday on occasion and if your case goes to trial you will need to attend. The second has to do with certain attorney's *expenses*. Some civil attorneys take cases on contingency only, which means they will cover the cost of the expenses until a verdict or settlement is reached. Many, however, may want some sort of down-payment on the expenses they will incur before they begin. I do not say this to discourage you, because most attorneys can work with clients to find a solution, but civil cases can be expensive and some attorneys can require $1,000 or more to begin work, especially if the case seems like it will be especially difficult or long.

Prepared to Prove Your Case

You know what happened to you, and sometimes that is all that matters, but to put yourself in the best position to win, having evidence and corroboration beyond just your testimony is going to be important. Stop and think, right now, about what people, documents, and facts *prove* your case. Don't worry about the rules of evidence or anything law related, just think of how you would prove it to a friend who asked you to. Was one of your brothers or sisters also abused? Are there medical records of suspicious injuries from when you were a kid? Were there other victims? Did a church or a school know something about your abuse or your abuser? Did you tell anyone when you were young who could testify? Can you describe something from memory that proves your story? Think particularly hard about this section because it is important at every stage to have good evidence that proves your case. How strong the evidence is can be a big factor in deciding whether to go forward, the better your evidence is the better chance you have of winning. The less evidence you have, the harder you may have to fight.

Journal Exercise – What I Really Want

- This one is important. It's time to connect to what you want from a lawsuit.

- Write MONEY in all caps. Then do some stream of consciousness about what you will do with your abuser's money when you win.

- Then write HEALTHY, and stream of consciousness all the ways you want to be healthy.

- Then do the same for JUSTICE.

- Then for ACCOUNTABILITY - shifting the responsibility to the perpetrator.

- And finish by doing any other words or phrases that are important to you.

CHAPTER THREE*:* **Can I Sue After All This Time**
Paths to Justice

Sue [soo]

> verb

> to seek justice or right from a person by legal process, to go after

Time [tim]

> noun

> method of reckoning; an appointed fixed moment for something to happen, begin or end.

"We must use time wisely and forever realize that the time is always ripe to do right."

- Nelson Mandela

Time, Memory, & the Law

Time and the law have a complicated relationship even in normal circumstances, and when it comes to dealing with child sexual abuse, it is even more complex. The bottom line is, that if the *statute of limitations* (aka the "time-limit") for suing your abuser has run out, you will have a very hard time suing your perpetrator.

So, I'm going to do my best to give you common sense explanations and practical understandings of legal concepts like *statutes of limitations, tolling, delayed discovery and window legislation.*

The rules for sexual abuse are special. They are an *exception* to the normal rules. They are different because of the special circumstances of *memory repression.* Because CSA victims often forget they were abused, it is a much different process for them to get justice from the legal system than for the average person. In many states, the statutes and rules themselves are different for victims who repressed their abuse! For this reason, to understand the law, we have to understand the science behind the memory problems many victims face.

Why People Forget Abuse

"Amnesia for childhood sexual abuse is a condition. The existence of this condition is beyond dispute."

- Jim Hopper, Ph.D., Clinical Instructor in Psychology, Harvard Medical School

Trauma is powerful, and when a human undergoes trauma the effects can manifest in many different ways. You may be familiar with something called "PTSD," also known as *Post-Traumatic Stress Disorder*, which we commonly associate with war veterans who have been through traumatic combat. PTSD is a severe anxiety disorder that can cause nightmares, flashbacks, bouts of anger, insomnia, paranoia, and memory loss, among many other symptoms. The way trauma affects each unique individual is so vastly different that very broad, catch-all diagnoses like PTSD are needed to properly identify their symptoms. The following are clinical symptoms associated with PTSD:

- Recurrent re-experiencing of the trauma (for example, troublesome memories, flashbacks that are usually caused by reminders of the traumatic events, recurring nightmares about the trauma, reliving of the trauma)

- Avoidance to the point of having a phobia of places, people, smells, sounds and experiences that reminds you of the trauma or a general numbing of emotional responsiveness

- Chronic physical signs of paranoia, including sleep problems, trouble concentrating, irritability, anger, poor concentration, blackouts or difficulty remembering things, increased tendency and reaction to being startled, and hypervigilance (excessive watchfulness) to threat

Every human being on Earth is affected by violations of (or threats to) their physical, sexual, and psychological integrity. Think about it, even the best and brightest of *soldiers* can have their foundations rocked by trauma. If trained warriors can be psychologically affected in so many strange ways, it makes perfect sense that the young victims of sexual abuse can have memory loss and repression among their symptoms.

Let's be clear: memory repression due to childhood sexual abuse is as real as any other mental or psychological ailment. Don't let anyone tell you it isn't. When I was a litigator in this field the science behind this condition was attacked from all angles on a regular basis. We faced constant skepticism and attempts to discredit and skew the science. Even then, we were able to show judges and juries the scientific truth. These days, *memory repression* and *dissociative amnesia* have been recognized again and again in scientific journals and vindicated by studies that prove they are legitimate psychological conditions.

So *why* do survivors repress the memories of their abuse? There are many theories, some scientific, some anecdotal. Some psychologists see memory repression, especially in cases where it is caused by severe trauma, as an extreme coping mechanism. When normal coping mechanisms become overwhelmed and are unable to process an event, natural "emergency" coping mechanisms kick-in so we can keep operating and functioning even in the face of overwhelming stress. One of the strongest coping mechanisms we have is *dissociation*, where the brain "turns-off" some aspect of outside experience so that they are not experienced as part of the "self" and are not accessible the way normal memories are.

Put very unscientifically, it's like the brain makes an executive decision that these particular memories are too painful, too horrific, and too damaging to your daily life to let them be remembered, and so the brain puts them in a secret vault and goes about its business. Dissociation represents the very human capacity to adapt and to do what's necessary to survive. Survivors of every type of human tragedy, especially children, have been known to experience dissociation and repression of memories. It is nothing to be ashamed of and it's perfectly natural. Think of it like this, if you had been getting beaten with a stick, your skin would have protected itself with a callus, this was like a very thick callus on your mind.

If you believe you have repressed memories from your childhood, you need to proceed responsibly and with caution. Many people who hear of repression and dissociation in the media and who believe they may themselves have been victims often feel the urge to go "digging" through their memories through various methods. I cannot urge you strongly enough to find a qualified therapist who has experience in safely uncovering these memories in a controlled environment of support. A qualified professional will use techniques like free association, guided meditations, visualizations, age regression, and projective drawings to safely bring any memories to the surface.

Never expose yourself to "triggers" or attempt hypnosis without the guidance of a therapist or psychologist. There is double danger in trying to "dig up" your memories on your own. First of all, when memories come back it can be an intense and traumatic experience. I remember how I felt when certain memories flooded back from wherever I had locked them away. They wracked me with anxiety and filled me with overwhelming emotion when they floated to the surface. It was a necessary part of the healing process, but a painful one that I am forever thankful I had a comfort and guidance of a trusted therapist to see me through. The second danger is that your memories could be tainted or influenced by the method they were uncovered with, or at least someone could *argue* that they were, like when you want to testify at trial.

Be careful, be responsible, be gentle, and remember to ask yourself the reasons that you want to uncover your memories before you do.

When People Remember

We know the mind can bury and quarantine memories that are overwhelmingly traumatic, but what makes those memories come back? If they are so painful, why do they bubble to the surface instead of staying locked away forever?

The physical and psychological reasons that these memories return are as complicated as the reasons they are buried in the first place.

There are again many theories, but one that I find resonates with many survivors is that these repressed or dissociated experiences surface when the mind becomes strong enough and mature enough to fully process them.

Besides, any survivor who has had to confront repressed memories, like myself, knows that just because a memory is "quarantined" in your mind does not mean you aren't affected by it. We suffer from anxiety, neurosis, depression, we feel anguish, we act out, and we don't feel that our sexuality is healthy, all *because* of what happened to us. Just because we've locked the basement doesn't mean that our memories aren't screaming and pounding behind the door. It just means we don't know why we feel this way!

"Having repressed memories doesn't mean you don't have a problem, it means you have a hidden problem"

- Leonard Ludovico

We are fooling ourselves when we pretend that our repressed memories aren't affecting us. We are confused, have gaps in what we remember, and we can *feel* something missing, something wrong, like a slow leak of toxins contaminating the system. I know survivors who had years of therapy before they ever fully remembered being abused, and they always thought that the "root" of their problems was hidden. It was! They were treating the symptoms, not the source. Only when their minds were ready did the "root" show itself.

Shari Karney

"It was terrible knowing that something was wrong but not knowing what it was. I would hyperventilate and panic around certain men, even nice ones that I knew. I had an overwhelming feeling that something wasn't right for years before my memories finally came up."

- Beth, CSA Survivor

Sometimes dissociated experiences or repressed memories can come back spontaneously, other times they are brought back by *triggers*. I have worked with countless survivors in my career, and in my experience, especially in women, memories tend to begin to return in the early and mid-thirties. Many landmark events typically happen around this phase as well, and often they trigger a release of memory.

I have talked to women whose memories returned when they gave birth, when they got married, or when their small children reached the same age of their own abuse. In reality it can be anything, a certain cologne, a taste or a texture in the mouth, certain foods, smells, the feel of a certain fabric, a body position, a sexual event, being restrained, every trigger is different. To this day, I cannot bear the smell of an overripe banana. A fellow survivor I know can't stand peanut butter; her abuser put peanut butter on her as a child and licked it off.

Film and television are also common triggers. Years ago, it was in the news that many World War II veterans were having flashbacks while watching *Saving Private Ryan*, because of how realistically it depicted the landing on Omaha Beach. The very same thing can happen to a rape or abuse victim when watching a graphic movie such as *"The Accused"* where Jodi Foster gets gang raped in a bar, especially if the scene is reminiscent of a traumatic event. If you suspect you have repressed memories of abuse, be mindful of how triggers work and be careful to protect yourself. If you find yourself in a flashback or experiencing a memory, try not to panic, let it come, and do your very best to remind yourself it's going to be okay.

No matter what brought your memory back, try not to fight against it. There is wisdom in your body. Your brain did what it had to do to protect you when you were young. Trust that wisdom. If your memories have returned, it is your body's way of telling you that it is time to begin to heal, and pain is a natural part of that process.

"There is no coming to consciousness without pain."

- Carl Jung

Remember this: The pain is not meaningless, you do not suffer just to suffer. Pain is the impetus for change. When we touch a fire, it causes pain, and that pain makes us yank our hand back. If we didn't feel the pain, it may not hurt, but our hand would be burned so badly we couldn't use it. Psychological pain is there for the same reason, to urge us to correct what is wrong, to seek therapy, to deal with the abuse, to become who we want to be. I heard an interview with Lance Armstrong that put it in a beautiful perspective, he said "Pain is temporary. It may last a minute, or an hour, or a day, or a year, but eventually it will subside and something else will take its place. If I quit, however, it lasts forever." I think survivors can relate to that concept; that when you are moving *through* it, pain is temporary, but if we let it beat us we will sit with it forever...

What Happens When Adults Tell

Adult survivors who want to tell their stories face many challenges, especially within their families. One thing I always try to explain to survivors that come to me is how hard people will fight to protect their illusions. Abusers will fight to keep secrets hidden, to maintain the control that they have held, to continue to be able to abuse, and to preserve the images of themselves that they have created. Mothers, grandparents, siblings, and extended family can potentially be in severe denial or can be viciously protective of their *illusion* of being part of a healthy harmonious family. Here are some of the common negative responses to an adult revealing their story of abuse

- *"Let it go. That was years ago."*
- *"The past is in the past. You got over it, you're fine."*
- *"Why do you want to tear this family apart?"*
- *"I don't believe you, you never said anything back then."*
- *"This is just an excuse for your problems."*
- *"He could never do that, he's a great guy!"*
- *"He's just an old man now, leave him alone."*

Not a single one of those is an appropriate response from a family member. Do not let them get to you. It doesn't matter how long ago it was, it doesn't matter that you overcame it, it doesn't matter that your family didn't want to hear it, it was wrong, it was a crime, and the truth needs to be told. *You* are not hurting the family by telling the truth, *they* hurt the family by abusing you and *they* hurt the family by keeping quiet and allowing it to happen. It doesn't matter how nice a predator is to everyone else, or how he supports them financially, or how respected he is, *he is still a predator.*

As an attorney, I worked with a beautiful young woman named Allison. She classically pretty and always very well put together with her shoulder length brown hair done up in different styles, but she was also always withdrawn. She had been abused and molested by her uncle from puberty through most of high school. The uncle was beloved by the family, everyone thought he was funny and gregarious and successful and fun. He would get her alone and force himself on her, sometimes while her parents were in the house. When she was in her late twenties, she finally came forward with the abuse. Her family members hated having to see their favorite uncle for what he was, and not see him as the guy they had always liked. When she told her father, this was his first response:

"You're lying. He doesn't need you to get women. He's married! How f***ing dare you lie about my brother."

The first one to believe Allison was actually the Uncle's wife! Then her mother believed her, and finally, the rest of the family. Unfortunately for most of us, Allison is the exception, most of us face an even harder road when trying to tell our stories as adults.

As adults we get less sympathy. Because we are grown up and seem capable of protecting ourselves, it is harder for those we tell to see us as victims, they don't see us as the children we were when these crimes were committed. I learned a powerful trial technique from a California sexual abuse litigator when I started taking a lot of CSA cases. He gave his closing argument in every abuse case standing in front of a picture of the victim at the age when they were abused. He would tell the jury "see this child, *this* is who was abused." It was a good reminder that the people we tell see us as the adults we are now.

Whatever the reaction is, you can handle it better if you understand the difficulties that come with telling as an adult. You can be better prepared if you are mindful of other people's interests and issues, and you can feel better about your difficulties in telling if you know you are not alone.

Finally, adults that expose past abuses face the challenges that come from the passage of time. The truth is harder to prove once memories fade and physical evidence disappears. Law enforcement agencies face more challenges and are more reluctant to investigate old cases. Plaintiffs' attorneys know that old cases are harder to recover for and are more hesitant to commit their time and resources.

Despite these hurdles, with some thought and some planning, you can have the best chance possible to sue and find justice, especially if you know what to expect from the legal system.

> **Journal Exercise – Spot the Nonsense**
> - **Write down 3 negative responses you got when you came forward about your abuse.**
> - **Then, write why each reason is total BS!**
> - **Chantelle's list looked like this:**
>> **Why are you doing this to me?**
>> **Do you know what this will do to your father?**
> **I don't want to know. You are a liar.**
>
> - **Then she did a stream of consciousness about why each of those responses were wrong, unfair, and hurtful.**

Legal Basics of Time & The Law

This is where we begin to get into the law itself. I'm going to do my best to give you common sense explanations and practical understandings of legal concepts like *statutes of limitations,* hopefully without sounding like a law professor. Always remember that I am teaching you basic legal principles, and that the laws are different in every state. The things I say may not be the law where you live, I am just trying to show you the ropes so you can understand your own case.

The laws in every state for survivors of sexual abuse are different, and some are so complex and convoluted that even *I* am stumped at times when reviewing all the state statutes. What I have explained below may *not* be the law where you live, I am just trying to show you the ropes so you can understand your own case. Here we go.

Statutes of Limitations - A Critical Issue!

Every state has statutes of limitations for when a lawsuit may be filed for personal injury. (Child sexual abuse is a personal injury, it is also a crime, but we will cover that later). Put very basically, statutes of limitations (or SOLs) tell us what the maximum amount time after an event has occurred that one can bring a lawsuit based on that event. For example, the statute of limitations for a personal injury claim in the state of California is 2 years. That means the following: if you are run-over in the crosswalk by Debbie Distracted (she didn't see you because she was texting) and her Buick breaks your legs on February 1st of 2012, you must officially file your claim in court before February 1st of 2014, or else you are forever barred from bringing a claim. Of course there are some exceptions, this is the law after all! A big one is for things that happen before the victim is of adult age, usually 18, but most exceptions aren't important for understanding the basics.

Statutes of limitations (SOLs) are also not just one-size-fits-all. In California, the SOL for medical malpractice is 3 years. Let's take a similar example: unlike when Debbie Distracted hits you with her car, when Dr. Clumsy leaves a towel inside you after surgery you have 3 full years to bring a claim before it is barred. That makes sense because it usually takes longer to figure out that your doctor treated you improperly than if you were hurt in an accident.

The reason that these laws exist is *efficiency*. If everyone with a claim could wait as long as they pleased to bring their claim, it would cause problems. Memories fade, records get destroyed, witnesses die or move away, businesses need to know when their liability ends. All of those are good, logical reasons for SOLs.

Why Having a SOL for Childhood Sexual Abuse is Unfair

Each and every reason that they make sense comes crashing down when the statutes are applied to sexual abuse survivors. When a child represses memories of abuse that only reemerge later in life, having a time limit works *against* justice. In California, the statute for intentional torts, which are basically harmful, intentional acts, is only 1 year! For survivors, these statutes were padlocking the courthouse doors, which is why we fought tooth and nail to change the law in 1990.

If it were up to me, I would abolish all statute of limitations for child sexual abuse and treat it as we do murder. But it is not up to me, so my goal is to help you maneuver through a broken legal system. Because every time a survivor brings a case, it can break a vicious cycle, protect other victims, help other victims come forward, stop perpetrators, hold organizations and companies responsible, help stop child sexual abuse, and compensate the survivor for the damages caused by the abuse.

Tolling of the Statute Until You Reach Your 18th Birthday

Almost every state stops the running of the SOL ("tolls it") for victims of child sexual abuse until your 18th birthday. After you reach 18, in most states, the clock starts ticking for when you can file a lawsuit against your abuser. For survivors, some states give victims anywhere from 2 years past their 18th birthday, to 30 years past their 18th birthday, to file a suit. The average number of years that most states stop the running of the statute of limitations (toll) is 5 years.

Therefore, in many states, you have to file your lawsuit for child sexual abuse by your 23rd birthday or else you are forever barred from bringing a claim. Of course there are some exceptions, this is the law after all! A big one is delayed discovery.

Three Legal Methods for Defeating the Statute of Limitations

Delayed Discovery

Delayed discovery is normally used in asbestos type cases, where toxic materials that cause cancers lay undiscoverable for decades. This doctrine was created because it was unfair that the statute of limitations was barring cases when the plaintiffs didn't even know they were sick for years! We argued that repressed memories of sexual abuse were like those undiscoverable toxins, and that victims had no way of knowing about the abuse until the "cancers" surfaced. Mary Doe had repressed the memories of her abuse until adulthood and she deserved her day in court.

Think about it, the court said she was "*sitting on her rights*" by not filing a lawsuit by age 19. What were most of us doing before age 19? Going to prom, doing college applications, living at home (often with our abuser), and living life! Mary didn't remember her abuse until she was 25. I didn't remember being abused until I was almost 30! The exact same principle applies, our abuse was undetectable until many years after it happened, just like the carcinogens (cancer causing substances) were in asbestos cases.

If you can successfully argue delayed discovery in your state, you might be able to toll the SOL on your claim for the time that you didn't remember your abuse.

Fraudulent Concealment

Fraudulent concealment is another very interesting legal theory that can be applied to sexual abuse cases, here's how it works: When someone lies about a fact, hides a fact, or conceals a fact, the law punishes them for the damage their dishonesty causes and/or does not allow them to be protected by their lies. The law is much more complex that that, but at its heart that's how it works. It is mostly used in cases that involve a legal *relationship* that carries duties, such as a lawyer-client, doctor-patient, and buyer-seller relationships.

Here's an example: If we make a contract for me to buy your house, and I tell you there is no mold, then I paint over the mold and make a fake mold inspection certificate, and then (obviously) there turns out to be all sorts of mold in the house, you can't enforce our contract against me because you lied. Now let's make it more relevant, let's say you buy the house and don't find the mold for 3 years because I painted over it. When you finally do find it - the statute of limitations has passed. If I allege fraudulent concealment the courts can toll (or pause) the SOL because you couldn't discover the mold *because I lied and covered it up*.

Now that is obviously way oversimplified! But let's look at the principle and apply it to child sexual abuse. Almost always there is some sort of legal-duty relationship between abusers and victims: parent-child, teacher-child, clergy-child, etc. If the perpetrator took steps to keep his young victim from telling, remembering, or understanding, it's a lot like painting over the mold – he is destroying the evidence that the damage is there, growing and getting worse all the time.

- *"If you tell you'll get in big trouble."*
- *"It'll hurt your mommy if she finds out."*
- *"This is our secret. If anyone finds out, I'll throw you out of this house."*
- *"I will kill you if you tell anyone."*
- *"What we do is God's will and you will not betray God."*
- *"This is between us, if you tell anyone, I won't love you anymore."*
- *"This is perfectly normal, this is what Daddies do, don't worry."*
- *"You are such a good girl for keeping our secret."*
- *"I'm your father and I have the right to do whatever I want."*

Some of these are outright threats and some of them of them are more subtle. All of them are an *abuse of the relationship of trust* and are attempts to *hide or conceal the truth*. Young victims are inexperienced and don't know what duties the adults around them carry, and so very commonly the relationship is taken advantage of by predators. That's why fraudulent concealment can be a viable method for overcoming SOLs, especially in cases when the abuser took steps to silence their victim.

Window of Opportunity - "Window Legislation"

Window legislation is special legislation enacted by state lawmakers to permit survivors' to file a claim during a limited time period even after the SOL has expired. It's a "fix-it" strategy. Recognizing that survivors of sexual abuse have long been denied justice, some state legislators have passed a law giving survivors a "window of opportunity" to sue for money damages even after the SOL has run out.

The "window" period is usually short and fixed. For example, California and Delaware have both opened "windows" which revived the ability of victims to bring suit. In California, the window was opened in 2003 for one year and about 1,000 new suits were filed which identified approximately 300 perpetrators. Delaware opened a two-year window in 2007 that expired on July 10, 2009. Ask your lawyer to look into this type of legislation in your state.

There is a downside, however, because legislators use these windows to "close the book" on old sexual abuse cases, and if you "miss the window" it may be harder to find another exception to the SOL of your case.

The Next Great Idea - Get Creative

The three legal concepts above have been accepted in many jurisdictions (but not all) as valid exceptions to the standard statutes of limitations. It is important to be aware of these concepts no matter what your state's law is. If your state doesn't recognize either, remember that the law can be changed by the right case.

In the law, sometimes justice takes creativity. My two suggestions to overcome SOLs are only the beginning, maybe your lawyer can think even further outside the box; challenge them to do so! The bottom line is: if *fairness* is on your side, you always have a chance, it just may take hard work.

State By State Statutes of Limitations Reference Chart

To give you a general idea of Statutes of Limitations across the country, we have included a state by state reference guide for you to refer to. As of the writing of this book, there is relevant pending legislation in New York, New Jersey, and Georgia that could change the information contained in this chart.

DISCLAIMER: This guide is for informational purposes only, and is not legal advice. These laws are subject to statutory change and court interpretation. You should consult an attorney when making a determination about any legal claim. No matter whether the chart indicates the Statute of Limitations has expired or not on any claim you have, we recommend you consult an attorney. The purpose of the chart is to give general information to help survivors and their supporters in assessing whether legal means will aid healing from childhood sexual. The authors and publishers shall have neither liability nor responsibility to any person or entity with respect to any loss or damage caused, or alleged to be caused directly or indirectly by the information in this book.

STATE CIVIL STATUTES OF LIMITATION ON CHILD SEXUAL ABUSE CLAIMS

Useful Terminology:

Statute of Limitations: The statute of limitations is the maximum amount of years that someone has to bring a lawsuit, starting from the date of injury. This time limit varies from state to state and depends upon what type of lawsuit someone wants to bring. There are special rules for victims of child sexual abuse.

Special rules for victims of child sexual abuse:

1. **Age of Majority:** In circumstances of child sexual abuse, most states allow a victim to sue after they become an **adult**, which is called the "**age of majority.**" The age of majority varies from state to state. Once a person reaches the age of majority, *then* the statute of limitations begins to run. **For example: In the state of Arizona, if a child was molested at age 9, that child, once he/she reaches age 18 (age of majority), he/she has 2 years, until age 20, to bring a lawsuit for injuries as a result of the molest.**

2. **Delayed Discovery Rules:** In some instances, victims may not know or realize until many years later that they were injured by an act or acts of molest done to them as children. In those cases, the law allows a victim to sue once he/she **discovers** the repressed memory of the injury or harm caused by childhood sexual abuse. The statute of limitations, then, does not begin to run until after the date they discover the harm. **For example: In the state of Arizona, if a child was molested at age 9 and doesn't realize the harm caused until age 45, he/she has 2 years, or until age 47, to bring a lawsuit for injuries as a result of the molest.** Not all states apply the special discovery rule.

STATES	AGE OF MAJORITY	STATUTE OF LIMITATIONS	DELAYED DISCOVERY
Alabama	19 years old	In Alabama, you have **2** years from age **19** to file a lawsuit. You can sue by your **21**st birthday.	Alabama does not make allowances for repressed memory for childhood sexual abuse by stopping the clock from running.

STATES	AGE OF MAJORITY	STATUTE OF LIMITATIONS	DELAYED DISCOVERY
Alaska	18 years old	In Alaska there is no time limit for suing where there has been **felony sexual abuse** of a minor. The ages of the perpetrator/victim; extent and seriousness of injury; relationship between perpetrator/victim, can change time periods. *See website below for actual law. The law in Alaska is very complex. Contact an attorney for details. For **misdemeanor sexual abuse** of minors you have **3** years from age **18** to bring a lawsuit. You can sue by your **21**st birthday.	Yes, if you are older than 21, a lawsuit may be brought within **3** years from the date you discover the injury/harm caused by childhood sexual abuse.
Arizona	18 years old	In Arizona, you have **2** years from age **18** to file a lawsuit. You can sue by your **20**th birthday.	Yes, if you are older than 20, a lawsuit may be brought within **2** years from the date you discover the injury/harm caused by childhood sexual abuse.
Arkansas	21 years old	In Arkansas, you have **3** years from age **21** to file a lawsuit. You can sue by your **24**th birthday.	Yes, if you are older than 20, a lawsuit may be brought within **3** years from the date you discover the injury/harm caused by childhood sexual abuse.
California	18 years old	In California, you have **8** years from age **18** to file a lawsuit. You can sue by your **26**th birthday.	Yes, if you are older than 26, a lawsuit may be brought within **3** years from the date you discover the injury/harm caused by childhood sexual abuse.

STATES	AGE OF MAJORITY	STATUTE OF LIMITATIONS	DELAYED DISCOVERY
Colorado	18 years old	In Colorado, you have **6** years from age **18** to file a lawsuit. You can sue by your **24**[th] birthday.	Yes, if you are older than 24, a lawsuit may be brought within **6** years from date you discover the injury/harm caused by childhood sexual abuse.
Connecticut	18 years old	There is no time limit for suing where the perpetrator has been criminally convicted of 1st degree sexual assault (i.e. forced sexual intercourse or sexual intercourse with a person under the age of 13). *See website below for actual law. For all other offenses, (i.e. personal injury, including emotional distress, caused by sexual abuse, sexual exploitation or sexual assault) you have **30** years from age **18** to file a lawsuit. You can sue by your **48**[th] birthday.	Connecticut does not make allowances for repressed memory for childhood sexual abuse by stopping the clock from running.
Delaware	N/A	In the state of Delaware, there is no time limit for suing where there has been sexual abuse of minor.	There is no time limit from the date you discover the injury/harm caused by childhood sexual abuse.
District of Columbia	18 years old	In the District of Columbia, you have **7** years from age **18** to file a lawsuit. You can sue by your **25**[th] birthday.	Yes, if you are older than 25, a lawsuit may be brought within **3** years from date you discover the injury/harm caused by childhood sexual abuse.

Shari Karney

STATES	AGE OF MAJORITY	STATUTE OF LIMITATIONS	DELAYED DISCOVERY
Florida	18 years old	In Florida, there is no time limit for suing where there has been sexual battery against victims under 16 years old. *See website below for actual law. For all other sexual abuse claims you have **7** years from age **18** to bring a lawsuit. You can sue by your **25**th birthday.	Yes, if you are older than 25, a lawsuit may be brought within **7** years from date you discover the injury/harm caused by childhood sexual abuse.
Georgia	18 years old	In Georgia, you have **5** years from age **18** to file a lawsuit. You can sue by your **23**rd birthday.	Not certain; law is changing.
Hawaii	18 years old	In Hawaii, you have **2** years from age **18** to bring a lawsuit. You can sue by your **20**th birthday.	Yes, if you are older than 20, a lawsuit may be brought within **2** years from the date you discover the injury/harm caused by childhood/sexual abuse.
Idaho	18 years old	In Idaho, you have **5** years from age **18** to bring a lawsuit. You can sue by your **23**rd birthday.	Yes, if you are older than 23, a lawsuit may be brought within **5** years from date you discover the injury/harm caused by childhood/sexual abuse.
Illinois	18 years old	In Illinois, you have **10** years from age **18** to file a lawsuit. You can sue by your **28**th birthday.	Yes, if you are older than 28, a lawsuit may be brought within **5** years from date you discover the injury/harm caused by childhood sexual abuse.

68

STATE	AGE OF MAJORITY	STATUTE OF LIMITATIONS	DELAYED DISCOVERY
Indiana	18 years old	In Indiana, you have **2** years from age **18** to file a lawsuit. You can sue by your **20th** birthday.	Yes, if you are older than 20, a lawsuit may be brought within **2** years from the date you discover the injury/harm caused by childhood sexual abuse.
Iowa	18 years old	In Iowa, you have **5** years from age **18** to file a lawsuit where there is sex abuse or exploitation by a counselor, therapist or school employee. *See website below for actual law. You can sue by your **23rd** birthday. For all other sex abuse offenses, you have **2** years from the age of **18** to file a lawsuit. You can sue by your **20th** birthday.	Yes, if you are older than 20/23 (depending on the offense), a lawsuit may be brought within **4** years from date you discover the injury/harm caused by childhood sexual abuse.
Kansas	18 years old	In Kansas, you have **3** years from age **18** to bring a lawsuit. You can sue by your **21st** birthday.	Yes, if you are older than 21, a lawsuit may be brought within **3** years from the date you discover the injury/harm caused by childhood sexual abuse.
Kentucky	18 years old	In Kentucky, you have **5** years from age **18** to bring a lawsuit. You can sue by your **23rd** birthday.	Yes, if you are older than 23, a lawsuit may be brought within **5** years from the date you discover the injury/harm caused by childhood sexual abuse.
Louisiana	18 years old	In Louisiana, you have **10** years from age **18** to bring a lawsuit. You can sue by your **28th** birthday.	Yes, if you are older than 28, a lawsuit may be brought within **10** years from the date you discover the injury/harm caused by childhood sexual abuse.
Maine	N/A	In Maine, there is no time limit for suing where there has been child sexual abuse.	Yes, there is no time limit from the date you discover the injury/harm caused by childhood sexual abuse.

69

STATE	AGE OF MAJORITY	STATUTE OF LIMITATIONS	DELAYED DISCOVERY
Maryland	18 years old	In Maryland, you have **7** years from age **18** to bring a lawsuit. You can sue by your **25**th birthday.	Yes, if you are older than 25, a lawsuit may be brought within **7** years from the date you discover the injury/harm caused by childhood sexual abuse.
Massachusetts	18 years old	In Massachusetts, you have **3** years from age **18** to file a lawsuit. You can sue by your **21**st birthday.	Yes, if you are older than 21, a lawsuit may be brought within **3** years from the date you discover the injury/harm caused by childhood sexual abuse.
Michigan	19 years old	In Michigan, you have **2** years from age **19** to file a lawsuit. While there is no special statute addressing child sexual abuse, a lawsuit for personal injury can be brought by your **21**st birthday.	Michigan does not make allowances for repressed memory for childhood sexual abuse by stopping the clock from running.
Minnesota	18 years old	In Minnesota, you have **6** years from age **18** to file a lawsuit. You can sue by your **24**th birthday.	Yes, if you are older than 24, a lawsuit may be brought within **6** years from the date you discover the injury/harm caused by childhood sexual abuse.
Mississippi	21 years old	In Mississippi, you have **1** year from age **21** to file a lawsuit. While there is no special statute addressing child sexual abuse, a lawsuit for personal injury can be brought by your **22**nd birthday.	There is limited availability for latent discovery of injury/harm caused by childhood sexual abuse.
Missouri	21 years old	In Missouri, you have **10** years from age **21** to file a lawsuit. You can sue by your **31**st birthday.	Yes, if you are older than 31, a lawsuit may be brought within **3** years from the date you discover the injury/harm caused by childhood sexual abuse.
Montana	18 years old	In Montana, you have **3** years from age **18** to file a lawsuit. You can sue by your **21**st birthday.	Yes, if you are older than 21, a lawsuit may be brought within **3** years from the date you discover the injury/harm caused by childhood sexual abuse.

STATE	AGE OF MAJORITY	STATUTE OF LIMITATIONS	DELAYED DISCOVERY
Nebraska	20 years old	In Nebraska, you have **4** years from age **20** to file a lawsuit. While there is no special statute addressing child sexual abuse, a lawsuit for personal injury can be brought by your **24**th birthday.	In Nebraska, there is limited availability for delayed discovery.
Nevada	18 years old	In Nevada, you have **10** years from age **18** to file a lawsuit. You can sue by your **28**th birthday.	Yes, if you are older than 28, a lawsuit may be brought within **10** years from the date you discover the injury/harm caused by childhood sexual abuse.
New Hampshire	18 years old	In New Hampshire, you have **12** years from age **18** to file a lawsuit. You can sue by your **30**th birthday.	Yes, if you are older than 30, a lawsuit may be brought within **3** years from the date you discover the injury caused by childhood sexual abuse.
New Jersey	18 years old	In New Jersey, you have **2** years from age **18** to file a lawsuit. You can sue by your **20**th birthday.	Yes, if you are older than 20, a lawsuit may be brought within **2** years from the date you discover the injury/harm caused by childhood sexual abuse.
New Mexico	N/A	In New Mexico, a lawsuit can be brought by your **24**th birthday.	Yes, if you are older than 24, a lawsuit may be brought within **3** years from the date you discover the injury/harm caused by childhood sexual abuse.
New York	18 years old	In New York, you have **5** years from age **18** to file a lawsuit for 1st degree sex offenses against children. You can sue by your **23**rd birthday. For lessor offenses you have **3** years from age **18** to file a lawsuit. You can sue by your **21**st birthday. *See website below for actual law. The law is complex. Contact an attorney for details.	New York does not make allowances for repressed memory for childhood sexual abuse by stopping the clock from running.

71

STATES	AGE OF MAJORITY	STATUTE OF LIMITATIONS	DELAYED DISCOVERY
North Carolina	18 years old	In North Carolina, you have **3** years from age **18** to file a lawsuit. While there is no special statute addressing child sexual abuse, a lawsuit can be brought for personal injury by your **21**st birthday.	In North Carolina, there is limited availability for delayed discovery.
North Dakota	18 years old	In North Dakota, you have **2** years from age **18** to file a lawsuit. While there is no special statute addressing child sexual abuse, a lawsuit can be brought for assault, battery, false imprisonment by your **20th** birthday.	Yes, if you are older than 20, a lawsuit may be brought within **2** years from the date you discover the injury/harm caused by childhood sexual abuse.
Ohio	18 years old	In Ohio, you have **12** years from age **18** to file a lawsuit. You can sue by your **30th** birthday.	Ohio does not make allowances for repressed memory for childhood sexual abuse by stopping the clock from running.
Oklahoma	18 years old	In Oklahoma, you have **2** years from age **18** to file a lawsuit. You can sue by your **20th** birthday.	Yes, if you are older than 20, a lawsuit may be brought within **2** years from the date you discover the injury/harm caused by childhood sexual abuse.
Oregon	N/A	In Oregon, a lawsuit can be brought by your **40th** birthday.	Yes, if you are older than 40, a lawsuit may be brought within **5** years from the date you discover the injury/harm caused by childhood sexual abuse.
Pennsylvania	18 years old	In Pennsylvania, you have **12** years from age **18** to file a lawsuit. You can sue by your **30th** birthday.	Pennsylvania does not make allowances for repressed memory for childhood sexual abuse by stopping the clock from running.
Rhode Island	18 years old	In Rhode Island, you have **7** years from age **18** to file a lawsuit. You can sue by your **25th** birthday.	Yes, if you are older than 25, a lawsuit may be brought within **7** years from the date you discover the injury/harm caused by childhood sexual abuse.

STATE	AGE OF MAJORITY	STATUTE OF LIMITATIONS	DELAYED DISCOVERY
South Carolina	21 years old	In South Carolina, you have **6** years from age **21** to file a lawsuit. You can sue by your **27**th birthday.	Yes, if you are older than 27, a lawsuit may be brought within **3** years from the date you discover the injury/harm caused by childhood sexual abuse.
South Dakota	18 years old	In South Dakota, you have **3** years from age **18** to file a lawsuit. You can sue by your **21**st birthday.	Yes, if you are older than 21, a lawsuit may be brought within **3** years from the date you discover the injury/harm caused by childhood sexual abuse.
Tennessee	18 years old	In Tennessee, you have **1** year from age **18** to file a lawsuit. While there is no special statute addressing child sexual abuse, a lawsuit for personal injury can be brought by your **19**th birthday.	Yes, if you are older than 19, a lawsuit may be brought within **1** year from the date you discover the injury/harm caused by childhood sexual abuse.
Texas	18 years old	In Texas, you have **5** years from age **18** to file a lawsuit. You can sue by your **23**rd birthday.	Yes, if you are older than 23, a lawsuit may be brought within **5** years from the date you discover the injury/harm caused by childhood sexual abuse.
Utah	18 years old	In Utah, you have **4** years from age **18** to file a lawsuit. You can sue by your **22**nd birthday.	Yes, if you are older than 22, a lawsuit may be brought within **4** years from the date you discover the injury/harm caused by childhood sexual abuse.
Vermont	18 years old	In Vermont, you have **6** years from age **18** to file a lawsuit. You can sue by your **24**th birthday.	Yes, if you are older than 24, a lawsuit may be brought within **6** years from the date you discover the injury/harm caused by childhood sexual abuse.
Virginia	18 years old	In Virginia, you have **2** years from age **18** to file a lawsuit. You can sue by your **20**th birthday.	Yes, if you are older than 20, a lawsuit may be brought within **2** years from the date you discover the injury caused by childhood sexual abuse.

Shari Karney

STATES	AGE OF MAJORITY	STATUTE OF LIMITATIONS	DELAYED DISCOVERY
Washington	18 years old	In Washington, you have **3** years from age **18** to file a lawsuit. You can sue by your **21st** birthday.	Yes, if you are older than 21, a lawsuit may be brought within **3** years from the date you discover the injury/harm caused by childhood sexual abuse.
West Virginia	18 years old	In West Virginia, you have **2** years from age **18** to file a lawsuit. While there is no special statute addressing child sexual abuse, a lawsuit can be brought for personal injury by your **20th** birthday.	Yes, if you are older than 20, a lawsuit may be brought within **2** years from the date you discover the injury/harm caused by childhood sexual abuse.
Wisconsin	18 years old	In Wisconsin, a lawsuit can be brought by your **35th** birthday.	Yes, if you are older than 35, a lawsuit may be brought after the date you discover the injury/harm caused by childhood sexual abuse.
Wyoming	18 years old	In Wyoming, you have **8** years from age **18** to file a lawsuit. You can sue by your **26th** birthday.	Yes, if you are older than 26, a lawsuit may be brought within **3** years from the date you discover the injury/harm caused by childhood sexual abuse.

The information contained in this chart is not to be construed as legal advice and is provided for informational purposes only. While the information is intended to be accurate and up-to-date, no warranty is provided as to the accuracy of the contents of this information either implied or expressed. **We recommend you contact a competent, independent attorney for more details regarding your personal situation.**

*_www.ndaa.org_ Search within the website for _Statute of Limitations for Civil Action for Offense Against Children 2010._

CHAPTER FOUR: **Holding Your Perpetrator Responsible**

How to Build a Good Case

Perpetrator [**per**-pi-trey-ter]

> noun
>
> inflict, pull off, carry out, achieve

Responsible [ri-**spon**-*suh-buh*l]

> adj.
>
> to be called to account, liable, to be forced to answer for one's conduct

"Justice is not to be taken by storm. She is to be wooed by slow advances."

- Benjamin Cardozo, Supreme Court Justice, 1932-1938

Who Can I Sue?

Believe it or not, this question is more complicated than it seems. Clearly the person who abused you is the one at fault, but there are a multitude of reasons to sue responsible parties other than your actual abuser as well. If your perpetrator was an employee of an institution that was responsible for your care, then the institution might be responsible for his acts. As an example, look at all the high profile cases and settlements against the Catholic Church. Those settlements are not coming from the pockets of the abusing clergymen, they are coming from the Church itself. In those instances, usually the plaintiffs are prepared to prove that those with authority in the church ignored signs of child abuse, sheltered abusing clergymen, and took no action to root out or expose sexual abuse in their church. That made those authority figures *responsible* and their churches *responsible* along with them.

Take another example that comes from the front pages as I am writing this. Jerry Sandusky was the long serving defensive coordinator for the Penn State football team. In November 2011, Sandusky was arrested on 40 counts of molesting eight young boys over a 15-year period. After his arrest, it came to light that Joe Paterno, the legendary football coach for Penn State, and several other University administrators had heard graphic reports from a witness that Sandusky was raping a young boy in the shower facilities. None of them called the police, none of them reported anything to the authorities, and one administrator even lied to a Grand Jury. When this all came out, there was a wave of firings and resignations at the University and no one was immune, even the most accomplished coach in college football history had to pay the price.

That story illustrates how it is *everybody's* responsibility to protect children, and our legal principles echo that responsibility. I virtually guarantee that several lawsuits will stem from this whole ugly incident at Penn State. One of the biggest reasons that lawyers might be unwilling or unable to take a sexual abuse lawsuit is that the defendant abuser may not have enough money to be worth going after.

Lawsuits are expensive and time consuming for attorneys, and attorneys are far more likely to take a case when they know the defendant can pay any judgment that comes down against it. Universities, schools, churches, and organizations are just those defendants. In circumstances where they failed to meet their legal responsibilities to keep a child safe, they deserve to pay for the damage they allowed to happen.

Think about it. When a school counselor knows of abuse and ignores it, there should be liability for the school. When a Bishop knows there is a molester working in his parish, there should be liability for that church. When a Troop Leader knows a teenage Boy Scout is sexually abusing a much younger Boy Scout and fails to act, there should be liability for the Boy Scout organization.

I want real justice for you, and would never, ever, advocate that an organization or an institution be sued only because they can pay. But when an organization fails you (and fails all of us) by allowing abuse to happen or protecting those that sexually abuse children, they *deserve* to pay. Our tort and civil law system is set up to protect all of us this way, if schools know they are on the hook for the actions of their teachers – they wake up, start paying attention, and start protecting kids. Same with churches, daycares, youth groups, and any other institutions that have a responsibility to the children they serve.

That principle, *that those who allowed it to happen were responsible for your safety*, can also be applied to individuals as well. Even other adult family members who knew and took no action should be considered. If your abuser has passed away or has no money, other individuals and/or organizations may be able to compensate you so you can pay for your therapy and get your life back on track. You do not have to choose just one, you can file against everyone responsible. Speak to your attorney about who to sue.

Where Should I Sue?

Put simply, this is the question "What state should I sue in?" Many people who are unfamiliar with the law don't know how *jurisdictions* work, and don't know that they may have options in choosing *where* to sue their perpetrator. The different laws in different jurisdictions/states can make a huge difference, and can even make or break a case. Here is the general principle for civil law: you can sue your abuser in any jurisdiction/state where they abused you, or in any jurisdiction/state where they reside. If your family moved around the country or your abuse happened on trips over the state line, you may have multiple options. If you live in different states, it may be possible to sue in Federal court so they don't have "home-field advantage." There are also circumstances that may directly invoke Federal law, like if it happened on an Indian reservation or on a military base.

Let's look at a couple examples. Leilani's father owned businesses in Southern California and in Hawaii, and her family had homes in both states. Around age 10, her father began to fondle and sexually abuse her. The abuse lasted almost until she left home, and while she never repressed any memories, she was afraid to tell or take action. Her senior year of college, she was inspired by a Women's Studies professor to take action and reclaim her life, and began to think about suing her father. Although she spent most of her youth in Hawaii and lived in Hawaii, after consulting with an attorney she ended up suing in California, because the SOL in

Hawaii is 2 years after the injury or after reaching 18 – and she would have had to sue by the time she was 20, which had already passed. Her father had assets and a presence in California, so jurisdiction was proper and her case was able to move forward.

Field trips, church retreats, family vacations, camping trips, try to remember every place that abuse occurred. Even if the abuse only happened once in a particular jurisdiction, it can be enough to take your case there. Make sure to confer with your attorney about this point.

Journal Exercise – Where You Can Sue

Look online for a map of the United States with lots of blank spaces, then print it out. Mark on the map each place you remember being abused. Camping trip, vacation, military base, visiting relatives in another state, your childhood home — mark each state on the map where you remember being abused.

Then, mark on the map anywhere your perpetrator(s) live or lived back then.

Finally, mark anywhere you know your perpetrator "has assets." Mark every state in which they own a business, own a home, work, or have property.

The Bottom Line

When and where to sue and what to allege and what to say can really be a complicated problem to sort out. Attorneys build their whole careers on solving problems like this, and they do it every day. I didn't show you these realities to intimidate you by the process, I showed them to you to educate you and give you tools to work along side your attorney and give them a head start.

Shari Karney

"We fear what we don't understand. With understanding comes confidence and success."

-Diane Olson

Damages: Recognizing & Proving Them

"Survivors deal with a cauldron of emotions associated with their abuse. A molten, venomous pot of hurt, humiliation, and shame."

- Ray Boucher, Leading CSA Trial Lawyer

Because you are suing for money damages, a key element to success is proving how the sexual abuse damaged you. The general principal is, when you win, you are awarded money that is supposed to "put you in the position you would have been had the injury/abuse/tort not taken place."

For personal injury claims (like yours) the court will be concerned with three types of damages: *General Damages, Special Damages, & Punitive Damages.* Special Damages are the easy ones, they are the expenses you can prove you have had to take on to deal with the trauma: Like your expenses for therapy to deal with issues related to the abuse, or medical bills from any treatments you receive that are related to the abuse. General Damages are more abstract, they cover the "value" of the pain and suffering you had to go through. Punitive Damages, unlike the others, are not really about you, they are a punishment that your abuser must pay to teach them a lesson. Punitive Damages are supposed to show a moral condemnation of certain torts. In CSA litigation, often punitive damages represent the biggest part of the money awarded.

Let's take the example of a more simple case, a car accident. When Debbie Distracted ran over Peter Plaintiff in the crosswalk, he was hurt very badly, and at court he alleged $45,000 in *Special Damages* (He paid $15,000 for his E.R. visit, $15,000 for surgery, and $15,000 for physical therapy) which he proved with his medical records and bills. He also alleged $100,000 in *General Damages* for his pain and suffering, which he proved through his own testimony and the testimony of a doctor - they both talked about how badly he was hurt and how much he suffered. There probably would be no *Punitive Damages* in this case, because there is no heinous, intentional act by Debbie.

Unfortunately, we know the damage that child sexual abuse leaves behind is far more complicated than that.

"A fractured soul is much more difficult to heal than a broken bone."

- Chantelle, Incest Survivor

We have scars of a different nature. Our damages are hard enough for *us* to understand, let alone to prove in court. The first step is the most important (and sometimes the hardest), we have to understand the damages that were done to us and see them for what they really are. When you can be clear and articulate with your attorney about what you believe your damages are, that can tremendously help your case.

The law is just beginning to recognize the tremendous, whole-life impact child sexual abuse has on adult survivors. Lasting anxiety disorders and problems with intimacy are only the beginning. The ability to have sex, to enjoy it, and to feel comfortable being a sexual person is part of a natural human life. No one deserves to bear the physical scars and maladies of the abuse they suffered as children. But how do we quantify this damage? How do we prove it?

"How does a psychologist or an economist (or anyone) testify to how many dollars worth of pain we have suffered in our lives?"

- Jerry, Priest Abuse Survivor

This is how: Through personal understanding. I always tell my Barwinners students that you don't really understand something unless you can teach it to someone else. We have to understand our own pain and understand the way our pasts have shaped and colored our lives. We have to take the time to learn and understand ourselves in order to show others.

The Handprint of Abuse - Organizing Your Damages

Think of it this way, your abuse left a handprint on you and that hand has 5 fingerprints. Each finger represents one of the major categories of damage that sexual abuse causes.

1. Physical Damages (Your Body)
2. Emotional Damages (Self Esteem)
3. Sexual Damages (Sexuality)

4. Relationship Damages (Capacity for Intimacy)

5. Work, Career (Ability to Work)

We are going to develop your understanding of each one of those categories and prepare you to work with your attorney in proving them as part of your case. We'll start with the one that is the most clear, physical, and move on to the ones that are the hardest to recognize and prove.

Physical Damages (Your Body)

> *"Child abuse casts a shadow the length of a lifetime."*
> - Herbert Ward

Sexual abuse can leave a physical legacy on your body. Take for example Oliver's case. Oliver was sodomized by his father on camping trips for most of his childhood. In his deposition he reported:

> *"I'd be screaming when I tried to relieve myself on the john. It hurt so much. I remember my mother yelling at me to shut up and stop being such a baby."*

As an adult, Oliver suffered urogenital problems as well as sexual performance problems because of what his father did to him. Oliver experienced severe pain in his penis whenever he was aroused as an adult because of what was done to him as a child. Children that suffer like Oliver did are known to try to hold their bowel movements for days because of how traumatic it is for them to go to the bathroom. In adult life these survivors often experience colon problems, ulcers and other intestinal disorders that many clinicians see as directly caused by the sexual abuse they suffered.

Some survivors have chronic problems during childhood such as vaginal infections, yeast infections, spotting or bleeding. When these problems are chronic and constant, they can lead to long term scarring and other permanent complications. Abused children are being diagnosed with lasting STDs such as vaginal warts, herpes and AIDS. Some young girls become so scarred internally that as adults they cannot conceive children of their own.

I know women who were forced to get abortions when their abusers impregnated them, causing mental and physical trauma and risking a lifetime of harm. I've heard reports of women being so badly scarred vaginally they cannot have intercourse at all. One client I had would bleed and tear every time she tried to have sexual relations with her husband. Because of the amount of scar tissue that had built up as a result of her sexual abuse as a child she finally had to be operated on in order to open the vagina.

Be mindful of other conditions and disorders that may not seem like they are related to your abuse at first. Doctors have told me they believe the immense trauma and stress that is caused by sexual abuse can be related to immune system suppression, allergies, skin disorders, digestive problems, muscular and skeletal problems, and even migraines. I have worked with survivors who lived their whole lives and never "connected the dots" between their past and their health until a health professional helped them see their ailments and physical struggles in a new light.

What you need to do is really think about your body. Think "outside the box" and really consider the source of every physical ailment and complication you have. You are the number one person who can understand and explain anything and everything that is wrong with you physically. When you have that understanding, then you can communicate your physical damages to your attorney and then develop a plan to prove them together.

Journal Exercise – Physical Damages

- **Write down every physical ailment or problem you have ever been diagnosed with that you think could be related to your abuse.**

- **Now write down all the problems you think you have that have never been officially diagnosed.**

- **Finally, do some stream of consciousness about any and all health problems you have, regardless of whether you think they are related to your abuse.**

- **You can refer to this when talking to doctors who are treating you.**

Emotional Damages (Self-Esteem)

Let's get one thing straight: This was not your fault. Period.

As a child who was faced with sexual abuse, you did what you had to to make sense of what was happening to you. Because it is such an alien concept for young children to think that their parents or loved ones are *bad people*, the only thing that makes sense for them is to assume *they* are responsible and to blame themselves.

Children rationalize for survival by saying "My parent can't be bad. I must be bad and it must be my fault." In a letter Mary Doe wrote during therapy she says:

> *"Growing up I always felt like a fat, ugly, dirty whore. I could not stand living in my own skin. I felt like I had this aura around me and everyone could see it. I wanted to hide my face, my body, my being. I was ashamed to live, to breathe, to take up space on the earth. I felt I had no right to be alive. No right to walk and no right to be."*

That's what being a victim of child sexual abuse and incest felt like to her and what it feels like to many of us who are victims of these crimes. That is the *damage* left behind by her abuse. Once, a survivor told me she thought her sexual abuse was like *gunshot wounds* - when it happened, it hurt so badly she wanted to die. She said over the years the pain slowly faded, but she felt like she had been crippled by her wounds, and she felt like she carried thick scars that she would always have. Those are the type of damages that you deserve to be compensated for, the ones that the law says are *just*, and *fair*, and *necessary* for your abuser to have to pay for.

You are not bad or stupid or worthless or crazy - but child sexual abuse DOES have serious consequences that you have been burdened with.

I saw it put beautifully in a prominent journal of social issues: "The abused child begins to organize his world around his *wound*. The child develops what's known as a *victim mentality*. This is a view of how you fit yourself into the world.

The world is seen not as safe and predictable, but as dangerous, unpredictable, and uncontrollable. Even long after the abuse stops the victimized child continues to think of him or herself as powerless and worthless."

It is not uncommon for victims to have thoughts of suicide. There are different data sets about attempts and thoughts of suicide by survivors, but it is somewhere around twice as prevalent as in non-victims. I just want to say this about the "suicide option." It is the ultimate act of loyalty to your abuser and the ultimate act of self-betrayal. If you commit or attempt to commit suicide, your perpetrator has won.

Suicide is a permanent solution to a temporary problem.

If you follow through with this thought then he has silenced you forever. He never has to be accountable for his acts, his secrets will follow you to your grave, and you have taken all of the responsibility for the abuse. You have acted like the perfect victim. You have blamed yourself, destroyed yourself, and shown yourself to be unworthy, while your perpetrator walks around and finds himself another child to destroy. You abandon those that do love you on Earth and all your hard lessons go to waste.

You have community here with us. You never have to be powerless or alone again. You can begin to heal *today*. Please do not waste your life on suicide. If you have attempted suicide in the past, tell your therapist and your attorney, it could be relevant.

The psychological damage from sexual abuse can be crippling. Anxiety, post-traumatic stress disorder, depression, poor self-esteem, hypervigilance, eating disorders, self-mutilation, problems with addiction and even schizophrenia have all been associated with CSA. To be able to identify and quantify your psychological damages, you will need to work with a qualified therapist. Together you can identify and put labels on the current problems you have that may be related to your abuse. Be honest and forthcoming and try to look at yourself with a "fresh" eye. These are problems we have *lived with our whole lives*. Often, they have been hiding in plain sight, whether it is because of pride or repressed memories or confusion, we just don't make the connection. Don't be afraid to look at your problems in a new way, and try to look at where they came from.

Mirror Work (Emotional Damages)

This is something called "mirror work," the idea is that when you are shown other people's struggles, they help you recognize parts of yourself that can be hard to see. Look at the following list of statements I have heard from other abuse victims. Do any of them sound like you?

- <u>"I Hate the Way I Look"</u> – I think I'm ugly, or too fat, or too skinny, or my nose is bad, etc. I think about my appearance constantly. I obsess over the pictures of myself I see online. I can't get undressed in front of anyone. There are specific body parts of mine that I hate passionately. I don't believe people when they compliment me. I think about plastic surgery a lot.

- <u>"I Have An Addictive Personality"</u> – I struggle with alcohol, cigarettes, prescriptions like Oxycontin or Vicodin, hard drugs like meth or heroin, I do drugs of all types. Everything I do I do obsessively. I work out obsessively, obsess about food and my weight. I take everything to the extreme.

- "I'm Unlovable" – I don't deserve love or happiness. Sex is sex but it's not about love. I don't trust anyone but I'll do anything for love. I don't deserve a good relationship; I don't know how to be in one.

- "People Make Me Uncomfortable" - Nobody seems to like me, I have trouble making friends and people seem to drift away. I'm much more comfortable around animals than people. I have trouble connecting with people at work, I'm never in the in-crowd, and I'm afraid of people. People always expect too much.

- "I'm Sick All The Time" – I have immune system problems, constant colds, back problems and other ailments. Doctors don't help, I have migraines and headaches, low energy, chronic fatigue, etc. I have been called a hypochondriac but I'm not!

- "I Have An Eating Disorder" – I feel like I could never be too thin. I think about food constantly, and I calculate every calorie that comes in and every calorie that gets burned off. Every step of exercise, every bite of food, is controlled and calculated.

- "I Feel Like a Time Bomb" – I feel enormous pressure inside of me, and I'm worried I'm going to lose my mind eventually. Every day gets harder. I don't know how much longer I can hold on. I can't trust anyone. People are always trying to take advantage of me.

- <u>"Everything Makes Me Mad"</u> - I'm aggressive. I want everyone to hurt the way I was hurt. My boss makes me furious, nobody works like I do, and everyone else is dumb - I'm the only one who can do it right. My kids makes me furious, my partner makes me furious, men make me mad, woman make me mad, the government, the media, everything makes me furious. I have trouble controlling my temper. People say I'm overpowering and overbearing.

- <u>"I Can't Stand Being Disappointed"</u> - New situations are scary for me, I don't really take risks, I pick partners and friends who don't challenge me, I feel like I have no opinions, I am always the caretaker – no one takes care of me.

- <u>"I Can't Stand Myself"</u> – I don't like who I am. I don't want to be here anymore. I wish I could "turn off" my mind. I think the world would be better without me.

Sexual Damages (Sexuality)

Child abuse has been called the "darkest side of human sexuality." We were abused in very formative years. The lessons we learn as children or teenagers are the deepest and strongest we ever learn. It is no wonder that sexual abuse can tattoo itself on the sexuality of a survivor. If you have problems with sex and sexuality because of your abuse - you are not alone. We all deserve to have healthy, loving sexual experiences, to be in control of our own sexuality, and to be able to experience the physical pleasure of sex if we want to. But it is not so easy when you've been raped or sexually abused as a child.

In my own case I was about 6 years old when my teenaged uncle began raping me. I had vaginal tears, sores and bleeding. I would go to my mother complaining how much my "peepee" hurt and she would put Vaseline on it in front of our next door neighbor. She never once took me to a doctor, despite all the vaginal problems I had as a young child. When I grew up I experienced frequent vaginal infections and pain during sex. What should have been a pleasure was more often than not an *ordeal* for me. Sex became something I had to "*go through.*"

In my own life, it took decades for me to believe that sex and love could go together. I had trouble as an adult seeing that sex could be loving and that love could include sex. After all, the people who had supposedly loved me were the ones who had sexually abused me. Often when I engaged in sex I'd experience flashbacks and feel like I was being raped. I believe that the destruction of this part of our humanity, of the ability to be physically intimate with another person, is a terrible, tragic form of *damage*. It is not a damage from which there can be no healing, but it is *a damage the law can and does recognize.*

This damage can take many forms. For other women a form of tensing up called vaginismus occurs, during which the vaginal pelvic muscles constrict so tightly that intercourse becomes extremely painful if not impossible. One woman confided that before she got her memory back she couldn't understand why she was responding to her husband's advances by tightening so much that he could not enter her without struggling. For her, sex hurt and was mostly unwanted. Her marriage became a repeat of the painful sexual experiences she'd suffered as a young child.

Shari Karney

"Once they tear you apart they just keep tearing you apart even after their game is over."

- Oliver, Incest Survivor

Some survivors become totally celibate and are absolutely terrified by the idea of having intercourse. They totally shut down when healthy, loving partners want to be with them physically, even if they may want to as well! Other survivors internalize their abuse by engaging in promiscuous and risky behavior, having unprotected, violent, or anonymous sex. Abuse survivors are known to even become full-blown sex addicts. Sometimes abuse survivors get so disconnected from the act of sex it becomes meaningless, nothing more to them than a tool to get what they want. Some get indoctrinated by their abusers into believing that sex is *the only way* to be deserving of love or affection! In some tragic cases, abuse by one person can start a vicious cycle:

"I'd rather say yes and give in than to be raped again..."

- Neta, CSA Survivor

Often times the damage is even worse if the sexual abuse was non-violent or "consensual." Victims often feel that if they did not fight back, did not say no, or enjoyed even the smallest part of the abuse, then they were complicit and consented. That is absolutely false! Medical organizations and legal systems around the world are clear on this point: children cannot knowingly or freely consent to sexual acts. If you were sexually abused, you were taken advantage of and the fault rests completely with your abuser.

92

"Pain stabbed through my body. The most horrible form of pleasure."

- Anonymous Survivor

In my experience, survivors who felt any level of physical enjoyment during the acts have to deal with a unique type of guilt: I call it *response guilt*. The normal, natural bodily response to physical stimulation is arousal and pleasure. But when that pleasure comes from unhealthy, unwanted abuse, the result is feelings of shame, guilt, and self-loathing. A victim's body will respond with pleasurable sensations even though the victims mind and soul are confused or terrified or horrified (or all 3). I remember struggling with myself over this issue. When I was abused by my father, it was non-violent. I was six months old when it began, pre-verbal. It had a pleasure aspect that left me feeling responsible. The only way not to feel guilty and responsible was to cut myself off entirely from my body. That way, he could take my body, but he couldn't take me. I had to separate my body from my *own identity* because of the shame and guilt I felt about my memories of that pleasure aspect.

A male client of mine was orally abused by a grandfather as a child and during the abuse he desperately tried (and succeeded) in holding back his orgasms as his way of not participating. He was afraid if he had an orgasm he would be equally responsible. A lot of clients tell me this. The whole dynamic of feeling physical pleasure from non-violent sexual abuse is both painful to admit and extremely confusing for all victims. They feel that if pleasure was experienced, they were responsible for the sexual abuse.

"What I now know is that the physical body does not distinguish between good and bad stimulation, even if the act is bad, when you

touch a child's genitals, it will feel good. The child is not responsible."

- Jerry, Priest Abuse Survivor

The adult is responsible. Always. Offenders, victims, and society in general think that erection, ejaculation, and orgasms are proof that the victim must have wanted or enjoyed the sexual contact, and therefore no actual abuse took place and no treatment is necessary. That is a ridiculous, anachronistic idea and you should reject it outright, both in your own mind and if anyone ever tries to tell it to you.

Response guilt can transform itself into anxiety, sexual disorders, or any of the other psychological conditions mentioned above. It is one thing among many that you need to explore with your therapist when you are organizing and labeling all the ways your sexuality may have been affected by the abuse you suffered.

Relationship Damages (Capacity for Intimacy)

We all should be able to talk to, relate to, love, and trust those we want to connect with in those ways. But love, trust, and communication do not come easily to sexual abuse survivors. Psychologists believe this happens for the following reason: We are supposed to learn about trust, love, and communication from our parents and loved ones, but sexual abuse massively disrupts that learning process. The *foundation* that our understanding of trust is built on is cracked and unstable.

The capacity for intimacy is related to our ability to experience someone else's needs, desires, and feelings on equal footing with our own. The ultimate expression of intimacy is to engage in a significant relationship, with a partner, which evolves over time and is based upon a deep emotional commitment and trust. I know from personal experience and speaking to countless survivors that that kind of relationship can seem out of reach for us.

We adapted to protect ourselves, and so we never developed healthy abilities to love, trust, and share with other people. This *radiates* into every corner of our lives, especially ones that have to do with personal relationships. The majority of survivors, myself included, have their friendships, family relationships, and romantic relationships impacted by their experiences of abuse.

If you believe you have trust or intimacy issues, share these with your therapist. If you have been divorced one or more times or had to seek relationship counseling, these could be important points in determining your damages. Maybe you just can't be "present" and intimate with your spouse, significant other, or lover. The important thing is to be reflective about the ways in which your abuse experience may have affected your capacity to trust and be intimate, because those are damages that the law recognizes if they can be proved.

Damages to Education, Work, Career (Ability to Work)

Sexual abuse can also interfere with your ability to hold a job and be productive. If any of the physical or psychological conditions you have been diagnosed with substantially affect your ability to work and make money, that could be a form of economic damage. Many survivors I meet are unemployed or under-employed – they feel unworthy of a good job with high pay. A significant number of them had immense difficulty in school due the stress and volatile emotional states they were in at the time. Some dropped out of college, some didn't go to college, and some never even finished high school. I have worked with other survivors who were well educated and talented and despite that still couldn't keep a steady position. Some of our careers have suffered due to cycles of victimization that repeat in our lives, we allow ourselves to be mistreated by coworkers and employers.

We all manifest our damages differently, some survivors are wildly *successful* in business or in their careers, but they may use their work as a shield against intimacy. Some survivors' lives are *all about work*, because that is the only place they may feel powerful or in control. It is important to look at your damages holistically for just this reason, your weaknesses can explain your strengths and sometimes *your strengths can reveal your damages.*

Tell your lawyer and your therapist about the ways in which you feel your work life has been affected, and especially limited, by your history of abuse. Apply the principles of the other forms of damage to your work life, and be mindful and reflective about how your abuse has affected you in this way.

Journal Exercise – The Handprint of Sexual Abuse

This is where you put everything you just learned about damages together.

On a blank page, draw a hand with 5 fingers. Then label the fingers for each type of damage you just learned about: PHYSICAL, EMOTIONAL, SEXUAL, RELATIONSHIP, and CAREER.

On the drawing, creatively list every way you believe you are affected by your abuse under the appropriate part of the handprint.

You can use this as a memory device when talking to your lawyer or whenever you need to remember your damages – just look at your hand.

CHAPTER FIVE: **How Do I Start My Case**
Finding an Attorney & Identifying Assets

Start [stahrt]

>   verb

>   to come into being, to stand up, to begin a course or journey, to
>   begin action

Case [keys]

>   noun

>   a situation requiring investigation or action

>   *"I don't know that there are any short cuts to doing a good job."*

>   -Sandra Day O'Connor, Supreme Court Justice 1981 – 2006

How Do I Find an Attorney

First of all, as much as I wish in my heart that I could take each and every one of your cases, in my practice I no longer take individual cases. Instead, these days I teach, speak, write, lobby, and advocate for survivors' and children's rights throughout the United States and worldwide. That is why I have written this resource on finding, screening, and hiring the right attorney for you and your case.

Finding the right attorney is a critical step! Once you have determined that you are physically and emotionally ready to take action, you need to find the best lawyer possible to handle your case. I want to use my own experience as an attorney who handled sexual abuse cases to give you the "inside scoop" on how to find an attorney, make sure they are qualified, and make your case an attractive case for them to take.

> *"When you work with adult CSA, you are helping survivors peel away those layers of fear and shame and guilt while at the same time finding a way to extract the truth of what happened, and also beginning the process of healing simultaneously. Our job as attorneys is to help the fire dissipate."*

- Ray Boucher

Your goal should be to find an advocate who cares about both the legal process and the healing process, someone who will fiercely represent you but who also understands the issues you face daily. It's going to require some searching.

Attorneys are like any other cross section of people, most are talented hardworking people, but some are not! In my career I have met attorneys who were absolutely brilliant and other attorneys for whom I couldn't figure out *for the life of me* how they graduated law school! Everything matters, education, experience, personality, intelligence, even gender can matter in sexual abuse cases. But at the same time, it's not any one factor. I've known attorneys who went to the best schools that I didn't feel were competent, I've also known young attorneys with almost no experience that had the intelligence and passion to be great advocates.

Geography matters. Lawyers are usually licensed only to practice in the state they are located in. You should probably find an attorney in the state you plan on suing your abuser, which will probably be either the state you live in or the state your abuser(s) live in. Refer to the "Where Should I Sue?" section above for more information about jurisdiction. Also, an attorney in your area is going to be much easier to work with on a regular basis than one whose office is far away from where you live.

So how do you find the right lawyer?

A couple different ways. The internet is chocked full of attorney referral services, local attorney contact information, and the personal advertising material of different law firms. We have also included our own list of plaintiffs attorneys who take sexual abuse cases in the reference section of this book. That's a great place to start. Begin to familiarize yourself with the plaintiffs law firms in your area. After that, I recommend three things:

1. Contact your local bar association (city or county) and ask them to help you find an attorney who specializes in sexual abuse litigation.
2. Begin calling reputable local plaintiffs law firms and ask them for referrals to attorneys who specialize in sexual abuse litigation.
3. Ask for personal referrals from trusted friends, or especially the members of your local support group. If you are not in a local support group, I recommend you join one.

These three resources are a great first step. You should end up with a list of names and contact information of recommended attorneys. If you want to build that list further, use the internet extensively, talk to other survivors, get on online message boards, and expand your geographical area of search (an attorney being local makes things easier, but it might be worth commuting to find the right attorney for you). Once you have a list of references you are happy with, the next step is contacting them.

Be Open & Honest With Potential Attorneys - Attorney Client Privilege

I want you to be confident and comfortable telling the whole and full truth to the attorneys you speak to, even in the initial interview stage. When you speak to an attorney, everything you say is protected in two ways: through attorney-client privilege and the duty of confidentiality.

Attorneys have ethical duties they must abide by. They can get in professional trouble if they breach those duties, including fines, mandatory classes, and disbarment (revocation of their attorney license). One of those duties is *confidentiality*, attorneys must keep secret all the information clients and potential clients tell them about their legal matters. When you, as a potential client, tell your attorney your private information, they are legally bound to keep it private and confidential.

The attorney-client privilege is something different. It covers basically the same information, but it means no one can ever *make* your attorney testify about the things you tell them in confidence.

As always, these laws are more complicated than I can explain in a few paragraphs, but the bottom line is you can tell your attorneys (and potential attorneys) *anything* and they *must* keep it secret, so you can fee confident to do so. If I feel like my clients are holding back when they talk to me, sometimes I tell them the following:

> "Have you ever seen an episode of *House M.D.*, where the patient either doesn't tell, or twists the truth about his symptoms, and then gets worse until House figures it out. Pretend I'm House, and tell me the whole truth. I promise that you can tell me anything, and you *never know* what might make a huge difference in your case. Be honest with me, and don't ever feel embarrassed or ashamed to tell me anything."

You wouldn't (or you shouldn't) conceal things from a doctor, and the same rule applies for lawyers. Always answer your lawyer's questions honestly and be forthcoming about the information that crosses your mind.

How to Make the Calls

I know that this step is tougher than it sounds, you are going to have to pick up the phone and actually talk to these professionals about difficult stuff. But you can do it! I have developed a list of questions that you can either read beforehand or read right off the page if you are nervous. Try to make appointments to talk and consult with the attorneys you want to speak to (for the *vast* majority of reputable attorneys these consultations will be free). Think of it like buying a car, the more research and effort you put into the search, the better car and better deal you get out of it, it is critical to your case and worth the effort.

Here are the questions you can use:

When asking these questions, pay attention to not only the content of the answers, but also to the way the person responds overall. You want to find an attorney who is a fighter, is experienced, and who has a good heart and cares. You don't have to ask all these questions, just the ones you feel are important. When you sit down with an attorney, they will almost certainly ask you questions as well, plan on having a back and forth conversation with any potential attorney you sit down with, these questions can help you fill out your side of the conversation.

37 Questions You Can Ask Potential Attorneys

Questions About Experience With Child Sexual Abuse Cases

1. Can you tell me about your experience handling sexual abuse cases, especially child sexual abuse cases?

2. Can you also tell me about your overall litigation experience?

3. Does the law in my state allow for bringing suits for childhood sexual abuse, after the normal statute of limitations has run?

4. What is the statute of limitations for bringing suit in my state for childhood sexual abuse?

5. Does this state allow for "delayed discovery?"

6. If the state of limitations in my case has expired, and this state does not have a "delayed discovery" type statute, will you take my case anyway to establish new law in this state. A test case, perhaps?

7. Have you taken any adult survivor cases to trial? How many cases have you won or gotten a money settlement for your client?

8. Do you represent victims only or do you also defend perpetrators as well?

9. Are you familiar with the physical, emotional, mental, and behavioral effects of childhood sexual abuse?

10. How aggressively do you pursue these types of cases? Are you a "fighter?"

General Questions About The Attorney and Their Feelings About Adult Survivor Cases

11. How do you feel about childhood sexual abuse? How comfortable are you in discussing the details of what happened to me?

12. What is your definition of sexual abuse? What is the definition of sexual abuse in this state?

13. What made you get into this area of the law?

14. Are you a survivor yourself?

15. If so, have you been in your own therapy to deal with your own abuse?

16. Did you yourself sue your perpetrator - why or why not?

Questions Regarding Costs of Suit and Attorney's Fees

17. How much will this lawsuit cost me, up front and at the end?

18. Will I be charged your hourly rate for the time you spend on my case or will my case be taken on a contingency fee arrangement. (a contingency fee arrangement is where the attorney does not charge you hourly for her time but if you win your case, the attorney will take a percentage of your recovery. Most attorneys will take 33 1/3 percent.)

19. If the fee is contingency, what percentage of my recovery will you take as your fee?

20. Who pays the cost of my lawsuit such as court costs, expert testimony fees, deposition fees, research, and office and secretarial fees? Do you provide a fee schedule for office, research, and secretarial fees?

21. If I am responsible for paying all costs, what is the minimum monthly amount I can pay? If I am not able to pay all costs up front, will you pay them? What method do you recover the costs you have paid and how is the accounting for such costs done?

22. Does your percentage of my recovery increase if the case goes to trial or is appealed?

23. Will you be the only attorney on my case. How many others will be working with you? Do the attorney fees go up if more than one attorney is working on my case?

Communication With Your Attorney

24. How often will I hear from you about my case?

25. What is the best way to reach you? By phone, email, etc.

26. If I have questions, who will be responsible for answering them? If it's you, how long will it take you generally to return my call? Is there a paralegal or assistant who might be able to respond to questions if you are too busy?

27. How close a working relationship do you generally have with your clients on a case like mine? How involved with my case can I be? How involved in my case *must* I be?

28. Will you work with my therapist or do you plan on hiring someone else to be the expert?

29. What emotional problems do you think I will experience while going through my suit? Is there anything you can warn me about? Anything you can prepare me for emotionally?

30. Will you protect me from my perpetrator and my perpetrators attorney?

31. Should we decide to work together, will you at some point lay out for me the process of suing, the stages, and what I can expect to help reduce my anxiety?

32. Will I have to face my perpetrator? Will he be in court or at my deposition? Do I have to be present at his deposition? What do I do if he calls me and asks me questions about the lawsuit?

Outcome of The Case

(Many of these outcome questions will be very difficult for your attorney to responsibly answer in an initial phone meeting. If they say "I can't really answer that right now" it's totally normal. These questions can be revisited later if the attorney can't answer them.)

33. Do you handle appeals? How many of your cases of adult survivors of sexual abuse are appealed?

34. How long do you think my case will take until I recover from my abuser?

35. I know it is difficult to assess at this point, but can you give me some idea of how much, given my situation, you will ask for and what do you think is the realistic financial outcome for me. Give me a ballpark figure, that I will not hold you to, as to what my case is likely to recover? (They are very unlikely to be able to answer this at all until they have been working on your case for some time.)

36. What are my chances of winning?

37. Are you in favor of, and comfortable with working with the news media should that be the outcome?

After The Interviews

When you are done with the initial interview, check out how you feel. Ask yourself how comfortable you felt with the attorney - was he or she sensitive, caring, confidant?

• Did the attorney seem to care about you? Did the attorney answer your questions willingly? Did they seem annoyed at you or at your questions?

• Did the attorney seem positive about your case?

• How was your attorney at handling strong emotions?

- How comfortable was the attorney with the details of your case?

- What do your instincts tell you? Are they the one?

The "Practice" of Law

There is something I want you to remember when trying to find an attorney:

The "practice" of law is just that: practice

There are hundreds of thousands of laws, and no attorney alive knows them all. What we are trained to do is learn and then act, a good lawyer doesn't have to *know* the answer, they have to *know how to find* the answer. Even an attorney who has handled 15 sexual abuse trials may never have dealt with the particular facts and circumstances of a case like yours. Attorneys are learning all the time. The law is so diverse and every case is so different, that you shouldn't let it surprise you if your lawyer needs to do some research or look up a statute while handling your case.

Gender Issues

If you are female, and were sexually abused by a male as a child, you may have some discomfort in working with a male attorney. You may have trust, fear, and compatibility issues. Similarly, if you are male, and were sexually abused by a male, you may also have issues in trusting a male attorney.

Trust me when I say, even as an advocate of gender equality, that gender can matter in sexual abuse representation. Basically, the bottom line is that the gender of your attorney may be very important in your level of comfort with that person.

Because comfort and trust are so important in the lawyer-client relationship, I want you to be aware of your own gender comfort level.

Making the Decision

After you have found the names and numbers, done the phone calls, and asked the questions, you will come to a point where you feel comfortable hiring the attorney of your choice. Meet with them and say "I would like to hire you to represent me." Congratulations! Once you sign the representation agreement, you will have an attorney and can begin working towards the resolution of your case.

How Much Will My Case Cost?

"It is the trade of lawyers to question everything, yield nothing, and to talk by the hour."

- Thomas Jefferson

Every case is different, and many attorneys have different fee structures. The representation agreement your prospective lawyer will give you should spell out in detail how they are to be compensated for their work. If there is any part of the representation agreement you disagree with or don't understand, you can (and should) ask the attorney about it.

Typically, there a few ways lawyers ask to be paid for their legal services: *hourly*, on *contingency, & flat fee*. Attorneys who are paid by the hour keep track of the hours they work and bill their clients at a set amount per hour. Certain types of cases are handled on a flat fee for all the work.

Attorneys who work on contingency (who are almost always plaintiffs attorneys because it is unethical to do work like family law or criminal law on contingency) are paid a different way. They are not paid up front, not paid by the hour, and have a stake in the outcome of the case. Typically these attorneys will keep 33% of any settlement or judgment you win and more if the case goes to trial, they also are not paid *unless* they win. These fees aren't cheap, a third of the judgment is a lot! Contingency fees reflect the fact that clients aren't paying anything up front and the lawyer is taking a big risk.

So what does this mean for you? You are most likely going to find an attorney who will take the case on contingency, especially if your perpetrator has assets you can collect a judgment from, but I think the majority of the out-of-pocket *cost* to you will come in the form of expenses. Your attorney will either advance the expenses (for copy service, court reporter for depositions, filing fees, etc.) and later deduct them from your award OR bill you for the expenses as they arise. Some attorneys may ask for a deposit for expenses, something like one or two thousand dollars up front which they will deposit in a trust account and deduct their expenses from as they go. You have the right to be very clear about who pays for the costs of the case and when. Here is an example of a good question to ask about billing: "If you get 33.3% of any settlement, is that before or after expenses are deducted?"

If money is an issue, talk to your lawyer about paying nothing up front, or getting on a payment plan. Many attorneys will work with clients who are open and forthcoming about their payment issues, especially clients who have valuable plaintiff's cases. So what will your case cost? There is a chance it will cost nothing up front, but you might need to cover at least a few thousand in costs. In almost any case, what it will really cost you is a percentage of your total recovery.

Assessing the Perpetrator's Assets

Here is a cold hard reality of litigation: Defendants without assets or insurance are not worth suing. You can have all the truth, justice, and evidence in the world on your side, but if a defendant has no assets to go after your victory will only be symbolic. It will be hard, if not impossible to get an attorney to pursue a case on a contingency basis if the defendant has no assets and no insurance. Understanding what assets (even potential assets) your perpetrator owns is critical to weighing the costs and benefits of your own lawsuit and to making your case enticing for your potential lawyers.

There are a number of ways to determine what kind of reachable assets your abuser may have. First, what kind of financial assets do you personally know he owns? A home, a business, a pension, a 401k? Does he own land anywhere? Does he have a job? How about a bank account? The first step of the "detective work" is writing down what you know about your abuser's finances.

But how do you dig deeper? A lawyer will have the know how to search for your abuser's assets. Here is the catch 22, you are far more likely to convince an attorney to take your case on contingency if you can show them, with documents, that your perpetrator has assets. Find ways to prove he has a good, steady job, or that he owns property, or that he has an interest in a profitable business.

How do you find it? Go to the public information. Go to the County Tax Assessor's office or Recording Office (or similar governmental entity) and run his name through their records. A lot of information about what property he may own is available there. You can use paid internet investigative services, but you should always confirm their results, they are not always 100% accurate. If nothing else, they can provide good leads. The final option is to actually hire a private investigator. Lots of them specialize in searching for assets; just don't expect them to be cheap. No matter what, the more identifying information you have about the person, the better results you will get. Having a full name, date of birth, and social security number will really cut down on getting inaccurate results.

Insurance

This is a sticky, tricky issue in child sexual abuse cases. Here is some basic law. Insurance policies are contracts, the insured pays money in exchange for the insurance company's promise to pay for damages suffered by *beneficiaries* of the policy. Generally, these policies only cover the innocent or "*negligent*" conduct of the insured (policyholder). Here's an example: Danny Dangerous has insurance. When he accidentally rear ends someone in his car, the damage will probably be covered by his insurance; it was his fault, but he didn't intend to rear end anyone. Later that night, still in a bad mood from his fender bender, Danny gets in a bar fight and breaks a stranger's nose with a punch. His insurance will NOT cover that damage, because he intended to hurt the person he punched.

This is why insurance is complicated. Most people think of sexual abuse as an intentional act, meaning the damage is not typically covered by insurance. There are strategies to get an abuser's acts considered negligent (and thus more likely to be covered by insurance) which we will discuss below.

If you were abused before the mid nineteen-eighties, many insurance policies did not exclude coverage for child sexual abuse at that time. If you were abused during that time period, you have a better chance of collecting from an insurance policy. I have known attorneys who were successful in arguing that a drunken molester acted without intent (thus negligently) who were able to collect from insurance. The most powerful and common way to reach insurance is to sue a non-abusing but non-protecting spouse, usually the mother, for negligently failing to protect her children from a predator.

Collecting from an insurance company will most likely be a complicated and bitterly defended course of action. Insurance companies have expensive, talented attorneys on their side. If your asset search reveals little else other than a homeowner's insurance policy (or something like it), collecting from insurance should be a big part of what you talk about with your prospective attorneys.

CHAPTER SIX: **The Art Of War**
Understanding Your Abuser - So You Can Beat Him!

Understand [uhn-der-**stand**]

> verb
>
> to be thoroughly familiar with his character and propensities

Abuse [uh-**byooz**]

> noun
>
> misuse, deceive, revile, to maltreat, to use so as to injure or
> damage

"Know your enemy"

- Sun Tzu, The Art of War

Knowing What Makes Your Abuser Tick

Understanding the way abusers operate can be incredibly helpful in winning lawsuits against them. You can see through their tricks, guess what they will do next, and stay one step ahead. Understanding the *psychology* and *pathology* of child abuse can help you heal and help you *win*.

115

"I will probably never know what made my step-father sick the way he is, but I understand more about him now than I ever have before. I see him for what he is."

- Madison, CSA Survivor

Survivors know what child abusers are capable of. Unfortunately for us, we know it *all too well*. As well as we knew our fathers or brothers or priests or coaches, whoever hurt us, I find almost universally that child sexual abuse victims don't understand how their abusers can possibly do the things they do. They don't understand how someone who should love and protect them could hurt them in such a selfish and dark way. Here is a breakdown of abuser statistics from the U.S. Department of Veterans Affairs:

Who Commits Child Sexual Abuse?

- Most often, sexual abusers know the child they abuse but are not family. For example, the abuser might be a friend of the family, babysitter, or neighbor. About 6 out of 10 abusers fall into that group.

- About 3 out of 10 of those who sexually abuse children are family members of the child. This includes fathers, uncles, or cousins.

- The abuser is a stranger in only about 1 out of 10 child sexual abuse cases.

- Abusers are men in most cases, whether the victim is a boy or a girl.

- Women are the abusers in about 14% of cases reported against boys and about 6% of cases reported against girls.

- Child pornographers, pedophiles, and other abusers who are strangers may make contact with children using the Internet.

Every pedophile is different; each one is a unique monster. But there are certain motivations, actions, and thought processes that the majority of them share. Over the course of my career I have done my best to understand them, and throughout my talks with survivors, negotiations with abusers, and interviews with psychologists I believe I have come to know what makes them tick (most of them anyway).

"Abusers are usually men who are trying to meet other needs or to avoid other issues in their life – feelings of inadequacy. Financially, physically, sexually, for example..."

- Dr. Wes Maram, Ph.D. Forensic and Clinical Psychology

The first major point of understanding is that *it's mostly not about sex*. This is a difficult concept to believe, I know. These acts and violations are sexual by their nature, but their motivations usually have different roots: *Power* and *Control*. This is a point of consensus among the psychologists and therapists I have spoken to over the years. That's why gender matters far less than age to pedophiles; heterosexual male predators will often abuse male children if given the opportunity. Children are the ultimate symbol of *powerlessness*, they cannot fight back or argue against the will of an adult, and adults who feel a need for *total control* can assert that control over a child.

Dr. Wes Maram, Ph.D. is a tough, no-nonsense, former probation officer and therapist. In his earlier career, he saw a total lack of prevention and rehabilitation for abusers in the justice system. They got *weak* treatment (if they got treated at all) before they were sent back into their homes and onto the street. Before he was even a therapist, he ran support groups and treatment programs for offenders through the probation office. As a licensed practitioner, he has seen hundreds of offenders in his treatment program. He was an amazing source of insight into the minds of perpetrators.

Very generally speaking, child sexual abusers can be divided into a few common subgroups:

The Typical Incest Perpetrator

"I do things for my daughter and this is something she can do for me."
- Father of a former client

In terms of prediction, this is an otherwise "normal" guy in every sense of the word. He cuts across every racial, social, and economic demographic. His capacity to deal with intimacy and stress is impaired in some way, and he doesn't approach choices with maturity; instead he is *reactive*. He has a very stereotypical, almost cliché, view of masculinity and sexuality and he regards sex in a very immature, dirty, almost primitive way. He struggles with intense feelings of *inadequacy* in one or more arenas. Maybe at work he feels pushed around by his boss or deserving of a raise, but he won't stand up for himself. Maybe he is married and wants to experiment in the bedroom, but he is afraid to bring it up. Maybe he feels ugly or weak, or feels like a failure in some way. He feels intense *internalized frustration* and *lack of control* in his life.

"If you could see what you put me through would you still rape me?"

- Anonymous Survivor

Many of the therapists I have talked to believe that some fantasies or thoughts of aggressive sex or sex with young partners occasionally pop up in the minds of normal men, but are quickly dismissed, but in *these* men they are focused on and obsessed and fantasized about. Over a period of time, the pressure of his desire to feel in control and to feel dominant will strip away his inhibitions. He will begin the process of sexualizing children in his mind. First seeing them more and more as little adults, then gradually stepping up his sexual contact (going from tickles to touches to deliberate sexual acts) stepping up his fantasies (younger and more childlike subjects and more intense sex acts) and stepping up his rationalizations (they want it, it's okay, I deserve it).

This "evolution" unfolds in numerous ways. Some feel intense guilt when they act upon their urges, but then they begin to associate that feeling of *taboo* with sexual excitement, and will start to fantasize about it while masturbating or having sex with an adult partner. Some will almost immediately disconnect from reality in their minds, and think that their behavior is normal. Almost always, subconsciously these men sexualize their new form of "control" until it becomes intense, compulsive, and radically interferes their ability to have normal sexual relationships.

Some of these men feel inadequate because of their "failures," aka they do not have the life/job/money/looks/relationship they want. Others feel inadequate because they are more like "control addicts," and no amount of money or success can fill the void inside them. These are typically the perpetrators who have the money and power and the good reputation in the community, but have a dark, abusive side feeding their addiction to power and control.

One subtype of the typical incest perpetrator uses something Dr. Maram and other professionals call "Toxic Faith," which is a perverted and misappropriated religious authority that they use to abuse children.

"Some of these guys, the only way they know how to talk to people is to quote scripture."

- Anonymous Therapist

This usually occurs when the man recognizes a void within himself and he feels like he is internally chaotic or without a set of "internal rules." They then use a rigid, contorted version of religious beliefs as sort of a prosthetic moral code, except it is a code that allows for them to act upon their impulses. They make the code fit their conduct, instead of making their conduct conform to the code. Not only that, but they wield their religious "authority" as a tool to get their way and even as leverage to intimidate, confuse, and silence the children they abuse.

The Situational Abuser

"You're really special to me, no one listens to me like you. You're my princess."

- Father of a former client

This guy shares many qualities with the Typical Incest Perpetrator, but isn't quite the same. This is usually a guy in his 20s or 30s, married or with a girlfriend, not usually successful. He is typically "everybody's friend" and dabbles with drugs and alcohol in his life. Maybe he's into sports, or basically *into* something that isn't really about communicating or understanding other people. The problem he has is an intense immaturity or inability to deal with and relate to people his age.

Usually some "breaking point" arrives and confronts this person with their own immaturity. It could be bills, loss of a job, the end of a relationship, being cut off from sex, something that requires adult tools to handle and overcome. He won't be able to handle it like a mature adult, and this will cause enormous stress and he will look for an outlet. If this person is around, for example, a niece or a cousin, he'll approach that child and he may want to verbally confide in her, sort of elevating her to adult status. The child will actually like this because she will feel mature and trusted. A woman in an incest group said:

> *"I was my Dad's lover from when I was 7 until I was 14. He bought me more clothes and jewelry than anyone else. We'd go out on dates. He treated me special, especially after we started having sex when I was 12. I was his sweetheart."*

The Situational Abuser will begin to sexualize the child, but in a "caring" and "loving" way (I mean that very ironically), as if there could be a relationship between the two. These perpetrators tend to fixate on specific children instead of all children in that age group. They will eventually overcome their guilt through denial and rationalization, and act on their impulses.

The Sociopath

Some child abusers can truly be defined as *sociopaths*. The American Psychiatric Association defines that condition as "...a pervasive pattern of disregard for, and violation of, the rights of others that begins in childhood or early adolescence and continues into adulthood." These individuals generally aren't even capable of remorse, and feel no sympathy or empathy with the suffering of others. They act out it a way that is primitively selfish, and are capable of unspeakable acts against others. They are motivated by uninhibited self-gratification, and whatever violent or sexual impulses they have, they will act on if they can.

The Hardcore Pedophile

The Hardcore Pedophile is best summed up by this quote by an anonymous therapist:

> *"We have some individuals out there whose best therapy is a bullet through the head because they will not stop. Their whole purpose and function in life is to re-offend, and it's not so much like a sexual addiction, but just their total aspiration."*

Hardcore pedophiles can be, and often are, sociopaths, but not always. Sometimes they compulsively re-offend despite terrible guilt and terrible self-punishment. What makes them hardcore is an overriding addiction to sexually abusing children. They constantly obsess about it, fantasize about it, masturbate to thoughts of it, and *define* themselves by it. They are the classic fixated pedophile, and most typically abuse boys.

How to Spot a Perpetrator

People always ask me how to identify perpetrators before they act. Understandably, we all want to protect our loved ones, especially our children, from the worst life has to offer. The problem is, this is a hidden epidemic for a reason: *it is hard to "spot" an abuser*. If every molester wore an overcoat, had tattoos, or was a "creepy loner," it would be easy to predict and protect ourselves from this type of crime. But unfortunately, abuse pathology cuts across every demographic; whether rich or poor, in their 20s or 70s, married or single, religious or non-religious, there is no single way to categorize and identify likely abusers.

> *"The best protection is to be mindful about the **behavior** of the people who have access to children."*

\- Shari Karney

Look at what people *do* instead of who they are. Remember that many child abusers work incrementally, and if you see things like wrestling, tickling, or touching increase in frequency and/or get less innocent, pay attention. A big red flag should go up when someone seeks to have alone time with a child or disappears during a family gathering with a child in tow. Though that behavior can be perfectly innocent, it is also a common abuser tactic.

Also, be aware that child sexual abusers tend to pick "easy" kids to prey upon. Those who won't tell, say "no," run away, or fight back. Abusers look for kids who are bullied at school, who are neglected by their parents, or who are already being sexually abused by someone else. In my experience, predators can "sniff" these kids out. Loners, kids with low self-esteem, and kids with absent fathers are at risk as well. If the "victim mentality" already exists, it is much easier to victimize someone and get away with it. Like the animal kingdom, *opportunistic* hunters always separate the sick and weak from the rest of the herd to get them alone.

Prevention can be as simple as paying attention to how a man looks at young children. What is the look in his eyes? Is he an attentive caretaker, or is it more like "checking them out." I think it is risky to allow much private interaction of the kind that is normal between adult friends between an adult and child, like texting. You should be wary of someone who regularly texts or has private cell phone conversations with a child. If you ever find child pornography or suspicious pictures of young children, this is a critical warning sign and they should be permitted NO contact with children (and you should call the police or other authorities).

Be especially wary of your child's use of the internet, it is a notorious hunting ground for child predators. Lay down ground rules and always try to be aware of who your child is talking to online. Dr. Maram, also recommends a strict "No male babysitters" rule, he believes that boys and men, whether uncles, brothers, neighbors, friends, should not be allowed to babysit because it creates opportunities for situational abusers.

This is a world filled with many wonderful people with wonderful intentions, and I do not encourage unreasonable paranoia. But we do not live in a perfect world, and there is more good than harm in a watchful eye. Child sexual abuse is also a generational problem. Children whose parents were abused are much more likely to experience abuse or be abusers. If you were abused, you owe it to yourself and to the children in your life/family to break the cycle. Don't be afraid to watch over and be protective of the children in your life, you know firsthand what can happen when adults don't protect children. That way, some good can come out of your abuse, and it can motivate you to be a protector of the next generation.

CHAPTER SEVEN: **The Lawsuit Walkthrough**
Litigation: What to Expect, Every Step

Expect [ik-**spekt**]

> verb

> to look forward to, to consider, to anticipate

Step [step]

> noun

> advance, proceed, succession, to be on one's way,

> to provide with steps

"First they ignore you, then they ridicule you, then they fight you, and then you win."

- Mahatma Gandhi

What To Expect - One Step At A Time

I am going to explain to you, as clearly as I can, what each step of the litigation process is like, in chronological order. I am going to spare you some of the boring details and teach you the things I think you need to know, understand, and be ready for as a survivor who is preparing for a lawsuit.

I have organized this chapter into *steps*, so we can walk through everything together. You will find I have focused my attention on the parts of the process that *you* will play the biggest roles in. You do not need to be an expert in *voir dire* (jury selection), motions, or the details of every little phase of a trial. If you really want to know the nuts and bolts of trial procedure in your state, there is a wealth of information available online. The *steps* that are covered in detail are what you as a survivor need to know to get through (and win!) your trial.

The Demand Letter

The demand letter is the equivalent of firing a warning shot. It is a letter that states the basis of a valid claim and *demands* certain terms of settlement of that claim. They usually, in essence, sound something like the following (with much more content, detail, and legal language, of course):

> You have wronged and hurt the Plaintiff. You are legally responsible, and she is asserting her right to compensation. We estimate that her damages equal X dollars in total. We demand that you settle this claim by paying X dollars to the Plaintiff within a certain time limit, if you do not, we will file a lawsuit against you and force you to pay.

> - Plaintiff's Attorney

These letters are more of a custom than a rule. In some jurisdictions, making an effort to settle the case is a mandatory prerequisite to filing a lawsuit, which the letter satisfies. Sometimes, the opening "shot across the bow" is simply filing the lawsuit and serving (delivering notice of the lawsuit) the defendant. These letters should be sent to each and every person or entity you plan on suing or believe you have a valid claim against. If you plan on making a claim against any insurance, notify the insurance companies as well, don't rely on the opposing party to notify them for you.

Look at that rough sample of a demand letter above. Your own demand letter will really reflect whether or not you are ready to begin a lawsuit. If you are unsure what your damages are, how can you make a demand to be compensated for them! Remember to really see these letters as *adversarial*. When these letters go out, people stop acting friendly (or stop pretending to be a loving family). If you are still on "good-terms" with the abuser, plan on the letter changing that. Get all the evidence and cooperation that you can out of them before sending it. You need to see the letter as a turning point you must be ready for, because you are finally rejecting silence and taking action.

*"When my attorney showed me a copy of the demand letter she sent, everything was finally real. This was happening. It felt so good to know he would have to read that letter and deal with me as a **person** for the first time."*

- Brittany, CSA Survivor

Consult with your attorney about strategy issues that may arise from the sending of a letter. Do you have enough time to wait for a response while your statute of limitations runs? Will they hide evidence? Will they try to preemptively counter-sue? All of these are important considerations.

Finally, the demand letter should contain contact information and a time limit for responding. It is rare that gravely serious cases like sexual abuse cases settle at the level of the demand letter. After the time period has expired and you have gotten no response (or a negative response) it is time to move forward and file the *complaint*.

Filing the Complaint

"A lawyer is a person who writes a 10,000 word document and calls it a "brief."

- Franz Kafka

A "lawsuit" does not technically start until a proper *complaint* is filed with the court clerk in the jurisdiction you are bringing the action in. "Complaint" is not used in the normal sense (you don't walk up and start complaining to the court clerk!), it is a formal legal document which states the facts and the laws your claim is based on and meets the technical requirements to start a lawsuit.

In order to have the factual information they will need to write the complaint, you will have to work and talk with your attorney, and tell he or she all the specific facts that make up your abuse. You will have to talk about times, dates, frequencies, specific facts, and describe the abuse in detail. If your attorney asks you about difficult details of your abuse, this may be one of the reasons why; they need to know what happened to write the complaint with a sufficient level of specifics.

The body of the complaint will contain the elements of each tort (wrong) you allege the defendant committed, state alleged facts that satisfy those elements, and have a *prayer for relief*, which will inform the court of what you believe your damages to be, like medical expenses, therapy expenses, pain and suffering, etc. It may also ask for non-monetary remedies. It is important to remember that you can't get what you don't ask for, and what you plead and ask for at the beginning can limit what is available to you in the end.

The complaint must then be filed with the court, and importantly, *served on the defendant.*

Service of Process

Everyone has the right to know that they are being sued. It would be really unfair to be able to go down to the courthouse and sue someone without them knowing. In our legal system, we go through the procedure of *service of process* to make sure that doesn't happen.

When the complaint is drafted, one copy of it is taken personally by a *process server* (basically a courier for legal documents) directly to the defendant. The process server records that the pleadings were delivered and states that they are prepared to testify to prove that they did. At the initial stage, a *summons* is usually also sent, which is official notice from the court of the legal action. In many states, the summons literally says "Notice! You have been sued" at the top. This process is repeated with almost every major document during litigation to ensure that both sides have equal notice of the pleadings, motions, and evidence.

After the complaint has been filed with the court and all defendants have been properly served, the next step is to wait for them to respond with either an *answer* or a *motion* of some kind.

How Your Abuser Can Respond

Your abuser must respond through at least one of a few ways. If they do nothing, they go into default after a certain amount of time and you can proceed against them without their participation. This is what is known as a *default judgment*. Most commonly they will respond by filing a *motion* or an *answer*.

They Can Respond With a Motion

A *motion* asks for a ruling on a specific point of law from the judge, and certain motions can even kill a case right at the beginning. That is why they are strategically deployed as "weapons" in litigation. The most critical type of motion your claim needs to be able to survive is a *motion to dismiss*. In that situation, the defense either attacks the validity of your pleadings, asserts that the statute of limitations has expired, or tries to invalidate your lawsuit of some other grounds. Other motions include privacy/gag orders which attempt to keep the court proceedings secret and non-public. Many plaintiff's attorneys see this phase as one of the most critical and fragile of all of the stages of this type of litigation.

"In most CSA cases, one of the biggest hurdles is surviving the tangle of legal technicalities in beginning the actual suit, aka demurrers and motions to dismiss. If a case can survive those, the plaintiff has leverage, credibility, confidence, and the case has a lot more value. Especially when the statute of limitations is involved."

- Shari Karney, Esq.

In response to hostile motions, your attorney can file *oppositions*, official arguments against that proposed action the defense is moving for. And it doesn't even stop there! Then, the defense can file a *reply* to rebut the arguments. Ultimately, either the judge will just read all the paperwork and make the ruling, or there will be a *hearing*. At the hearing, the judge hears arguments from both parties, asks questions, and then makes a ruling on the point of law. Motions can happen all throughout the trial, not just at the beginning, and can be brought by either side. They are one of the reasons that litigation is so intense and technical.

They Can Respond With an Answer

After any motions (if there were any) are dealt with, your abuser will have to file an *answer*, which is the term for the defendant's pleadings. The answer can do a lot of things, lay out the defendant's version of the facts, assert *affirmative defenses*, argue a different interpretation of the law, or even include a counter-claim (a lawsuit sent back against you!).

Once the complaint and answer are both officially filed, in the absence of any gag-orders or special identity-protecting statutes, they become public records. Child sexual abuse cases can garner media attention, or just a lot of community attention. Be aware that this is the stage where things "go public" and confer with your attorney about how you want to handle it, you can embrace the coverage or work to keep the details of your case private. There are many options available for keeping the proceedings secret, in almost every state there are ways you can ask the court to keep the case or the documents non-public, don't be afraid to fight for this if it is important to you.

As a survivor who is a public figure, I've gotten used to being open and frank about my abuse, but that doesn't mean I don't understand how sensitive and painful this issue can be. I advise you to "go with your gut," and manage your "publicity" in whatever way your instincts tell you to do so, it really is a matter of personality and no one but you can make that decision.

At this point, the two sides have engaged and laid out their versions of the facts. Next comes the step where each side uses the power of the court to gather evidence through *discovery* and prepare for trial.

The Discovery Process

Discovery is an official exchange of information between the parties. It is the process through which each side gathers evidence from the other parties in order to present its case at trial. Be prepared for the discovery process to be the *longest* and often most *difficult* (and boring!) part of the case.

There are some main parts of the discovery process that I want you to be familiar with: *Interrogatories, Requests for Admission, Requests for Production of Documents, Depositions*, and *Medical Exams*. I'm going to give you a common sense understanding of each of those processes individually, so that you can know what to expect, know how to react, get the best information, and protect yourself and your case.

Interrogatories

Interrogatories are essentially questions. Since they are part of the official proceeding, each side has the right to ask certain questions of the other side and to be answered honestly. The questions range from extremely basic (What is your full name? What is your mailing address?) to extremely specific and personal (Asking for details of the abuse). Some of these will be standard forms with boxes checked next to the questions you are to answer, others are questions carefully crafted by the opposing attorney.

As the plaintiff in this kind of litigation you will have to work with your attorney in answering these questions. The questions will be long, repetitive, boring, and sometimes offensive. You have to hang in there. Remember that not all of them have to be answered! Sometimes the questions ask for privileged (protected by the attorney client privilege), irrelevant, or legally protected information.

Your attorney should be diligently protecting you from improper questions. Your goal when responding to interrogatories should be the following: Answer only the questions they are entitled to ask, give short, honest answers when you must, and always tell the truth, even if a particular fact is bad for you. Answer the questions literally, and don't give or offer "extra" information that wasn't asked for. Be honest, but also smart, don't give any gifts to the defense.

I've litigated and advised these cases for over a decade, and one of the worst problems a plaintiff can have is being caught in a lie. At the end of the interrogatories, you must sign and affirm to the court you are telling the truth. Take that seriously! Getting caught in even a partial lie will really hurt your **credibility**, which is priceless during this process. I tell my clients "lying is like giving your abuser a gift, because if they catch you in that lie, they'll feel like it's Christmas."

Your attorney will also be able to write interrogatories for the defendant/s to answer. This is a time consuming process, the language has to be written and responded to with precise language. Lawyers can endlessly argue about the meanings of words, so clarity and precision are critical

Requests for Admission

These are questions of a different type. If you have ever taken a True/False test at school you are more familiar with these than you may think. They look something like this.

"From 1990 to 1993, you and the Defendant both resided at the same residence."

There are only 3 answers: Admit, Deny, or a state that you can neither Admit nor Deny (most commonly for lack of knowledge).

These questions make you commit to positions that are relevant at trial. The same rules apply that applied to interrogatories, these will be carefully worded by your abuser's attorney, so be careful and work with your attorney to give careful, limited, honest answers.

Requests for Production of Documents and Other Evidence

These are just what they sound like, an official process for each side to get access to the documents and physical evidence held by the opposition and others. These requests are much more commonly used in business litigation, where business records are very important, but they can still be quite relevant here too! Generally, the parties will request some combination of insurance records, financial records, property records, and/or medical or psych records if they exist. If you know of any documents or evidence your abuser has in their possession, you can subpoena it, and they have to produce it. If they don't, they face serious consequences from the judge.

This process of document exchange makes it is so important to make absolutely sure that your journal work is protected. I wish it was different, but there is some real danger of your candid thoughts and feelings being "discovered" by the other side if it isn't completely protected by the attorney client privilege. That's why, although I wish I didn't have to, I must recommend you not start the journal work until you have discussed it with your attorney.

Documents can also be obtained from third parties through a *subpoena duces tecum*. Third parties are individuals or entities like doctor's offices, schools, churches, businesses, etc. who are *not* parties to the lawsuit. Being able to use the power of the court compel entities like churches and hospitals with is an amazing tool for gathering evidence. You can't "fish" for evidence with third parties the way you can with opposing parties because you have to be very specific when subpoenaing documents, but it is still an important power to have.

A Quick Vocab Lesson

When you are working with your attorney to deal with all the discovery issues you face, sometimes it will really start to sound like another language! Attorneys use a lot of abbreviations and nicknames when talking about discovery, here are a few translations:

ROG (Rawg): Interrogatory

S-ROG (Ess-Rawg): Special Interrogatory

FROG (Frog): Form Interrogatory

RFA: Request for Admission

RPD: Request for Production of Documents

SDT: Subpoena Duces Tecum - Request for Production of Item

Depo (Depp-O): Deposition

Depositions

The deposition. The holy grail of the discovery process. This is the most difficult, yet in this lawyer's opinion, most valuable part of the discovery process by far. A deposition is the taking of the out-of-court oral testimony of a witness. The judge and jury are not there, but the witnesses are under oath and a precise, verbatim record of every question and every answer is kept. Each party chooses witnesses it would like to question, then notice (and often a subpoena) is sent out, and the deposition is arranged.

To understand the process, picture this scene from a deposition:

Several people gather in the conference room of your attorney's office, today your attorney is deposing your childhood doctor. You are there (though your lawyer told you that you didn't have to be) because you wanted to see this through. Your attorney is also there, as is her paralegal taking notes. There is a court reporter, who in a moment will sit down and set up to record everything that is said once the deposition goes "on record." There is also a videographer, because your attorney thinks this deposition is important and wanted to video it as well.

This lawsuit is against your father, and although he is not there, his lawyer is. The doctor arrives, with his own attorney, and everyone sits down. The deposition begins, the doctor is sworn in, and your attorney begins asking him questions. Periodically the doctor's lawyer will interrupt and say "objection," and your father's lawyer does it once or twice as well. Around noon everyone takes a break and you go "off the record." After about a half hour break or so, everyone sits back down, your attorney finishes her questions, the other lawyers each ask a handful of questions, and everybody breaks for the day.

In a week or so your attorney's office is sent a perfect copy of the transcript of what was said and the video from the deposition, which your lawyer will use to shape his case in preparation for trial.

Although this was just a quick fictional story of a mid-day deposition, it really gives you an idea about how the whole process works. It is very similar to the way testifying in a trial works, except the questions are not as limited by the judge and the rules of evidence. Depositions are really about asking open-ended questions and finding information. Here in California, you can ask any question reasonably calculated to lead to the discovery of admissible evidence. The deposition transcripts aren't strictly *evidence*, because they are not by themselves admissible at trial (with many exceptions of course).

Depositions are unique in the discovery process, anyone who has relevant testimony can be deposed, it isn't just limited to the opposing party. Eye-witnesses, siblings, doctors, teachers, neighbors, anyone who has relevant personal knowledge can be *subpoenaed* and compelled by the court to be deposed.

Being able to question someone face to face is such a powerful tool. I have had molesters admit their crimes on record, heard incestuous fathers make devastating self-incriminating statements, and found game-changing evidence in depositions, all from asking questions, truly listening to the answers, and following where they took me. From the moment the deposition starts, you are laying the foundations for your trial, because witnesses can be *impeached* on the stand with their deposition testimony. Your lawyer gets to pin your abuser to certain positions, then have time before the trial to collect evidence and prepare to question them in front of the jury. As useful of a tool as it will be for you and your lawyer, the deposition is also a tool of the defense, and you must be prepared to get deposed as yourself.

Your Deposition

Giving a deposition and testifying at trial are the two biggest confrontations you face during this whole process. I prefer to think of them as your time to shine. You will be on center stage, and it will be the moment where you stand your ground and tell the truth for the world to hear. Successfully handling a deposition is a major transition point in the journey from victim to victor.

What should you expect? If the case proceeds through discovery you will almost certainly be deposed by the defendant's attorney. He or she is *not your friend*, do not try to help them, even if they seem nice and friendly, they will try to use anything and everything you say against you at some point. He or she will ask you tough questions that have tough answers.

You should expect a lot of topics to be fair game. You will probably be questioned about your sexuality, sexual history, medical issues, emotional problems, marital problems, finances, and childhood. It is likely you will be asked detailed questions about the abuse itself. They will try to take your medical records and therapeutic records and rake them over the coals. In the worst-case scenario the defendant's attorney will ask you disgusting, embarrassing, invasive questions and press you for answers. Many survivors want to know if their perpetrator will be at their deposition and in most cases the answer is yes (sometimes just to intimidate you).

Hang. In. There.

You can do this, even if the opposing counsel's questions get more aggressive and pointed. Your attorney is your backup, and they should be doing everything they can to shield you from improper questions. Remember you can stop and get support and advice from your attorney any time you need.

There will be times when you will have to give ugly answers to ugly questions. It can't be avoided, you just have to hang tight and give short, accurate, honest answers. Depositions can last several hours, and maybe even multiple days, but you can take it at your own pace. If you need a break, take one. If you need water or food or a breath of fresh air, you are entitled. Take care of yourself. Talk to your therapist and attorney, and when scheduling the depositions, expressly limit the questioning to a few hours a day.

Answer the question. Then shut up.

Talk too little, not too much. Also, make sure to answer slowly to give your own attorney time to say "objection" and protect you. If you don't understand a question, say "I don't understand the question" and make them work for the answers. You don't have to explain yourself, you don't have to justify yourself. This is NOT your day in court. The jury is NOT in the room. Your job in the deposition is to answer the questions and nothing else. So don't answer questions that are not asked. Here is a quick lesson on staying on point, look at the following two examples:

You are being deposed, your abuser's attorney is asking you questions

Attorney: "Do you know Mark Molester?"

You: "Yes. He was my neighbor when I was in elementary school. My family lived two doors down from his house, he used to abuse my sister and I when his wife was supposed to be babysitting us!"

Believe it or not, that was the <u>wrong</u> answer. Here is the right answer:

Attorney: "Do you know Mark Molester?"

You: "Yes."

Make your abuser's attorney do the work. You have *no idea* what they know and do not know and you also have *no idea* what is going to be relevant for them. Do not throw them information and quotes that they can pick apart later when they read your deposition transcript eight times looking for contradictions, lies, and information they can use to their advantage. If they ask, tell them the answer. If they don't, that's their problem, period. I am also not telling you not to tell your story! Be strong and stick up for yourself in your deposition. I am just saying save your rage, your righteousness, and your explanations for the witness stand at trial.

Be aware that this may be an intense event. If you are prone to flashbacks or panic attacks, you need to take special precautions to protect yourself. If you can make arrangements to have your therapist with you at the meeting. Strongly consider videotaping the deposition, in my experience lawyers seem to mind their manners more when they are on tape. If you expect your abuser's presence to cause you serious problems, look into the possibility of getting them excluded or working out a solution. In some states there are options for keeping them away from your deposition.

Above all don't fear your deposition. It will be tough, but it is a chance to teach the opposition that you aren't afraid anymore. You can show them that you are an articulate, smart, and sympathetic witness that knows how to testify. Stay focused, rely on your attorney for backup, answer the questions, and it'll be over before you know it.

"I had no idea what to expect in my deposition. At first it was okay but then BAM the attorney started asking me about [my abuser's] penis and what did it look like and could I identify it and to describe it and stuff and it got really bad. Shari kept stopping the record and objecting and we took a break. I calmed down and we started again and now I wasn't scared, I was mad! We finished and I did really well. Now I am not scared at all by testifying, I'm more like "bring it on.""

- Sandra, CSA Survivor

Your Abuser's Deposition (and the Depositions of Other Parties)

These are also important to be aware of. Your attorney can use the power of the court to depose almost anyone who has relevant personal knowledge of important facts. Your abuser, neighbors, siblings, doctors, therapists, teachers, and other witnesses can all be brought in for deposition. The beauty of this is that you don't have to attend *any* of these if you don't want to, your attorney can handle them on her or her own. But you have the *option* of being there if you choose to (most of the time).

You might want to consider going. As well as your attorney may learn your case, there is no substitute for *your* knowledge. I have had clients come sit in on depositions and talk to me during breaks, letting me know the person I was deposing was lying or giving me info that helped me ask the rest of my questions. That can be extremely helpful! Your attorney can know your case inside and out but they will *never* know the facts as well as you do, being able to slip them a note or meet with them during a break and let them know your version of the facts could lead to great deposition questions or new evidence.

You absolutely must, however, take seriously the prospect of having to confront your abuser. If you are prone to breakdowns or flashbacks, seeing them in a tense situation might be difficult. Confer with your therapist and your attorney, and trust your instincts, when choosing whether or not to try to attend the depositions of others.

The Physical/Psychological Exam

Almost always in child sexual abuse litigation, the defense wants medical and/or psychological exams. These will be formal medical examinations by licensed doctors, who you probably do not know. Like depositions, exams can be friendly (arranged by your attorney) or unfriendly (arranged by the defense). Friendly exams are relatively easy, they are a trip to a doctor or psychologist who was chosen by your attorney to check you out. What I want to make sure you are well equipped for is defense medical exams. Like your deposition, there are several things you should know about and be prepared for.

The idea is that a "neutral" doctor, who doesn't know you, gets to examine you to verify your claims of damage to your body. The defense often has the right to ask for these because you have raised the issues of your body and your psychology in alleging the way your abuse damaged you. Be mindful of what you say to your examiners, they may end up testifying for the defense at trial. Treat their questions like deposition questions and answer only what you are specifically asked.

These exams will be just that: exams. In a physical exam a doctor, who will be a licensed and board certified professional, will examine you to form an opinion about your health. Depending on what kind of information the exam is intended to find, it may be fairly personal. The doctor may need to examine your genitals and other private areas, and it may feel embarrassing or invasive.

The psychological exam will be the mental version of the physical exam. You will sit with a psychologist or a psychiatrist over one or more sessions and they will ask you questions and talk to you. It will probably be stuff like "Do you ever have thoughts of suicide?" "Do you have nightmares or flashbacks?" "Talk to me about a typical day for you." In both types of exams, the doctor will have probably reviewed your medical records and may ask you some questions about your history.

The thing that makes these exams unique is that they are not for the purpose of making you better, only verifying the truth about your body. Depending on who you are, your level of body comfort, the type of exam, and the doctor who administers it, this could be anything from a pain in the neck to a very difficult, invasive ordeal. My clients have run the entire gamut of dealing with these exams, from terrible to not-that-bad. For example, Susan, who was a funny firecracker in her early twenties, did very well in her physical exam and in several sessions with an independent psychotherapist.

> *"At first I was dreading it, but when I got there I realized that these are just normal doctors. I had gotten it in my head that they worked for my dad. The nurse and the doctor were both nice and everything went fine. The therapy exam was more boring than anything else."*

Susan was able to take it in stride. She was the type of client that got more confident after every successful step. But not every survivor has that experience. I represented a 30-year-old woman named Paloma who had a very difficult time through during her physical exam. Paloma was rendered infertile from being repeatedly penetrated as an infant, and she alleged infertility and vaginal scarring in her complaint. She had to endure a full pelvic exam from a male doctor and had to suppress a panic attack during the examination.

> *"I just wanted to close my legs and run. I couldn't breath. It was only a minute or two but it felt like an hour. I threw up in the bathroom in the waiting room and I had to call my cousin to drive me home. I wanted to shower when I got home but I couldn't because I didn't want to be naked."*

Paloma had to experience the worst-case scenario, but that doesn't have to be you. I just want you to understand that these exams can potentially feel like a major invasion of privacy. I know first hand how sacred and intimate a survivor's body is! Every woman's body is sacred, but for us, there is another level of memory and meaning and need for sanctity in our bodies. For years I didn't even like it when my boyfriend touched me, let alone a strange doctor!

Every survivor understandably has issues with personal space, privacy, body image, and body comfort. Use this to your advantage! The opposition does not just get to choose any doctor they want, you get to have a say in the matter. Make sure that your attorney fights for the things that are important to you, a female doctor, a limited exam (non-relevant body parts are off-limits!), excluding certain medical records, a doctor that has experience treating abuse survivors. Those demands are reasonable and you have a right to protect your privacy.

The Settlement Process

This step is relatively simple, once discovery is finished or has progressed far enough, each side begins to have enough information to make realistic evaluations of your likelihood of success at trial. Most of what would be admissible evidence has been identified and exchanged by the parties, and the attorney's can begin to "see" the trial and its outcome. Settlement can happen at any time, but this is a common time for complicated cases (like CSA cases) to settle, if they are going to.

After discovery has unfolded, the attorneys can really negotiate *realistically*. Each side can see the strengths and weaknesses of their case and their opponent's. The "stronger" a case, the more money it's worth and the more likely the success at trial is because of the strength of the evidence, appeal of the plaintiff, procedural advantage, etc. As a long time plaintiffs lawyer I can tell you this: No one can see the future and read the minds of twelve jurors no matter how strong a case is or how weak, there is always risk for both sides. That is what makes these negotiations so hard. They are complex and dynamic, with nearly unlimited factors to consider.

This is a great time to take stock of your case and your priorities. If you have strong evidence and can't wait to testify, you may want to accept settlement on your terms only. If you really want your day in court, you should go have it even if your case has challenges. If you have holes or weaknesses in your case, like no corroborated physical or medical evidence of the abuse, it may be in your best interest to take even a modest settlement, especially if you need the money.

"I was abused by a family friend. I had hired an attorney and filed a lawsuit against him. My attorney and I had rejected the first two settlement offers before he finally offered me something that made me feel satisfied. My goal was to hold him accountable and to pay for my therapy, and I did that." - Valentina, CSA Survivor

In any case, settlement is up to YOU. Your attorney has an ethical duty to report each and every settlement offer to you, and they will probably make a recommendation to take or not take each respective offer. The choice is yours and yours alone. If you want to be vindicated at trial, that is your choice, and you can proceed no matter what the opposition offers you. At the same time, even if your attorney suggests rejecting an offer, you can choose to accept it. I recommend giving great respect to your attorney's recommendations; they are less likely than you to be tricked, scared, or intimidated into settling, and also know when to *take* an offer to avoid a greater loss.

If you do choose to settle, a contract called a *settlement agreement* will be drafted and re-drafted by the attorneys. Its terms will probably include a payment by your abuser to you (or whatever they agreed to settle the case for) and your waiver of claims and promise not to sue in the future. There may also be a provision of confidentiality, called a gag provision. This may prevent you from speaking publicly about your abuse, and is definitely something to think about when you consider settling. Nothing is final until you sign the contract, so get your attorney to push for your rights to speak, and if the settlement agreement is unacceptable to you, push on with your case.

Finally, a lesson it took me decades of law practice to learn: Never expect your case to settle. Cases that look like open and shut slam-dunks can end up being long fought battles to the end. It ends up being a catch-22: The more you prepare for and expect trial, the more likely it is your case will settle (if you want it to).

Alternatives to Trial - Mediation

There is another side to the settlement process, *alternative dispute resolution*, also known as ADR. These are processes that help settle the case or decide it without going through with the actual trial. *Mediation* and *Arbitration* are common forums for ADR. A mediation is a special negotiation between the parties that is overseen by a *mediator*, usually a retired judge or a very experienced attorney who can value the case and help guide the parties toward a settlement. In mediation, the parties are still negotiating with one another and still control the actual decision to settle or not, but the presence and the advice of the mediator can be very influential. Also, the rules of evidence are not the same, they are more flexible, and often this works in the favor of survivor plaintiffs.

Arbitration is like trial-lite. Again, an ex-judge or a very experienced attorney will sit and preside over a hearing, will hear testimony, read the parties' paperwork, and see all the evidence. Unlike in mediation, in arbitration the arbitrator will make a decision and it will be like the final verdict. It is basically like going to trial, but it is less expensive and one or more arbitrators decide the case instead of a jury.

Both mediation and arbitration have advantages and disadvantages. They are cheaper and quicker than going to trial, they have more flexible rules of evidence, and you get to have some say in who your arbitrator or mediator is (both sides come to an agreement about who it will be). On the other hand, they are non-public/unofficial forums and cannot officially vindicate you the way a trial can. Both of these ADR options are very common these days, and are getting more widely used every year as the courts clog up. It's important to have a working understanding of your possible trial alternatives.

Trial—General Considerations

Not to be overdramatic, but trial is a beautiful thing. As a trial lawyer, I think the trial is a beautiful snapshot of our democracy and civilization; instead of violence, instead of might making right, we have a mechanism where adversaries clash their versions of the facts, and truth rises to the surface. Trial is where a victim can become a victor. Our system isn't perfect, but it what it represents is beautiful and powerful.

Trial is a complex, consuming, intense process. Be prepared for it to be confusing and exhausting. When a lawyer is "in trial" usually they are working 12 hour days (or more) and are totally focused on the trial the whole time. If they are not in court they are preparing or reviewing, when they are in the courtroom they are razor focused on every word and every detail of the proceeding.

At the end of the day, the goal of the trial process is to determine what the facts were and to decide how the law applies to those facts. The *fact finder* in a case can be either a jury or a judge (depending on many factors), who will hear all the evidence and then determine what the "facts" of the case are. The stages of the process will flow something like this:

The attorneys will screen potential jurors and select them in a process called *voir dire*, possibly followed by some *motions* (like in discovery) about evidence or other issues, then the lawyers will give their *opening statements* to the jury and introduce them to the facts, then the plaintiff's (your) attorney will present their *case in chief*, aka their evidence, meaning people will testify and evidence will be offered.

During the plaintiff's case your attorney will give *direct examinations* to his own witness (ask them questions so they can tell the jury what they know) and the opposing attorney will probably *cross-examine* them to try to hurt their credibility.

Then the defense will present its case and its own evidence and witnesses. In the end, the lawyers will give their closing arguments, the jury will be given instructions to follow and deliberate in private, then they will return to give the verdict.

Trials can be as short as a day or two or longer than a week, depending on the amount of evidence that will be presented. Litigation is like a marathon, the hardest steps are going to be the last ones, you have to finish hard, but then you are done. Every trial is different, and you are going to need to rely on your attorney and your therapist to tell you what to expect and how to prepare.

Experts – Finding Them

Finding expert witnesses to testify for you at trial is something you should trust your attorney to handle. In fact, it can be problematic if you have been in contact with a potential "expert" outside of the process of their expert review of the evidence and testimony and I recommend against you trying to find your own experts without your attorney.

That said, I believe you should know the basic process so you can assist your attorney in finding experts if necessary. There are many databases where experts in different fields advertise their services, and these are a great place to start from scratch. Both online and in print, databases can be a great place to find medical experts of all kinds. Hopefully, your attorney will be well connected and able to get recommendations from his colleagues for highly trained, reputable professionals who can testify for you. You can help by connecting your attorney with your therapist and/or your support group leadership for referrals and recommendations. Don't ever hesitate to offer your attorney a head start, it may be very helpful to them.

"When it comes to experts, never underestimate the power the right expert, like a handwriting expert to verify old notes or letters. A computer expert can get into the bowels of computer systems of 3rd parties. A research expert, like a librarian, can look back 20 or 30 years, especially in small towns, to place the victim at the same time and place as the perpetrator.

- Ray Boucher

Ray is right. It can be powerful simply to prove that you were with your abuser at the same time and place you claim you were abused. He uses the example of a camping trip, if you claim you were abused on a church camping retreat, then a newspaper clipping about that trip from the date you claim it happened can be strong corroborating evidence of your abuse.

Sometimes attorneys will have "go to" experts that they use in all of their cases. Both you (and your attorney) should be aware of the danger of expert witness "overuse." I have seen defense attorneys execute devastating cross-examinations based on the number of times an expert has testified for an attorney (or law firm) and how his testimony might be tainted by his having a long term working relationship with the lawyer that hired him. Hopefully your attorney will be well aware of that pitfall.

Finally, experts are very expensive. If you are covering expenses up front, you should expect these professional experts to be paid a very high hourly wage for their work, sometimes many hundreds of dollars an hour. Experts are only experts because they are highly educated and extremely experienced, and they don't testify for free. If money is an issue, be aware that these witnesses can be one of the most expensive parts of the litigation process.

Your Performance and Behavior at Trial

When it comes to trial, survivors frequently ask me "what can I do?" They understandably feel like the process is out of their hands. It can be tough to sit and watch quietly as the trial unfolds in front of you. If someone is lying about you or what happened, you can't just jump up and scream "Liar" and point at them! You have to trust and rely on your attorney to do the fighting for you. Believe me, I know first hand how hard it is to *trust* someone else to take this on for us. The good news is there are ways you can help.

> *"The Common-Sense rule is in effect!"*
> - Shari Karney

First, as simple as it sounds, you can help through your appearance and demeanor. *Credibility* is crucial in every civil case, and it is established in many different ways. The jury is going to see you and size you up, and you have to do everything you can to make a good impression. You don't need to be anything or anyone you aren't, but they need to see you for who you are: a good person who was victimized and deserves empathy.

Dress nicely and especially non-sexually, pay attention to your appearance and do your best to look like an upstanding friend, neighbor, sister, or daughter, whoever you are. If you struggle with alcohol or drug problems it is critical you remain 100% sober and alert during your trial. Do whatever you need to do to be clean and sober while you are in the plaintiff's chair or on the witness stand.

Be respectful to everyone. From the moment you leave your house in the morning on trial days you should be on your "best behavior." If you are cutting people off in traffic or cutting into the security line, you never know when it might be a juror that you just cut off. There are also certain universals about in court etiquette: no chewing gum, cell phones on silent or off, no texting, etc. I know this process is tough, but you can't lose touch with your common sense.

Be aware of your expressions and gestures – remember that the jury sees everything! I always tell my clients a helpful story from the 2000 presidential election: There was a famous debate between George W. Bush and Al Gore. Whenever Bush made a point Gore didn't like, Gore would roll his eyes or sigh or look exasperated. Throughout the same debate, George Bush kept checking his watch.

When audiences were later polled for their reactions, many responded with negative feedback about those small gestures, instead of judging the candidate's actual answers! They felt Gore was immature and Bush was acting like he had somewhere to be. Juries will be the same way, they are people too, and for good or bad, small things like your smile or your frown or sighing or checking your watch will matter to them. Be attentive, be mature, be real. If you feel the need to cry, let it out, you don't have to pretend you are happy when you aren't, just remember that your gestures and your expressions matter.

Testifying

Taking the stand is truly your time to shine. There is not a purer, truer moment of vindication in the entire trial process. I have watched my clients swell with strength on the stand and reclaim their lives. There is no better way to make your story known, set the record straight, and shine the truth on your abuser. They have to sit in silence and listen to you tell the world exactly who they are and what they have done. They have to watch you take the stand and break their control forever. But it's not a cakewalk, you have to know what to expect.

First things first: forget everything you've ever seen on TV and in movies about testifying.

Your testimony will have two main phases: *Direct Examination* and *Cross Examination*. "On direct" is when you get to tell your story, "on cross" is when the defense will try to tell their story through you and hurt your credibility. Testifying is not really an optional thing for you, you have brought the case, the best evidence will come from you, and the jury needs to hear you get up and say what happened to believe you. The better you understand and prepare for these phases of testifying, the cleaner and clearer and more compelling your testimony will be.

Direct Examination

Direct examination is "friendly" questioning. Unlike your deposition and cross-examination, *your* attorney will be asking you questions on direct. The goal is to *tell your story*; to speak from your heart and tell the jury in your own words what happened and how it has affected your life. Your attorney will need to guide you towards particular facts to satisfy certain *elements* of the claims you are trying to prove, but mostly it is just you telling your story. This will be easier than you may think, because you can just let the truth *flow*. Your attorney will ask you open-ended questions like "what happened on that camping trip?" and you can answer however you want. Even though your attorney will be asking you questions, the focus is no longer on them, it will be on you and your answers; you will be in the driver's seat.

Don't embellish and don't exaggerate. Getting caught in even a small stretch of the truth hurts your credibility, and credibility is your key to victory. Every plaintiff has facts that aren't perfect for their case, and it's okay. If you have a difficult or embarrassing fact, bring it out on direct. An old trial mentor of mine taught me to always "take the sting out" of bad facts. If you have addiction problems, have made past accusations, or have a sexual history you know the defense will bring up, the smartest and most credible thing you can do is to *bring it up on your own terms*. You can't hide anything in litigation, and if you try to it looks like you are trying to hide the truth, which is devastating to your case. Trying to hide a fact just gives the defense an opportunity to have a "gotcha" moment, and those are powerful.

Here is how to take the sting out: I represented a young woman named Shelly who had been forced to give her grandfather oral sex for years. Shelly had two children and her ex-husband had full custody of both of them because of Shelly's alcoholism. Shelly had lied about her 2 DUIs during their custody battle, and had been caught on record in a lie. Shelly had made a mistake, no question about it, but she didn't deserve to lose her case against her grandfather because of it. We knew the defense would attack her credibility on those grounds, so we decided to bring it out on direct. It went something like this:

SK: Shelly, do you currently have custody of your children?

Shelly: No I don't

SK: Why is that?

Shelly: My husband, my ex-husband, has them because I used to have a drinking problem.

SK: What happened, why did they get taken away?

Shelly: During our divorce my husband told the court that I would cut my arms and that I would drink around my kids, he accused me of leaving them alone. He called me an unfit mother to the court.

SK: Was that true?

Shelly: At the time some of it was true. I pray about it every day.

SK: Why were you drinking during that time?

Shelly: I was depressed. I was suicidal. I wanted to die. I couldn't handle anything.

SK: Why did you feel that way?

Shelly: That's just my life since I was in middle-school, I've always felt that way.

SK: When did your grandfather start abusing you?

Shelly: I moved in with him when I was 13.

SK: What grade were you in in school?

Shelly: About to start seventh grade.

SK: What was the custody hearing like?

Shelly: Horrible.

SK: Why?

Shelly: They told me I was gonna lose my kids because of my problems with drinking.

SK: How did that feel?

Shelly: It was the worst I had ever felt in my life.

SK: Shelly, did you tell a lie to the court about getting DUIs at that time.

Shelly: Yes I did.

SK: What was the lie?

Shelly: I had gotten 2 DUIs in Nevada but when my husband's lawyer asked me if I had been driving under the influence in the last few years I said no. Then he asked me about the DUIs and I said I never got them.

SK: Why did you deny that you got them?

Shelly: I was desperate. I thought that if I told the truth I would lose my kids, and I did lose them when my husband's attorney pulled out my Nevada record.

SK: Do you regret lying about the DUI?

Shelly: Every day. I have now been clean and sober for 2 and a half years and I still can't even visit my kids without a social worker watching me.

SK: Why should we believe you are telling the truth now if you told a lie then?

Shelly: I started drinking when I was 14 so I could get messed up enough to not think about what my grandfather used to do to me. I got my first DUI at 18. My life was a giant mess and I tried to numb it all out by drinking. At that time I lied because I would have said anything to try to keep my kids with me. I have been sober for almost 3 years,

and I'm not lying about what my grandfather did to me. I'm afraid he
is going to do it to my children.

Shelly went on to win her case despite a terrible flaw in her credibility. We
showed that she told that lie *because of the damage her grandfather's abuse caused.*
Not only was it a far less damaging fact to come out on cross-examination, she had
already explained it in a way the jurors could understand and sympathize with. We
turned a negative into something that was possibly even positive, we showed the
jurors just how desperate and damaged her life had been as a result of her
grandfather's actions. In the end we reinforced her credibility. Just remember that you
can't blame *everything* on the abuse, because jurors won't buy that. Ray Boucher puts
it this way:

> *"The trick of a trial lawyer is to take a weakness and turn it into a*
> *strength, because every weakness can be turned into a strength if you*
> *really chew on it. For example, if the family makeup was chaotic, you*
> *can show the jury that that chaos created the vulnerability and opened*
> *the victim up to the perp. In every case, there will be aspects of the*
> *case where you have to ask the jury to take the leap of faith. Explain it*
> *with experts, but don't try to excuse everything. Create credibility.*
> *Understate - don't overstate."*

So be real. Be emotional *if it is real.* Cry if you need to cry, be angry if you
are angry, get righteous if you feel righteous. Testifying is not about acting, that is a
dangerous misconception from TV. Jurors can smell the truth, and sometimes all you
need is for them to believe you. This is the time to be thorough in your answers, the

"answer the question and shut up" rule from depositions is not in effect during your direct exam (but it will be again in your cross!). Don't ramble, and pay attention to your attorney, they will guide you and lead you where you need to go if you listen.

Finally, remember that the most important people in the room are in the jury box (or the judge's seat if it is a judge-only trial). Look at them, make eye contact with them, talk *to* them, and turn your head towards them when you answer - it forms a connection with them that can be very powerful.

Be confident, be honest, be strong, and you will do an amazing job.

The Cross-Examination

The cross exam is the opposing attorney's opportunity to poke holes in your story, attack your credibility, highlight inconsistencies, and bring out facts that are bad for your case. It's gonna be tough. It can be bad, but I find often it isn't as bad as my clients have thought it was going to be. Here is the reality: attorneys can be real jerks during this part of your trial, and they are highly motivated to make you look bad, but the judge and jury know you are a victim, and they will be protective of you. Most attorneys know that being "hard" on a victim-witness can easily backfire. Many judges are also very protective and will quickly shut down badgering or harassing questions. Your attorney will also be there, shielding you from inappropriate questions and conduct by objecting.

Sometimes you should treat your cross examination similar to your deposition, giving short, honest answers to exactly what was asked (with an important exception, see below). Unlike your direct exam, you will be asked *closed questions*, meaning questions that imply the answer. Unlike the open question "What happened on that camping trip?" the closed question "You claim your father assaulted you on that camping trip, don't you?" calls for a very specific answer. Many of the questions you will be asked will be "yes or no" or "correct or incorrect" questions.

This is a double-edged sword, cross questions are easy to answer, but they make it easy to fall into traps and get *impeached*. Getting impeached means the attorney who is questioning you tries to challenge your honesty or your credibility through showing inconsistencies in your testimony. If you do get impeached, it's okay, just be calm and confident, it happens frequently in trials and it is one of the biggest reasons for cross-examination. You will have the chance to explain yourself when your attorney asks you more questions on *re-direct*.

Here are some tips. Even though the questions are "closed" you can answer them *however you want* – as long as you are actually answering the question asked. You are allowed to answer with context, explain yourself, and give more information (within reason of course). The lawyer may squawk and complain and sometimes the judge may tell you to answer yes or no, but don't think that the other attorney is in control: *you* are still the one on the stand! Remember Shelly? She was a great witness because she was strong and passionate, but was still thoughtful and in control of her answers. Take a look at these samples from her cross-examination:

Defense: You claim you were being abused the entire time you lived with your grandfather, correct?

Shelly: I was.

Defense: Yet you never reported any abuse to anyone during that time?

Shelly: My grandfather told me that no one would understand "our secret" and that no one would ever believe me if I told.

Defense: Ms. Donatelli, during the 5 and a half years that you lived with your grandfather, you never told anyone you were being abused, not even your parents isn't that correct?

Shelly: I didn't tell anyone because my grandfather swore he would kick me out if I told <u>anyone</u>. I didn't tell my dad because I didn't want him to think his father was a monster! I wanted to be in the house so he wouldn't hurt my little sister Olivia!

She could have easily answered "Yes. No. Yes." But look at how powerful her answers were when she stood up and defended herself. It was like a second opportunity for her to testify. Now take a look at how she handled herself when the attorney tried to pin her to yes or no answers.

Defense: At that time you had been living on your own for almost a year?

Shelly: Yes.

Defense: And yet you chose to move back in with the man you now say was abusing you, isn't that correct?

Shelly: I had nowhere else to go. I had no financial support if I wasn't living at home.

Defense: You chose to voluntarily return home didn't you. Yes or no?

Shelly: I moved back in with my grandfather because I had absolutely nowhere else to go. Moving back in with him was a nightmare and I cried and I had so much anxiety my hair fell out by the handfuls when I realized I had to go back. So yes I "voluntarily" returned home.

Shelly let herself be emotional, but she didn't fall apart, and even though she gave so much additional information she "answered" the question, which is proper. The defense attorney tried to make it look like if she was abused, she never would have moved back in with her grandfather. She gave such a vivid answer that she put the jury in her shoes and showed them both why she would move back in and how she felt about it.

Don't be combative and don't be rude, but answer the questions the way they need to be answered, the way that is *fair*. The attorney who is questioning you doesn't make the rules, the judge does, so listen to the judge's instructions but say what you need to say no matter how the attorney frames his questions. Otherwise be strong, be smart, and hang in there.

Closing Statements & Verdict

When all is said and done and all the evidence has been presented by both sides, the attorneys will give their closing arguments. They will passionately argue the facts and evidence that they have presented and talk about how the law applies. This is the last chance to influence the jurors on both sides, and both speeches will hit the jury hard.

After they are done, the judge will instruct them on the law and the process of coming to a verdict, and they will go confer in private (sometimes for a few days even) until they return a verdict to the judge. In many states it is the jury that decides what your damages are, and they fill out forms awarding general, specific, and punitive damages.

The jury will return to the courtroom when they have finished, and the jury foreman will stand and read the verdict aloud.

Congratulations. No matter what happens, this phase is over. You did it. Win lose or draw you stood up and spoke out, and you can always take pride in that.

Win, Lose, Heal – From Victim to Victor

You have reached the end of this stage of your journey, I hope with all my heart that you were vindicated in the eyes of the law, and won an award to compensate you for the pain and the heartache that was inflicted on you. If you were, I hope that this victory and the money you were awarded will buoy your spirit and help you along the road to feeling healthy and whole. Pay for therapy, pay for comfort, pay for education, pay for fun. Honor your journey by spending your money wisely and treating it as an opportunity to heal and live the life you want. I also encourage you to help other survivors navigate the process and reclaim their own lives.

If the outcome was something less than the victory you wanted, I'm so sorry. I know how hard the process was, and it is salt in a painful wound to have come so far and not walk away with victory. Even if you didn't win, you made the choice to sue because you knew it was something you had to do. You knew that taking action and speaking out was an important part of your healing process. You did it. You took the initiative and you spoke out. Win, lose, or draw this was a part of your personal journey of healing, and the benefits may surprise you in the end. An attorney colleague represented a male survivor in a bitterly contested trial, and in the end they only convicted the perpetrator on one of the lessor included claims and the damages awarded were pretty low. Months after the case ended, the survivor called his attorney's office and left the following message:

> *"I'm calling because I thought I should let you know how I've been doing. I thought you deserved to know. I've been doing really well with my therapy. I'm doing better with my daughter. I don't feel like I have an open wound anymore. So thank you."*

Even if you lose, this process still is a cleansing process. Even if the system didn't work for you, you still used the process to disinfect your wounds by bringing in light and fresh air. You stood up for yourself and are now a role model and mentor for other survivors. Keep your head up, stay on track, and try to see the loss as a necessary part of a greater process.

How to Collect a Verdict

We plaintiff's lawyers have a saying: You haven't won until the check clears. Unfortunately, collecting a judgment often isn't as easy as just getting a check in the mail. Many plaintiffs believe that as soon as the trial is over, the defendant will have to write a check the same day, and that's simply not the way it is. The collection process can be a long pain in the neck, and sometimes judgments turn out to be worth only the paper they are printed on. Hopefully the defendant(s) will pay what they owe, but if not, you have options.

Here is the good news: your lawyer will be highly motivated to help you collect on the judgment (especially if they took the case on contingency). That's pretty critical, because the collection process is different in every state, even county by county. If the defendant has a home, a business, land, a steady job, any access to a stream of income, you can probably go after it. For example, here in California the law allows for wages to be garnished or property to be *attached* (confiscated) and sold to satisfy the debt if you have a valid judgment. This is the bottom line of why identifying the assets we discussed earlier is so important: assets are like a guarantee of getting paid.

Judgments are powerful. In California and many other jurisdictions, the money owed from punitive damages cannot even be wiped clean in bankruptcy. If the verdict included punitives they will follow your perpetrator to the grave, part of every cent he earns in the state will go to you if you follow up closely.

Like everything else, if the defendant resists the judgment, it will require work and attention to make them pay. But your job is long done, let your attorney go after the money, if it's there a good attorney will find it. Between you and me, trying to collect a judgment is the fun part, you've already won and now you are playing hide and seek with money. Remember the story about the guy hiding his money in his backyard – I'm the only non-pirate I know who has ever found buried treasure.

Having a judgment executed against your abuser puts *you* in control of him, which is a powerful and empowering thing for a sexual abuser survivor.

CHAPTER EIGHT: **It Can Stop Today**

What To Do If You Or Someone You Know Is Being Sexually Abused

Stop [stop]

> verb
>
> prevent, obstruct, to hinder, restrain

Today [t*uh*-**dey**]

> adv.
>
> now, this day

"Doing the best at this moment puts you in the best place for the next moment."

- Oprah Winfrey

How to Deal with Ongoing Abuse

If you or a loved one are currently being abused, we have to put that "fire" out immediately and get you safe and out of harms way. Nothing else in this book matters until you are safe.

If You are a Teenager Living in an Abusive Home

If you are a child or teenager who is reading this while living in an abusive home, my heart goes out to you. Right now, you are enduring the worst that life has to offer.

Our first task is to get you safe, and that means taking on the complicated task of untangling you from your home and abuser. You have many different options, both short term and long term. Your options will vary based on what state and city you live in, because your legal options depend on state law and local help and resources vary by state, county, and city. **I would recommend starting with telling someone at your school.** Someone like a counselor, teacher, school nurse, or trusted coach or principal. Most states have laws that require schools to report sexual abuse and get help for victims. In my experience, most young CSA victims who are rescued from their abusers are rescued because an adult at school became involved. I believe telling someone at school is the simplest, safest, best place to start. If you have told adults at school, and no action has been taken, keep telling adults until someone help!! Believe me, eventually someone will help.

Other Than School, Where Else Can I Turn

The Police: These days, the police take charges of sexual abuse from children very seriously. If you are currently suffering from ongoing abuse, your best option might be going to the police. Many states have special police forces dedicated to sex crimes and systems in place to protect and shelter you. The TV show "Law and Order: SVU" is based on a real police unit in New York, and those types of units exist all over the country.

<u>Your Doctor</u>: You can tell your doctor during an appointment, or even call them at their office. Many laws require them to report abuse and help you.

<u>Emergency/Runaway Shelters</u>: You may be able to find food and a safe place to sleep at a local shelter. Most of these cannot shelter you for more than a day or 2 without having to call your parents by law.

<u>Friend or Relative's Home</u>: In many states, you DO NOT need court permission to stay with a friend or relative under many circumstances. Go to a trusted adult for help, you might find a safe place to stay and an ally to help you get to a permanently safe solution.

Getting Out Of The Abusive Situation Permanently

<u>Legal Guardianship</u>: If there is an adult relative or friend that you trust, look into to changing your legal guardianship status. Many state courts have mechanisms that allow abused children to change who their guardian is, especially in cases of sexual abuse. It is usually harder to change your guardian to a non-relative as opposed to a relative, but it can be done.

<u>Emancipation</u>: States usually have a mechanism for minors (under the age of adulthood) to be declared legal "adults" for the purposes of making medical decisions, school decisions, and deciding where to live. Most of the time, this will be a complicated process that will be very hard without the cooperation of your parents, but it can be done.

<u>Become a Ward or Dependent of Court (Foster Care)</u>: This is the option with the biggest downside. This will make your guardian the state, meaning you will probably be placed in foster care or in a group home. If your current home is a

sexually abusive environment, I still recommend that you consider this. Every child in the state's care is entitled to a social worker and a lawyer, and you will be allowed to leave your home and go somewhere safe.

Believe me when I tell you that there is a brighter, better, safe, happy life waiting for you out there. Those who have gone before you have survived and thrived, and you have begun that journey by reading books like this.

I know that leaving home as a teenager is an incredibly difficult task. It is daunting and intimidating. It is a huge decision to call the police on your abuser or to leave home, but it is the right decision. It is made more complicated because every circumstance is different; your abuser may neglect you completely and not care if you leave or might become violent and dangerous. Each parent and each abuser has their own agenda, and it is possible you might face tough adult resistance if you try to escape. Some parents don't want the embarrassment, some know they face legal consequences, some want to preserve their illusions of a perfect family, and some abusers simply don't want to lose their object of sexual pleasure.

Not only that, but it is tough when you are dependent on the food, shelter, and money that comes from being at home. That is perfectly natural, in nature, animals take care of their young until the young can take care of themselves. What is happening to you is unnatural, and it is breaking that cycle and putting you in a difficult position.

"The best advice I can give you is to tell someone at your school and keep telling! Tell people, break the silence. No one can help you if they don't know what's happening. Be brave and don't quit, you have already survived the worst part."

\- Shari Karney

Use the resources that are available to make yourself safe. Go online and educate yourself about the government resources, church organizations, support groups, local non-profits, women's groups, and shelters that can help you. Make phone calls, talk to guidance counselors, call the police if you have to. You will get through this. You are not alone.

If Your Friend or Sibling is Being Abused

Again, tell trusted adults that this is going on. Tell a teacher, counselor, principal, nurse.

This is a very difficult situation for a brother or sister or friend to be in. I know that you may feel powerless to help, but you can. If you are a minor, like a kid or a teenager, the most important thing you can do is to *tell other adults* about what is happening. Another way of doing this is to convince your friend or sibling to tell other adults themselves. Sexual abuse withers in the light. When other people know it's going on, other adults will step in to help. I recommend telling a teacher, school counselor, school nurse, or a principal everything you know about your friend or sibling being abused. In most states, the law demands that they report the abuse to the proper authorities, who will step in and protect the person being taken advantage of.

This is the best way you can help, you don't have the power to step in and fix things yourself, but you can get help for them. If the first person you tell doesn't help, tell someone else, eventually the right authorities will get involved.

The biggest thing that gets in the way of friends and siblings reporting rape and molestation is actually *trust*. Usually, the victim has made you swear or promise that you wouldn't tell anyone. They have done this because they are traumatized or embarrassed or scared, maybe their abuser has threatened them, or maybe they just don't know what to do. Here is what you need to know: When the victim is a kid or a teenager, **that decision isn't up to them**. They need to be protected from their abuser, and that can't happen while it is kept a secret.

It is my opinion as a survivor and attorney that **child victims of sexual abuse don't have the legal authority, maturity, or experience to freely choose to keep their abuse a secret**. No matter what their perpetrator has told them, they are in greater danger while abuse is kept secret and is going on unchecked. The longer it goes on, the worse the damage is becoming, and the more powerful the hold the abuser has on the victim. If you have been told about sexual abuse, the most noble thing you can do, and the best way that you can be a friend, is to go to the police or to a school counselor. It may hurt your friendship with that person in the short or even the long term, but you just may save their life.

If Your Child is Being Abused

If you are an adult and you suspect your child or a child you care about might be getting abused, you need to take immediate precautions to keep them safe. If a child *tells* you that abuse occurred, even if they deny it or take it back later, they were almost certainly telling the truth the first time. If the suspected abuser is also a loved one, like a boyfriend, husband, brother, father, cousin, or female relative, you are in a difficult position - but you *cannot* allow that relationship to shield the abuse of a child.

When a child tells you something or you see something that indicates abuse, you have to keep a level head. The child's wellbeing is your number one priority, and you must act calmly and rationally. Talk to the child and tell them that anything that happened is not their fault, that you believe them, and that they are "good" for telling you. Make sure to say that you are there to keep them safe, and that telling adults is the way to be safe.

Then, if you are sure enough that abuse occurred, you need to take the child to the police and/or a sexual abuse medical professional right away. To contact the police, dial 911 or call or go to your local hospital emergency room or rape crisis center and tell them what you believe is happening. Some cities, like Santa Monica, California, have special centers which combine the services of law enforcement, social services, and medical professionals trained in helping and treating child victims of sexual abuse. The facility in Santa Monica is called the Stewart House. To try to find services like that in your area, do the following:

Here's how to do it:

1. Google this: "National Children's Alliance"
2. Go to their website
3. Click the "Find a local National Children's Alliance Member Location" link

4. Select your state

5. Begin calling the facilities in your area, talk about what happened and ask for help finding out what to do.

Many cities have child advocacy centers where children and family members can get help – ask them what you need to do. These centers know how to interview children and family members in a sensitive, warm place, give the child the medical care they need, and preserve evidence that can be critical to stopping the abuse. They can also help report the abuse to the proper authorities. If you cannot actually make it to a nearby facility, they can help you find a medical examiner and therapist skilled in child sexual abuse in your area.

The next step is, if you have the power to do so, end the child's contact with the suspected abuser. This may involve going to the police and telling them what has happened. If the abuser is a legal guardian of the child this is especially important. Many states have laws that are very protective of children when sexual abuse allegations are made, often there are programs that can get children out of an abusive home almost immediately.

Be *very very* cautious about making these allegations with only bare suspicion, I am 100% in favor of acting early to protect children, but making an allegation of child abuse without being able to prove it can be very damaging to proving it in the long run. It puts the abuser on notice that he needs to hide his conduct, he can more credibly claim you are just being malicious, and he can hide or destroy any evidence that does exist. It is not unheard of for parents in contentious custody battles to make false claims of child abuse to help their cases, that's one of the reasons why courts look at these allegations seriously, but also skeptically.

CHAPTER NINE: **It's A Crime – Can I Send My Abuser To Jail**
Navigating the Justice System

Crime [krim]

>noun

>grave offense against morality, reprehensible, disgraceful

Jail [jail]

>verb

>to take into or hold in lawful custody; imprison.

>*"True peace is not merely the absence of tension: it is the presence of justice."*

>- Martin Luther King

Child Sexual Abuse Is Also A Crime

The criminal law is very different to navigate than the civil law is. The criminal justice system can be far easier and more helpful for some victims than the civil law, and for others it can be a frustrating dead end. The most important difference is that *you have almost no control over the criminal process*. Other than taking the initiative to report the crime, give a statement, and press charges, the process is completely out of your hands. Unlike the civil system, you neither have control nor are responsible for the costs of a criminal prosecution. The state will prosecute and punish a criminal on behalf of the citizens of the state ("the people") for violating the laws. This means no cost to you. A state employee district attorney will be the prosecutor and the defendant will either hire a defense attorney or be represented by a public defender.

Your first step is going to the police. The police have the power to gather evidence and make arrests when they believe a punishable crime has been committed. If they believe, based on your statements, that your abuser has committed a crime that they can make a valid arrest for they will most likely open an investigation and/or arrest your perpetrator. They may search him or his property, question him and other witnesses, interrogate him, or detain him as well. Your involvement at this stage will probably be limited to making the initial report to the police, making a statement, filling out a victim impact report, and getting interviewed by a police investigator or a detective. Otherwise it is up to the police.

Whether it has been 10 hours, 10 months, or 10 years since you were abused - you should go to the police if you want your perpetrator prosecuted, but at this stage, the sooner you act the better.

If they do make an arrest, then the matter goes to the district attorney. The district attorney determines what laws they think were violated and uses their *prosecutorial discretion* to choose whether or not to attempt to convict the defendant on those crimes. For the crimes they choose to proceed with against the defendant, they initiate a criminal trial and begin to build a case. They work with the police (and possibly you) to try to gather as much evidence as possible to convict the defendant by a jury at trial.

But nothing is guaranteed, especially for old cases. The state has discretion at many levels to take or not take a case. The police can decline to investigate or make an arrest for a number of reasons, the age of the alleged crime, lack of proof, lack of jurisdiction, etc. They may also accept your complaint of wrongdoing but then do a weak investigation and fail to make an arrest.

The district attorney may also decline to prosecute your abuser's case for any number of reasons, this is the downside of the criminal process. Don't get me wrong, the police will take claims of rape and child molestation very seriously, but the older the claim is – the less likely they are going to be able to do anything about it.

Police procedure and the willingness of individual police officers and police forces to handle this type of crime is different everywhere, so don't hesitate to pick up the phone and call your local police force to find out what your options are.

Pre-Trial Stages

Criminal law unfolds in many different ways. The police might go directly to your abusers home or workplace and arrest him or they might issue a "soft" warrant, which means the police will arrest him if they find him, but they will not go *looking* for him.

If your abuser is arrested, he will be brought to the local jail, booked, processed, and will go in front of a judge for their *arraignment.* The judge will tell them the charges against them and set the bail amount, which gives the defendant the option of depositing that much money with the court as a guarantee they will show up for the rest of their proceedings. If they put up that much money, they will be out of jail while their trial is in progress. If your abuser is dangerous or a flight risk (likely to flee the state) the judge may deny them bail.

Once the proceedings have gone this far, you should seriously consider getting a lawyer who is familiar with the criminal process. They can be invaluable in asserting your rights. Sometimes, even in the law, the squeaky wheel gets the grease. Your lawyer can help protect your rights and interests and be a critical go-between for you and the prosecution.

Remember - if you are going to try to sue civilly (for money damages) *and* get your abuser prosecuted criminally (try to send him to jail) there are important procedural and evidence issues to consider. You need to work with your attorney to determine when and how to coordinate your civil and criminal cases to get the best results and not jeopardize either.

By this time, you will probably have someone from the District Attorney's office or a police detective who will act as your liaison to the prosecution and investigation teams. You are the victim, and your testimony will probably be the most powerful evidence that the prosecution has. You are critical to the case, and they should hopefully treat you as such. If you don't feel like you have someone from law enforcement you can call to get updates or to give information to, contact the investigating police or the prosecuting attorney to try to arrange a "point" person to talk to.

Preliminary Hearing

This stage of the pre-trial process has a few different names in different jurisdictions. In California we know it as the preliminary hearing or "pre-lim," other jurisdictions call it the "probable cause hearing." Basically, after the D.A. has filed a charge against your abuser, the prosecution and defense go before a judge to determine if there is enough evidence to warrant a trial. In the United States, the judge has to find that there is "probable cause" that a crime was committed in order to go forward.

You will most likely be involved at this step - this is the first time the prosecutor will need to show evidence of the abuse, and that means your testimony. This is a necessary step, and it's a *little bit* like the civil deposition, though not nearly as difficult. Mostly, it will be the prosecutor asking you easy questions to lay out the *prima facie* case for the judge, which means they are showing the judge they have a minimum level of evidence to justify a trial.

Defense counsel will get to question you as well, but it typically is brief and relatively limited. Do expect them to try to nail down your version of events, because record is kept of your testimony and later you can be *impeached* (not like a President; it means busted for inconsistency on the stand) if you give them a different version of the facts. Work with and listen to the District Attorney, they should work with you quite a bit and guide you before you testify. I also recommend reading the sections

above about giving a deposition and testifying in a civil matter, they will both help you prepare for this phase and testifying at the trial.

"Criminal Discovery"

There is no "criminal discovery" in the way we refer to it in the civil sense. Some lawyers and judges in some jurisdictions call it that, but there isn't really the same opportunity for asking questions and exchanging information. Because the burden of proving the sexual abuse rests squarely on the prosecution and the Constitution protects criminal defendants from testifying against themselves, criminal prosecutors can't just send a bunch of interrogatories to the perpetrator.

However, in most states, the prosecutor, who gets their evidence from you and the police, has ethical obligations to give most of that information to the defense. Here in California, prosecutors have to make the defense aware of "anything that may show innocence." The only thing the defense has to hand over is the names of people they have talked to, to give the prosecution a bare minimum level of info about likely witnesses.

For your purposes, this will be a totally different process and require way less from you than civil discovery did. Sometimes the defense will send an investigator to talk to you, and how much you have to cooperate with them varies from state to state. Your general rule should be do what the District Attorney advises you to do, and otherwise, say nothing to anyone from the defense without a court order that says you must do so.

Pre-Trial Conferences - Plea Bargaining

This is a meeting (or a series of meetings) between the DA and your abuser's defense counsel where they try to "hammer out a deal." This is what's known as a "plea-bargain" - reduced punishments in exchange for pleading "guilty" or "no contest" (not admitting guilt but not denying it). This is like a condensed version of the settlement process in a civil proceeding.

You need to know that statistically, *a plea-bargain is very likely to occur*. Sexual abuse cases are complex and hard-fought by abusers because of the seriousness and stigma of the crime, but even these cases settle at very high rates. This becomes a *very mixed* bag for survivors.

In civil actions offers to settle are generally good to see for plaintiffs, and you can also choose to reject them if they are unsatisfying. In my experience victims of crimes of all types, and especially sexual abuse victims, expect hardcore "TV style" prosecution, and they usually are disappointed.

Quite often, the terms of the plea-bargain seem pretty soft and forgiving. I find that sometimes victims feel like they are *sold out* by the prosecution at this phase and their criminal action ends anti-climactically. Depending on your prosecutor, it might really surprise you what offers will be on the table: no jail time, no sex offender registration, pleading guilty to smaller misdemeanors instead of their real crimes etc.

I hope that the District Attorney who leads your case will be a warrior, but I want you to be prepared for this kind of outcome. This is another time where it can be extremely helpful to be represented by an attorney of your own, because in many jurisdictions the judge has to approve proposed plea-bargains and you may or may not get to have a say at that hearing. No matter what, encourage your District Attorney to be firm and don't be surprised if your case doesn't make it to trial.

Criminal Trial

The criminal process unfolds at blinding speeds compared to the glacial pace of civil litigation. This is mostly because the Constitution guarantees a speedy trial to the accused and because there is only a fraction of the "discovery." Most criminal prosecutions, even complex ones, take as little as few months from start to finish. Expect the criminal trial process itself to track very closely to what you learned about the civil trial process. There are some differences: the burden of proof is different, the statutes and jury instructions will be different, and some evidence may be suppressed for constitutional reasons.

You will probably be asked to testify by the DA, and if you don't want to testify, they will probably drop the case. That sounds harsh, but you are probably their best evidence of the abuse. Besides, the jury has to be unanimous to convict and they will want to see and hear the victim of these crimes. Work with the DA, listen to their advice, and everything will be fine. Refer to the civil sections above for a guide to testifying and being cross-examined.

Once the jury returns the verdict, it is in the judge's hands to determine the sentence. At the sentencing hearing, you may get a chance to speak or your statement about how the crime affected you (victim impact statement) may be read. This can be one of the most pivotal moments for sexual abuse victims, because you can truly impact the severity of your abuser's punishment if you can move the court with your words.

I recommend working with your therapist and legal counsel to figure out how to truly sum up the damage that has been done and what it meant to you. The judge may return a sentence of state prison, county jail, sex offender registration, fines, probation, community service, mandatory classes or therapy, or some combination of those. Like before, hope for the best but be prepared for the sentence to be unsatisfying.

If you make it this far, congratulations. You are a warrior who has furthered the cause for all of us! You stood up, got help, and did everything you could to bring society's justice down on a sexual predator. Your heroism may very well have saved other children from the horrors of abuse.

Use The State's Power - Other Options For Stopping Your Abuser

Getting your abuser arrested and prosecuted isn't the only way to use the power of the state against them, you have other options for protecting yourself and protecting others as well.

One option is getting a *restraining order*. A restraining order makes it illegal for someone to come near you or contact you. You can go to the court or the police to find out what procedures you need to undertake to get a restraining order. In most jurisdictions they can be gotten relatively quickly based only on your statements to a judge about what kind of danger the person poses to you. They can be awarded as temporary or permanent. These are especially helpful and effective if your abuser is violent and/or you are trying to get away from them or protect yourself from them.

If there are other children you want to protect from your perpetrator you can contact your state's equivalent of Child Protective Services. It has different names in different states, but its function is to protect children from just this type of harm. These agencies take accusations of abuse deadly serious, and may take the children from the home they are living in. They will interview them and conduct an investigation into the abuser's conduct. They have the authority to even permanently remove children from their parents or guardians if evidence of abuse is found.

You can also consult an attorney to find out what other options you have in using the power of the state to help protect you and others.

AFTERWORD

How We Changed The Law

"Laws should be like clothes. They should be made to fit the people they serve."

- Clarence Darrow

Remember Mary Doe from before? Hers was the heartbreaking case we fought all the way to the California Supreme Court for, and it had everything to do with the statute of limitations. Mary Doe spent years being raped and brutalized by her father, and then came to us for justice.

As a child, unable to understand the significance of what was happening to her and overwhelmed by the trauma of the invasive sexual abuse, she blocked out all memory of it. She denied she was abused, repressed the memories, and disassociated from what her father had done to her. As a result, she grew up without remembering that these incidents had happened. Her mind blocked out all memories of her abuse for almost 20 years.

Mary Doe:

I went through my teens and early adulthood where I drank heavily, took drugs, was sexually promiscuous, and suffered low self-esteem. I attempted suicide 5 times. Finally, I got arrested for drunk driving and was court ordered into mandatory drug and alcohol rehab. Sobriety led to me to psychotherapy, and that process led me to the release of my repressed memories.

I decided to take her case because I was so outraged at what her father had done to her. Even more outrageous was that the law had let him get away with it. It meant that smart predators should select younger children to molest, because the younger the child, the more likely the child will repress the horrible memories in order to function and survive.

It was time for someone to fight back and stand up for victims. Perpetrators were getting a free ride in California and throughout the United States because of statutes of limitations, and it was their victims who were serving the life-long sentences of re-living trauma they didn't ask for.

We filed suit on Doe's behalf and, almost immediately, Doe's father filed a motion for summary judgment. Summary judgment means that a judge makes a decision about a point of law that seems clear on its face, and rules without a full trial. The judge agreed with Doe's father's argument that our case was "time-barred." It meant that we couldn't sue because we were *too late*, even though Mary had only recently uncovered her memories.

But we weren't finished. We argued that the legal doctrine of *delayed discovery* (explained below) applied to Doe's case. Basically, we made the argument that it wasn't fair that her "clock" was running before she ever even remembered the abuse! I had read a passage by Martin Luther King, Jr. in law school that always stuck with me, and we took its principles to heart:

"Law and order exist for the purpose of establishing justice and when they fail in this purpose they become the dangerously structured dams that block the flow of social progress."

We argued the dramatic unfairness of the system and the importance of delayed discovery, but the lower court ruled against us. The judge wrote "Although we sympathize with what Doe has allegedly gone through, she is too late for the law to provide a remedy for her. Not all wrongs can be righted by the law." He went on to say that the law in California required that Doe file suit before her 19th birthday. If she *"sat on her rights* she couldn't expect the law to help her."

In our legal system *precedent* is crucial, that means that the law tries to rule consistently with past decisions. When the trial court ruled that Doe was barred from suing her abusive father it meant that every subsequent survivor of child sexual abuse who didn't get a lawyer and file a lawsuit by their nineteenth birthday would also be barred. Not only would our abusers be able to silence us, but now there would be a conspiracy of silence - with the legal system inadvertently protecting those who had preyed upon us.

Who was the law protecting? As it was, it was working to protect the abusers and the wrongdoers. The statutes of limitations were punishing the victims. These laws are in place for reasons that make sense in most civil cases, but not in sexual abuse cases. My law partner and I decided we had to take Doe's case as a test case to get the law changed for all adult survivors.

I believed we were fighting for victims so they could get their day in court. We believed the law should be a path to justice. We took the stance that the sexual abuse against children is a crime against humanity and should be treated as such by the legal system. I still believe that today.

At the time, many people treated me like I was crazy. I fought tooth and nail in the courtroom. I had a reputation as a no nonsense, take-no-prisoners litigator. When I think about those days and how exhausting they were, I think my engine must have been running on pure passion, and my passion came from the empathy I had for the pain and injustice survivors were feeling in a legal system that was stacked against them.

We decided, with Doe's consent, to use her case as a test case to push the courts and the law to their limits. The perpetrators of this horrible crime were getting away with it, shielded by the law. Not on my watch!

We appealed the decision of the lower court to the California Court of Appeal.

With tremendous support from the California Women Lawyers Association, the ACLU Foundation of Southern California, the California Consortium of Child Abuse Councils, and the Youth and Family Coalition (filing Amicus Curiae briefs), we continued to stand our ground. In our supporting briefs, we made this argument:

> *"If the Court sustains the trial court's ruling, it will provide the perpetrators of the most heinous forms of child sexual abuse with the greatest protection from liability, by virtue of the fact that the severest abuse will be that which is most deeply buried and repressed by its*

victims. This was never the intended nor is it the purpose of the statute

of limitation."

On Nov. 30th, 1989, in San Jose, the California Court of Appeal, 6th District, made a revolutionary decision and wrote:

> *"Although her memory of the alleged abuse came long after the statute*
> *of limitations had passed, Mary Doe should not be denied her day in*
> *court. The doctrine of delayed discovery should be applied, for the*
> *first time in California, to survivors of childhood sexual abuse."*

Further, the court went on and said the old application was in direct conflict with the true purpose of the statute of limitations. The appellate court decided that Mary Doe was entitled to proceed against her father, and sent the case back to the lower court so that the trial of *Mary Doe v. John Doe* could proceed.

We were ecstatic with the decision of the Appellate Court; we filed twenty-five other cases on behalf of sexual abuse survivors in various courts throughout California. But before the ink had even dried on the Appellate Court's decision, Doe's father filed an appeal to the California Supreme Court challenging the Appellate Court's interpretation of the law.

Doe's father (an awful man, very aggressive, smart, devious, and unrelenting to the end) appealed the case to the California Supreme Court arguing that the statute of limitations should be applied strictly to his daughter's lawsuit and that her case against him should be dismissed.

I don't always trust judges, and at the time I didn't trust the California Supreme Court. I didn't think the legal system could understand what it is like to be a survivor. I told my law partner we had to work on changing the law through the state legislature as well. We were already working 17-hour days and lobbying for legislation is an enormous task. She thought it would split our energy and focus. For once in my life, my trust issues actually helped me succeed. I didn't trust the courts and didn't want to put all of our legal eggs, time, passion, and effort into one basket. We had to take it to the people.

It took us 6 years to finally accomplish what we set out to do. We fought with California legislators in a daily struggle. I was unwilling to accept the kind of compromises being pushed on us in order for the bill to pass. I could not do it. I could not sell out the survivors who were counting on us. I was not popular or well liked.

Often, I was treated very disrespectfully. The entire legislative team was furious with my stubborn position but I wouldn't agree to watering-down the bill. At one point, they didn't speak to me for over a year.

I realized we weren't going to win this case in the courts or the legislature until we won it with the people of California. That meant a full out media campaign. We had no other choice, so we funded it ourselves. We launched a grass roots movement for survivor's rights, and tried to raise resources and support to stay afloat when the opposition was attacking us. Finally, after all of our hard work and all the uncertainty, the Legislature passed and the Governor signed our bill, called SB108, and CCP 340.1, the statute of limitations section of the California Code of Civil Procedure was changed. Now survivors of child sexual abuse were going to have their day in court and finally be able to hold their perpetrators accountable. Survivors were taking their power back in California. It was one of the sweetest victories of my life. Finally, a victory for our team—team survivor!

I Wish You The Best In Your Journey

As you undertake this monumental task of holding your perpetrator accountable and in the process finding your own voice, please know that my heart and love are with you. As someone who knows what it means to walk your path, I know you have the strength and the courage to do what is best for you. I support you as sisters and brothers in this fight.

Like Oprah says *"turn your wounds into wisdom."*

With Love,
Shari Karney

Contact Shari

I would love to hear from you! To e-mail Shari about how Prey No Longer helped you or impacted your life, to write a review, to tell Shari or other survivors your personal story of how you took action against your abuser(s) e-mail: info@sharikarney.com

To receive Shari's newsletter or to read or post comments on her blog, go to www.sharikarney.com. There are links on the website to connect with her via Twitter, Facebook, Google+, and LinkedIn.

You can also take your power back by going to law school and passing the bar! These days she owns a company that helps law graduates become lawyers by helping them pass the bar. Go to www.barwinners.com for more information.

RESOURCES

To assist you in finding an attorney and navigating the law in your state we have compiled some references and resources for you that might be helpful in your research. We have included a list of plaintiff's attorneys you can contact about your case, organized by region, and a list of some local support groups you can contact.

Please understand that Shari Karney herself is no longer actively practicing law and is no longer accepting cases. She wishes she could take every case and help each of you individually, but she now devotes her time to fighting for this cause on a national and international level. We have also done our best to give you a basic guide to the law governing statutes of limitations in your state, organized state-by-state, at the end of Chapter 3.

Once again, the information we are providing you is just that: general information to assist you in finding legal counsel, finding support, and pursuing your case. We are not making any representations or guarantees about the lawyers, law firms, or groups listed, nor are we guaranteeing that they will take your case. Some of the contact information may not be current.

The information in the Statute of Limitations chart **is not legal advice** and is subject to change. Even if, based on the chart, you believe your statute of limitations may have expired, you should still seek legal counsel and pursue a definitive answer from a qualified, competent professional who knows the specifics of your case. In other words, the chart is just there for your information, not to be relied on instead of an attorney.

Attorney Listing (Alphabetical by State)

Alabama

Turner & Webb, PC
2312 University Blvd.
Tuscaloosa AL 35402
(205) 535-1034
http://www.turnerwebbroberts.com

Capell & Howard, P.C
150 South Perry St.
Montgomery AL 36104
(334) 241-8000
http://www.capellhoward.com

Clifford W. Cleveland, II
711 McQueen Smith Rd
S. Prattville AL 36066
(334) 365-6266
http://www.prattvilleattorneys.com

Melton, Espy & Williams, P.C
255 Dexter Ave
Montgomery AL 36104
(334) 263-6621
http://www.mewlegal.com

The Atchison Firm, P.C
3030 Knollwood Dr
Mobile AL 36693
(251) 665-7200
http://www.atchisonlaw.com

Proctor & Vaughn, LLC
201 North Norton Ave
Sylacauga AL 35150

(256) 249-8527
http://www.proctorvaughn.com

Hardwich, Hause, Segrest & Walding
212 North Lena St
Dothan AL 36302
(866) 409-4036
http://hhswlawfirm.com

Briskman & Binion, P.C
205 Church Street
Mobile AL 36601
(251) 433-7600
http://www.briskman-binion.com

Warren & Simpson, P.C
105 North Side Square
Huntsville AL 35801
(256) 539-7575
http://www.warrenandsimpson.com

Watson, McKinney & Artip, LLP
203 Greene Street
Huntsville AL 35801
(256) 536-7423
http://www.watsonmckinney.com

Redden, Mills & Clark, LLP
505 - 20th Street North
Birmingham AL 35203
(205) 588-2877
http://www.rmclaw.com

Sides, Oglesby, Held, Dick & Burgess
1310 leighton Ave
Anniston AL 36201
(256) 237-6611
http://www.sohdb.com

Wilkins, Bankester, Biles & Wynne
201 East Second St
Bay Minette AL 36507
(251) 937-7024

Vernis & Bowling of Birmingham, LLC
2100 Southbridge Parkway, Suite 650
Birmingham AL 35209
(205) 445-1026
http://national-law.com

Coumanis & York, PC
2102 Main st
Daphne AL 36526
(251) 990-3083
http://www.c-ylaw.com

Cassady & Cassady PC
201 Rural Street
Evergreen AL 36401
(251) 578-5252
www.southalabamalawyers.com/

The Anderson Law Firm
7515 Halcyon Pointe Dr
Montgomery AL 36117
(334) 694-1039
www.theandersonlawfirm.com/

Smith & Smith LLP
328 First Ave SE
Cullman AL 35055
(256) 841-4365
http://www.smithandsmithllp.com

Edwards, Belser & Smith
123 Less Street
Decatur AL 35601

(256) 353-6323
http://www.alaattorney.com

Helmsing, Leach, Herlong, Newman & Rouse, PC
150 Government St, Ste 2000
Mobile AL 36602
(251) 432-5521
http://www.helmsinglaw.com

Knight Griffith LLP
409 First Ave
SW Cullman AL 35056
(256) 734-0456

Alaska

Doherty & Stuart, P.C
750 West Second Ave, Ste, 105
Anchorage AK 99501
(877) 314-3301

Cook Schuhmann & Groseclose Inc
714 Fourth Ave, Ste 200
Fairbanks AK 99701
(907) 452-1855

Crowell & Morning, LLP
1029 3rd Ave, Ste 402
Anchorage AK 99501
(907) 865-2600

Arizona

Mushkatel & Becker, PLLC
15249 North 99th Ave, Ste A
Sun City AZ 85351
(623) 889-0691

Renaud Cook Drury Mesaros, PA
One North Central Ste. 900
Phoenix AZ 85004
(602) 307-9900
http://www.rcdmlaw.com

Karp & Weiss, P.C.
3060 North Swan Road
Tucson AZ 85712
(520) 325-4200
http://www.karpweiss.com

Piccarreta Davis PC
145 South Sixth Ave
Tucson AZ 85701
(520) 622-6900
http://www.pd-law.com

Marc J. Victor, PC
3920 South Alma School Rd. Ste 5
Chandler AZ 85248
(520) 413-4382
www.attorneyforfreedom.com

Law Offices of Robert M. Cook
219 West 2nd St
Yuma AZ 85364
(928) 782-7771
http://robertmcooklaw.com

Hawkins & Hawkins, PLLC
1930 North Arboleda, Ste. 216
Mesa AZ 85213
(866) 673-7952
www.hawkinsandhawkins.com

John C. Churchill
1300 Joshua Ave, Ste. B
Parker AZ 85344
(928) 669-6195
http://johnchurchilllaw.com

Burch & Cracchiolo, PA
702 East Osborn Rd., Ste. 200
Phoenix AZ 85014
(602) 388-1847
http://www.bcattorneys.com

Rothstein, Donatelli, Hughes, Dahlstorm, Schoenburg & Bienvenu
80 East Rio Salado Pkwy., Ste 305
Tempe AZ 85281
(480) 921-9296
http://www.rothsteinlaw.com

Borrowlec, Borrowlec & Russell, PC
4226 Avenida Cochise, Ste. 5
Sierra Vista AZ 85635
(520) 417-0221
http://borowiecrussell.net

Scott A. McKay, PC
7601 North 22nd Pl
Phoenix AZ 85020
(602)957-1612
http://scottamckay.com

Slaton Law Office, PC
6730 N. Scottsdale Rd., Ste. 233

Scottsdale AZ 85253
(888) 342-9450
http://sandraslaton.com

Arnold N. Hirsch
Apache Junction AZ 85117
(888) 865-1170
http://www.arnoldhirschlaw.com

McGuire Gardner, PLLC
2915 East Baseline Rd., Ste. 109
Gilbert AZ 85234
(623)208-6086
http://www.mcguiregardner.com

Sara J. Powell
550 West Portland St
Phoenix AZ 85234
(602) 996-4447
http://sarapowell.com

Curry, Pearson & Wooten, PLC
814 W. Roosevelt St
Phoenix AZ 85007
(602) 635-1726
http://www.azlaw.com

Rowley, Chapman, Barney & Buntrock, Ltd
63 East Main St., Ste 501
Mesa AZ 85201
(480)833-1113
http://www.azlegal.com

Law Offices of Jeffrey J. Rogers, PLC
177 North Church Ave., Ste 700
Tucson AZ 85701
(520) 505-5182
http://jrogerslaw.com

Shari Karney

Arkansas

Simpson, Simpson & Collier
200 N. Spring St
Searcy AR 72143
(888) 699-1844
http://simpsonsimpsoncollier.com

Taylor Law Partners LLP
303 E. Millsap Rd
Fayetteville AR 72703
(479)443-5222
http://taylorlawpartners.com

Hilburn, Calhoon, Harper, Pruniski & Calhoun
One Riverfront Pl., Eighth Fl
Little Rock AR 72119
(501) 372-0110
http://hilburnlawfirm.com

Hughes Law Office
400 W. Capitoal, Ste. 1700
Little Rock AR 72201
(888) 399-7051
www.myarkansaslawyer.com

California

Angeloff, Angeloff & Levine
910 North State St. Ste. C
Hemet CA 92543
(951) 652-2000
http://www.angelofflaw.com

Kestenbaum, Eisner & Gorin
333 S. Grand Ave
LA CA 90071
(877) 781-1570
http://www.keglawyers.com

Okabe & Haushalter
225 Aveue I, Ste. 201
Redondo Beach CA 90277
(310) 953-3700
www.southbaylawyer.com

Cartwright, Scruggs, Fulton & Walther
340 Soquel Ave, Suite 215
Santa Cruz CA 95062
(831) 457-1700
http://www.csfwlaw.com

The Law Firm of Brenneman, Juarez & Adam, LLP
625 East Chapel St
Santa Maria CA 93454
(805) 619-5060
http://santamarialawyers.com

Bley and Bley
555 Montgomery St., Ste. 605
San Francisco CA 94111
(415) 982-7311
http://www.bleyandbley.com

Scott Gailen, Inc
6322 Fallbrook Ave, Ste. 101
Woodland Hills CA 91367
(888) 354-1370
http://gailenlaw.com

Fischer Schrader, LLP
888 Munras Ave
Monterey CA 93940
(831) 920-4153
http://www.fs-legal.com

Murphy, Logan & Bardwell
2350 First St.
Napa CA 94581
(707) 927-0410
http://napavalleylawfirm.com

Mary Alexander & Associates, PC
44 Montgomery St., Ste 1303
San Francisco CA 94104
(415) 433-4440
http://www.maryalexanderlaw.com

Benjamin, Weil & Mazar, APC
235 Montgomery St., Ste 760
San Francisco CA 94104
(415) 421-0730
http://www.bwmlaw.com

Bohn & Bohn ,LLP
152 North 3rd St., Ste 200
San Jose CA 95112
(408) 514-5077
www.bohn-brain-spinal-lawyer.com

Boskovich & Appleton
28 North First St., Ste. 600

San Jose CA 95113
(408) 286-5150
www.bayareatrialattorneys.com

Glassman, Browning, Saltsman & Jacobs, Inc
360 North Bedford Dr. Ste. 204
Beverly Hills CA 90210
(310) 598-2163
http://gbsjlaw.com

Taylor & Ring
10900 Wilshire Blvd., Ste 920
LA CA 90024
(310) 584-7685
http://www.taylorring.com

Law Offices of Robert W. Ripley & Associates
14440 Civic Dr., Ste. A
Victorville CA 92392
(760) 780-1421
http://www.ripleyslaw.com

Bishop, Barry & Drath, PC
2000 Powell St., 14th Flr
Emeryville CA 94608
(510) 343-6961
http://www.bishop-barry.com

Scher & Bassett
465 S. Mathilda Ave., Ste. 210
Sunnyvale CA 94086
(408) 739-5300
www.scherandbassett.com

Law Offices of John H. Anderson
105 E. Mariposa
San Clemente CA 92672

Shari Karney

(949) 272-0953
www.johnandersonlaw.com

Ferguson Case Orr Peterson, LLP
1050 S. Kimball Rd
Ventura CA 93004
(805) 659-6800
http://www.fcoplaw.com

Kiesel, Boucher & Larson LLP
8648 Wilshire Blvd
Beverly Hills CA 90211
(800) 356-9898

The Zalkin Law Firm, P.C.
12555 High Bluff Dr
Suite 260
San Diego, CA 92130
California:
(858) 259-3011
http://www.zalkin.com/

Colorado

Prendergast & Associates, PC
1901 West Littleton Blvd., Ste 200
Littleton CO 80120
(720) 253-0031
www.criminaljusticeco.com

Mountain Law Group, LLC
70 Benchmark Rd.
Avon CO 81620
(970) 688-4144
http://www.mountainlawgroup.com

Anderson & Travis, LLC
121 East Vermijo Ave
Colorado Springs CO 80903
(719) 520-5011
http://www.andersonandtravis.com/

Stevens, Littman, Biddison, Tharp & Weinberg, LLC
250 Arapahoe, Ste. 301
Boulder CO 80302
(303) 443-6690
www.boulder-injury-attorneys.com

Richialno Shea, LLC
1800 15th St., Ste 101
Denver CO 80202
(303) 893-8000
http://www.richilanoshea.com

Helmer & McElyea, LLC
611 Main St
Frisco CO 80443
(888) 366-5679
http://www.helmerlaw.com

Karl J. Geil
621 17th St, Ste 2655
Denver CO 80293
(303) 295-6261
http://karlgeil.com

Anderson & Hughes, PC
7385 West Highway 50
Salida CO 81201
(719) 539-7003
http://anderson-hugheslaw.com

Kain & Burke, PC
225 North 5th St., Ste 611
Grand Junction CO 81501
(970) 241-2969
http://www.kainlaw.com

Metier Law Firm, LLC
4828 S. College Ave
Fort Collins CO 80525
(970) 237-5742
http://www.metierlaw.com

Rotole, Rotole, Blanchard & Lumbye, LLC
Two Steele St., Ste 202
Denver CO 80206
(720) 324-7482
http://rrbl.net

Roberts Levin Rosenberg, PC
1660 Wynkoop St., Ste. 800
Denver CO 80202
(866) 581-3430
http://www.robertslevin.com

Robinson & Henry, PC
757 Maleta Ln, Ste 104

Castle Rock CO 80108
(303) 731-3348
http://www.robinsonandhenry.com

Fahrenholtz Tucker & Wiens, LLC
100 West Beaver Creek Blvd, Ste 236
Avon CO 81620
(970) 949-6500
http://www.ftwlawyers.com

The Ward Law & Associates
2851 S. Parker Rd., Ste 550
Aurora CO 80014
(720) 324-7707
http://www.thewardlaw.com

The Law Firm of Springer & Steinberg
1600 Broadway Ste. 1200
Denver CO 80202
(303) 861-2800
http://www.springersteinberg.com

Howard Bittman
1113 Spruce St
Boulder CO 80306
(720) 259-8611
http://bittmanlaw.com

Law Offices of John kenneth Pineau, PC
2305 Broadway St
Boulder CO 80304
(303) 945-3493
http://johnpineau.com

Bell, Gould & Scott, PC
322 East Oak St
Fort Collins CO 80524

Shari Karney

(970) 237-5719
http://www.bell-law.com

Miller & Law, PC
1900 Littleton Blvd
Littleton CO 80120
(303) 731-0164
http://millerlawattorneys.com

Connecticut

Smith & Moore, LLC
24 East Main St., Old Avon Village North (Rte. 44)
Avon CT 06001
(860)678-1860
www.smith-lawfirm.com

Cramer & Anderson LLP
30 Main St., Ste. 303
Danbury CT 06810
(203) 744-1234
www.cramer-anderson.com

Wofsey, Rosen, Kweskin & Kuriansky, LLP
600 Summer St
Stamford CT 06901
(203) 327-2300
http://www.wrkk.com

Zeldes, Needle & Cooper, PC
1000 Lafayette Blvd, Ste 500
Bridgeport CT 06604

(203) 612-5296
http://www.znclaw.com

Berman & Russo
819 Clark St
South Windsor CT 06074
(860) 640-4204
http://www.brslaw.com

Kennedy, Johnson, D'Elia & Gillooly, LLC
555 Long Wharf Dr
New Haven CT 06511

Shari Karney

(203) 285-3614
www.kennedyjohnson.com

Ury & Moskow, LLC
883 Black Rock Turnpike
Fairfield CT 06825
(203) 610-6393
http://www.urymoskow.com

Moots Pellegrini, PC
46 Main St
New Milford CT 06776
(860) 355-4191
http://www.newmilfordlaw.com

Suisman, Shapiro, Wool, Brennan, Gray & Greenburg, PC
2 Union Plaza
New London CT 06320
(860) 865-0649
www.suismanshapiro.com

Cacae, Tusch & Santagata
777 Summer St.
Stamford CT 06901
(203) 327-2000
http://www.lawcts.com

Koskoff, Kosoff & Bieder, PC
350 Fairfield Ave
Bridgeport CT 06604
(203) 336-4421
http://www.koskoff.com

Gesmonde, Pietrosimone & Sgrignari, LLC
3127 Whitney Ave
Hamden CT 06518
(203) 407-4200
http://gpsp.com

The Law Offices of Frank J. Riccio, LLC
923 East Main St
Bridgeport CT 06608
(888) 349-1105
http://ricciolaw.com

Ferguson Cohen, LLP
25 Field Point Rd.
Greenwich CT 06830
(203) 742-1366
http://fahwlaw.com

Beck & Eldergill, PC
447 Center St.
Manchester CT 06040
(860) 646-5606
www.beckeldergill.com

Law Offices of Harold Burke
21 Sherwood Pl
Greenwich CT 06830
(203) 883-9414
www.burke-legal.com

Lynch, Traub, Keefe and Errante, PC
52 Trumbull St
New Haven CT 06506
(203) 787-0275
http://www.ltke.com

Silver Golub & Teitell, LLP
184 Atlantic St
Stamford CT 06904
(203) 325-4491
http://sgtlaw.com

Murphy, Laudati, Kiel, Buttler & Rattigan, LLC
10 Talcott Notch, Ste. 210

Farmington CT 06032
(860) 674-8296
http://mlklawfirm.com

Cicchetti, Tansley & McGrath, LLP
500 Chase Parkway
Waterbury CT 06708
(203) 574-4700
http://ctm-law.com

Jackson O'Keefe
36 Russ St
Hartford CT 06106
(860) 956-5242
http://www.jacksonokeefe.com

Delaware

Schmittinger & Rodriguez, PA
651 N. Broad St., Ste 104
Middletown DE 19709
(302) 378-1697
http://www.schmittrod.com

Prickett, Jones & Elliott, PA
1310 King St
Wilmington DE 19899
(302) 416-4608
www.prickett.com

Boudart & Mensinger, LLP
2323 Pennsylvania Ave
Wilmington DE 19806
(302) 428-0100

Stumpf, Vickers & Sandy, PA
8 West Market St
Georgetown DE 19947
(302) 339-8356

Mattleman, Weinroth & Miller, PC
200 Continental Dr., Ste. 215
Newark DE 19713
(302) 731-8349

McCarter & English, LLP
405 N. King St., 8th Flr
Wilmington DE 19801
(302) 984-6300

Schnader Harrison Segal & Lewis, LLP
824 N. Market St., Ste 800

Wilmington DE 19801
(302) 888-4554

Duane Morris, LLP
1100 North Market St., Ste 1200
Wilmington DE 19801
(302) 657-4900

Christie, pabarue, Mortensen and Young, PC
1000 N. West St., Ste.1200
Wilmington DE 19801
(302) 295-5000

Florida

Weil Quaranta, P.A
200 S. Biscayne Blvd, SE Financial Center, Ste 900
Miami FL 33131
(305) 372-5352
http://weillaw.net

Jay C. Howell
644 Cesery Blvd. Ste., 250
Jacksonville FL 32211

McFarland, Gould, Lyons, Sullivan & Hogan, PA
311 South Missouri Ave.
Clearwater FL 33756
(727) 461-1111

Jung & Sisco, PA
101 E. Kennedy Blvd., Ste 3920
Tampa FL 33602
(813) 225-1988
http://jungandsisco.com

Harrell & Harrell, PA
4735 Sunbeam Rd
Jacksonville FL 32257
(866) 764-7602
www.harrellandharrell.com

Genovese Joblove & Battista, PA
200 East Broward Blvd., Ste 1110
Ft. Lauderdale FL 33301
(954) 453-8000
www.gjb-law.com

Stephen J. Taminosian
2108 Monroe St

Ft. Myers FL 33902
(239) 244-8162

Law Offices of Douglas A. Oberdorfer, PA
432 East Monroe St., 2nd Flr
Jacksonville FL 32202
(904) 354-5454
http://www.oberdorferlaw.com

Hutchison, Mamele & Coover, PA
230 N. Park Ave
Sanford FL 32771
(407) 322-4051

Yanchuck, Berman, Wadley, Zervos
5453 Central Ave.
St. Petersberg FL 33710
(727) 822-6313
www.yanchuckberman.com

Law Offices of John M. Phillips, LLC
4191 San Juan Ave
Jacksonville FL 32210
(904) 834-4726

Ledford A. Parnell
1515 N. University Dr., Ste. 230
Coral Springs FL 33071
(954) 752-5587
http://llparnell.com

Elizabeth A. Amond, PA
811 W. Garden St.
Pensacola FL 32502
(850) 316-8110
http://elizabethamondlaw.com

Harper, Kynes, Geller, Greenleaf & Frayman, PA
2560 Gulf to Bay Blvd
Clearwater FL 33765
(727) 474-4379
http://www.harperkynes.com

Carey & Leisure
622 Bypass Dr., Ste. 100
Clearwater FL 33764
(727) 799-3900
http://careyandleisure.com

Ronald B. Smith, PL
807 SW 2nd Ave
Okeechobee FL 34974
(888) 220-8083

Arcadier & Associates, PA
2815 West New Haven, Ste. 304
Melbourne FL 32904
(321) 473-7379
www.melbournelegalteam.com

Robert E. Turffs
1444 1st St., Ste. B
Sarasota FL 34236
(941) 328-8215
www.sarasotatriallawyer.com

Payas, Payas, Payas, LLP
1018 E. Robinson St
Orlando FL 32801
(866) 918-7180
www.payaslaw.com

Joseph R. Kalish, PA
13153 N. Dale Mabry Hwy., Ste. 115
Tampa FL 33618

(888) 902-3104
www.josephkalish.com

Colodny, Fass, Talefeld, Karlinsky & Abate, PA
100 SE Third Ave
Ft. Lauderdale FL 33394
(954) 492-4010
http://www.cftlaw.com

Dell & Schaefer
2404 Hollywood Blvd.
Hollywood FL 33020
(954) 620-8300
http://www.cftlaw.com

Herman, Mermelstein & Horowitz, PA
18205 Biscayne Blvd, Ste. 2218
Miami FL 33160
(305) 931-2200
www.hermanlaw.com

Georgia

Catts & Brooks, LLC
1529 Reynolds St
Brunswick GA 31520
(912) 261-8448
www.cattsandbrookslaw.com

Whelchel, Dunlap, Jarrard & Walker, LLP
405 Washington St. NE
Gainesville GA 30503
(770) 535-4001
http://www.wdjwlaw.com

Brown Rountree, PC
25 North Main St
Statesboro GA 30458
(912) 225-6133
http://br-firm.com

Fortson, Bentley and Griffin, PA
2500 Daniells Bridge Rd
Athens GA 30606
(705) 548-1151
http://www.fbglaw.com

John D. Harvey
1126 Ford Ave, Unit 101
Richmond Hill GA 31324
(877) 412-7224
www.harveyandhendrix.com

Collins & Jones, LLC
7 West Croad St
Fairburn GA 30213
(877) 593-3997
www.collinsjoneslaw.com

Shari Karney

Sherrod & Bernard
8470 Price Ave
Douglasville GA 30134
(678) 840-9991

Timmons, Warnes & Anderson, LLP
244 East Washington St
Athens GA 30601
(866) 745-6361
www.classiccitylaw.com

Sanders, Haugen & Sears, PC
11 Perry St
Newnan GA 30264
(770) 253-3880
www.sandershaugen.com

Andrew H. Agatson, PC
145 Church St., Ste 230
Marietta GA 30060
(770) 795-770
http://agatstonlaw.com

Federal & Hasson, LLP
Two Ravinia Dr., Ste. 1778
Atlanta GA 30346
(678) 443-4044
www.federalhasson.com

Prior, Daniel & Wiltshire, LLC
490 North Milledge Ave
Athens GA 30601
(706) 543-0002
www.pdwlawfirm.com

Richard E. Allen
440 Greene St
Augusta GA 30901

(706) 724-4466
http://richardeallen.com

Melvin S. Nash
3340 Peachtree Rd. NE
Atlanta GA 30326
(770) 422-0878
www.melvinnashlaw.com

Ellis, Painter, Ratterree & Adams, LLP
2 East Bryan St. Tenth Flr
Savannah GA 31412
(912) 373-7765
http://www.epra-law.com

Gammon, Anderson & McFall
105 Prior St
Cedartown GA 30125

(770) 748-2815
www.gammonanderson.com

Andrew, Merritt, Reilly & Smith, LLP
Seven Lumpkin St.
Lawerenceville GA 30046
(770) 513-1200
http://www.amrslaw.com

Phillips & Sellers, LLP
411 21st St.
Columbus GA 31914
(760) 653-7151
http://phillipsandsellers.com

Perrotta, Cahn & Prieto, PC
5 South Public Square
Catersville GA 30120

Shari Karney

(678) 792-3213
http://www.perrottalaw.com

Haygood Lynch Harris Melton & Watson
119A West Washington St., Ste 311
Monticello GA 31064
(706) 468-8846
http://hlhmw.com

228

Hawaii

Crudele& DeLima
101 Aupuni St., Ste 133
Hilo HI 96720
(808) 969-7707
www.bigislandlawyers.com

Blake T. Okimoto
1580 Makaloa St., Ste 1020
Honolulu HI 96814
(808) 943-8899
www.honolulufamilylaw.com

Philip H. Lowenthal
33 North Market St., Ste 101
Walluku HI 96793
(808) 242-5000

Christoher D. Thomas
1001 Bishop St., Ste. 2925
Honolulu HI 96813
(877) 782-8183
www.hawaiianfamilylaw.com

Edmunds Verga & Omonaka
841 Bishop St.
Honolulu HI 96813
(808) 524-2000
http://ev-law.com

Starn O'Toole Marcus & Fisher
733 Bishop Street
Honolulu HI 96813
(808) 537-6100

Shari Karney

McCorriston Miller Mukai MacKinnon LLP
500 Ala Moana Blvd
Honolulu HI 96813
(808) 529-7300

Idaho

Hopkins Roden Crockett Hansen & Hoopes, PLLC
599 West Bannock
Boise ID 83701
(208) 336-7930
www.hopkinsroden.com

Aherin, Rice & Anegon, PA
1212 Idaho St.
Lewiston ID 83501
(208) 746-3646
www.aralawoffice.com

Clark & Feeney, LLP
1229 Main St.
Lewiston ID 83501
(208) 743-9516
www.clarkandfeeney.com

Manweiler, Breen, Ball & Hancok, PLLC
355 W. Myrtel St., Ste 100
Boise ID 83701
(208) 629-3739
www.mmbb-law.com

Gulstrom Henson & Petrie, PC
1009 W. Sanetta St
Nampa ID 83651
(208) 899-4631
www.nampalawyers.com

May, Rammell & Thompson Chartered
216 West Whitman
Pocatello ID 83204
(208) 233-0132
www.dialmayrammell-law.com

Roy, Nielson, Barini-Garcia & Platts
780 Eastland Dr., Ste 1
Twin Falls ID 83303
(877) 366-5909
http://www.twinfallsattorneys.com

Eberle, Berlin, Kading, Turnbow & McKlveen Chartered
1111 W. Jefferson St., Ste. 530
Boise ID 83701
(208) 344-8535

Keeton & Tait
312 Miller St
Lewiston ID 83501
(208) 743-6231
http://ktlewiston.com/

Racine Olson Nye Budge & Bailey Chartered
201 East Center
Pocatello ID 83201
(208) 232-6101

James, Vernon & Weeks, PA
1626 Lincoln Way
Coeur d'Alene ID 83814
(208) 209-3183
http://www.jvwlaw.net

Illinois

Petty Law Office, PC
702 Bloomington Rd., Ste 215
Champaign IL 61820
(888) 524-5343

Sivia Business & Legal Services, PC
217 South Main St
Edwardsville IL 62025
(618) 307-4340
http://www.sivialaw.com

Michael T. Schulenberg
428 South Batavia Ave
Batavia IL 60510
(866) 473-6592
http://www.calldui.com

Metnick, Cherry, Frazier & Savin, LLP
1 West Old State Capitol Plaza
Springfield IL 62791
(217) 753-4242
www.springfieldlawfirm.com

Law Offices of Zuba & Associates
6067 Strathmoor Dr
Rockford IL 61107

(815) 516-8105
http://www.zubalaw.com

Adamski & Conti, LLC
100 N. LaSalle St., Ste 1720
Chicago IL 60602
(312) 324-0206
www.adamskiandconti.com

Law Offices of Cooper Storm & Piscopo
117 South Second St
Geneva IL 60134
(866) 775-9178
www.cooperandstorm.com

Dixon & Giesen
121 East First St
Dixon IL 61021
(866) 770-8617
http://www.hsdixonlaw.com

Ryan, Bennett & Radloff
300 Richmond
East Mattoon IL 61938
(217) 234-2000
http://rbrkolaw.com

Spina, McGuire & Okal, PC
7610 W. North Ave
Elmwood Park IL 60707
(708) 628-5140
http://www.smolaw.com

Dreyer, Foote, Streit, Furgason & Slocum
1999 W. Downer PL
Aurora IL 60506
(630) 897-8764
http://www.dreyerfoote.com

Tabet DiVito & Rothstein, LLC
209 South La Salle St, Seventh Flr
Chicago IL 60604
(312) 762-9450
http://www.tdrlawfirm.com

Siemer, Austin & Fuhr
307 North Third St

Effingham IL 62401
(877) 821-1229
http://www.siemeraustin.com

Phebus & Koester
136 West Main St
Urbana IL 61803
(217) 903-5168
http://phebuslaw.com

Rathbun, Cservenyak & Kozol, LLC
3260 Executive Dr
Joliet IL 60431
(815) 730-1977
http://www.rcklawfirm.com

Regina P. Etherton & Associates, LLC
190 South LaSalle St., Ste. 1730
Chicago IL 60603
(312) 529-5500
http://www.rpethertonllc.com

Franks, Gerkin & McKenna, PC
19333 East Grant Highway
Marengo IL 60152
(815) 572-4562
http://www.fgmlaw.com

Craig & Craig
115 North 7th St.
Mount Vernon IL 62864
(618) 244-7511
http://www.craiglaw.net

Philip J. Berenz
134 N. LaSalle St., Ste 1515
Chicago IL 60602
(312) 445-9157

Collins Bargione & Vuckovich
One N. LaSalle St., Ste 300
Chicago IL 60602
(312) 445-9175
http://collinsbergione.com

Indiana

David C. Koble, PC
221 N. Washington St.
Warsaw IN 46580
(574) 267-5353
http://kolbelawfirm.com

Ned Tonner Attorney at Law
503 West Washington St.
Rensselaer IN 47978
(219) 964-4540
http://www.tonnerlaw.com

Campbell Kyle Proffitt, LLP
11595 N. Meridian St., Ste 701
Carmel IN 46032
(317) 846-6514
http://www.ckplaw.com

Stout & Wheeler, PC
118 W. Mumee St
Angola IN 46703
(260) 624-4282
http://swzlaw.com

Kiley, Harker & Certain
300 West Third St
Marion IN 46952
(765) 664-9041
http://www.khclegal.com

Cohen Garelick & Glazier, PC
8888 Keystone Crossing Blvd., Ste. 800
Indianapolis IN 46240
(317) 573-8888
http://www.cgglawfirm.com

Spanger, Jennings & Dougherty, PC
9200 Keystone Crossing Blvd., Ste 410
Indianapolis IN 46240
(317) 571-7690
http://www.sjdlaw.com

Yoder & Kraus, PC
515 Professional Way
Kendallville IN 46755
(260) 582-4035
http://www.yoderkraus.com

Ball Eggleston, PC
201 Main St., Ste. 810
Lafayette IN 47902
(765) 742-9046
http://www.ball-law.com

Braje, Nelson and Janes, LLP
126 East 5th St
Michigan City IN 46361
(219) 872-2100
http://www.braje-nelson.com

Bleeke Dillon Crandall, PC
8470 Allison Pointe Blvd., Ste 420
Indianapolis IN 46250
(317) 348-2294

Stuart & Branigin, LLP
300 Main St., Ste. 900
Lafayette IN 47902
(765) 423-1561
www.stuartlaw.com

Ruckelshaus, Kautzman, Blackwell, Bemis & Hasbrook
107 N. Pennsylvania St., Ste. 900

Indianapolis IN 46204
(317) 634-4356

Steward & irwin, PC
251 East Ohio St
Indianapolis IN 46204
(317) 639-5454
http://www.silegal.com

Hostetter & O'hara
515 N. Green St., Ste 200
Brownsburg IN 46112
(317) 852-2422
www.hostetter-ohara.com

Smart & Kessler
1648 Fry Rd., Ste. A
Greenwood IN 46142
(317) 885-9100
http://smartkessler.com

Barrett & McNagny, LLP
215 East Berry St.
Ft. Wayne IN 46802
(260) 440-7633
http://www.barrettlaw.com

Newby, Lewis, Kaminski & Jones, LLP
916 Lincolnway
La Porte IN 46350
(219) 362-1577
http://www.nlkj.com

Wilkinson, Goeller, Modesitt, Wilkinson & Drummy
333 Ohio St
Terre Haute IN 47807
(812) 232-4311
http://wilkinsonlaw.com

Shari Karney

Lockyear & Kornblum, LLP
555 Sycamore St
Evansville IN 47734
(812) 422-1199

Iowa

Heidman Law Firm
1128 Historic 4th St
Sioux City IA 51102
(712) 560-0384
www.heidmanlaw.com

Chuck Hannan Attorney, PLC
215 S. Main St., Ste 301
Council Bluffs IA 51502
(402) 218-4863
http://www.rphlaw.com

Meardon, Sueppel & Downer, PLC
122 South Linn St
Iowa City IA 52240
(319) 338-9222

Hudson, Mallaney & Shindler, PC
5015 Grand Ridge Dr., Ste. 100
West Des Moines IA 50265
(515) 223-4567

Swisher & Cohrt, PLC
528 West 4th St.
Waterloo IA 50704
(866) 765-2016
http://www.s-claw.com

Orsborn, Milani, Mitchell & Goedken, LLP
110 East Third St
Ottumwa IA 52501
(641) 682-5447
http://ommglaw.com

Shari Karney

Gallagher, Millage & Gallagher, PLC
3840 Middle Rd
Bettendorf IA 52722
(563) 388-8417

http://gmglawfirm.com

Law Office of Michael J. Winter
541 Sixth Ave.
Council Bluffs IA 51503
(402) 218-2324

Eells & Tronvold Law Offices
1921 51st St., NE
Cedar Rapids IA 52402
(319) 393-1020
www.eellsandtronvold.com

Hayek, Brown, Moreland & Smith, LLP
120 East Washington St.
Iowa City IA 52240
(866) 759-9229
http://www.hhbmlaw.com

Belin McCormick, PC
666 Walnut St., Ste 2000
Des Moines IA 50309
(515) 243-7100
www.belinlaw.com

Leff Law Firm, LLP
222 South Linn St
Iowa City IA 52244
(319) 338-7551
http://www.lefflaw.com

Gaudineer, Comito & George, LLP
3737 Westown Parkway, Ste. 20

West Des Moines IA 50266
(515) 327-1750

Hansen, McClintock & Riley
218 Sixth Ave
Des Moines IA 50309
(515) 244-2141
http://www.hmrlawfirm.com

Crary, Huff, Inkster, Sheehan, Ringgenberg, Hartnett & Storm, PC
614 Pierce St
Sioux City IA 51031
(712) 277-4561
www.craryhuff.com

Rosenberg & Morse
505 Fifth Ave
Des Moines IA 50309
(888) 366-3418

Murphy, Collins & Bixenman, PLC
38 First Ave
NW Le Mars IA 51031
(712) 546-8844

David R. Nagle
501 Sycamore St., Ste 704
Waterloo IA 50703
(319) 234-3623

Robberts Law Office
205 Washington St., Ste. 201
Burlington IA 52601
(319) 758-9800

Kansas

Case, Moses, Zimmerman & Martin, PA
200 W. Douglas Ste. 900
Wichita KS 67202
(319) 303-0100
http://www.craryhuff.com

Clark, Mize & Linville Charted
129 South Eighth
Salina KS 67402
(785) 823-6325
http://www.cml-law.com

Sizemore, Burns & Gillmore, PA
121 East Fifth St
Newton KS 67114
(316) 281-4159
http://www.sizemorelaw.com

Petefish, Immel, Heeb & Hird, LLP
842 Louisiana St
Lawerence KS 66044
(866) 485-7057
http://petefishlaw.com

Hubbard, Ruzicka, Kreamer & Kincaid
130 North Cherry
Olathe KS 66061
(913) 712-9132

McAnany, Van Cleave & Phillips, PA
10 East Cambridge Circle, Ste. 300
Kansas City KS 66103
(913) 232-2591
http://www.mvplaw.com

McDowell, Rice, Smith & Buchanan, PC
7101 College Blvd., Ste. 200
Overland Park KS 66210
(913) 338-5400
www.mcdowellrice.com

Krueger & Williams
501 Commerical St
Emporia KS 66801
(620) 342-2499
www.kruegerlawoffices.com

Weary Davis, LC
819 North Washington St
Junction City KS 66801
(785) 762-2210
www.wearydavis.com

Forker Suter, LLC
129 West 2nd Ave., Ste. 200
Hutchinson KS 67504
(620) 663-7131
www.fsrlegal.com

Woodard, Hernandex, Roth & Day, LLC
245 N. Waco Ste. 260
Wichita KS 67201
(316) 263-4958
www.woodard-law.com

Dreiling, Bieker & Hoffman, LLP
111 West 13th St.
Hays KS 67601
(785) 625-3537

Law Office of Geisert, Wunsch, Watkins & Graffman
410 North Main

Kingman KS 67068
(620) 532-3108

Kennedy Berkley Yarnevich & Williamson Chartered
1200 Main St., Ste. 102
Hays KS 67601
(785) 623-4110

Barber Emerson, LC
1211 Massachusetts St.
Lawerence KS 66044
(785) 843-6600

Hite, Fanning & Honeyman, LLP
100 N. Broadway, Ste. 950
Wichita KS 67202
(316) 265-7741

Sharp McQueen, PA
419 North Kansas Ave
Liberal KS 67905
(620) 624-2548

Kentucky

McMurry & Livingston, PLLC
333 Broadway
Paducah KY 42002
(270) 443-6511
www.lawyersforyourlife.com

Wellman, Nichols & Smith, PLLC
444 Lewis Hargett Circle, Ste. 170
Lexington KY 40503
(859) 368-8116
www.wnsattorneys.com

McBrayer, McGinnis, Leslie & Kirkland
402 Main St., Ste. 2
Greenup KY 41144
(502) 223-1200
www.mmlkadvantage.com

Middleton Reutlinger, PSC
401 S. Fourth St
Louisville KY 40202
(502) 684-1135
www.middreut.com

Gwin Steinmetz & Baird, PLLC
401 W. Main St. Ste. 1000
Louisville KY 40202
(502) 618-5700

Atkins & Atkins
462 S. Fourth St.
Louisville KY 40202
(502) 584-9714
http://www.atkinskylaw.com

Yewell Law, LLC
221 West Second St.
Owensboro KY 42303
(888) 896-5076
www.yewelllaw.com

Givhan & Spainhour, PSC
200 S. Buckman St.
Shepherdsville KY 40165
(502) 543-2218
www.givhanandspainhour.com

Lynch, Cox, Gilman & Goodman, PSC
500 West Jefferson St., Ste. 2100
Louisville KY 40202
(502) 589-4215

Gailen Wayne Bridges, Jr.
732 Scott St.
Covington KY 41011
(859) 912-7783
www.gailenbridges.com

Bell, Orr, Ayers & Moore, PSC
1010 College St.
Bowling Green KY 42102
(270) 781-8111
www.boamlaw.com

Phillips Parker Orberson & Arnett, PLC
716 West Main St., Ste. 300
Louisville KY 40202
(502) 583-9900
www.ppoalaw.com

Landrum & Shourse, LLP
106 West Vine St., Ste. 800

Lexington KY 40507
(859) 317-2031

Boehl Stopher & Graves, LLP
400 West Market St.
Louisville KY 40202
(502) 589-5980

Hogan Derifield & Perdue, PLLC
314 East Madison St
Louisa KY 41230
(606) 638-9900

Bunch & Brock Attorneys at Law
271 W. Short St., Ste. 805
Lexington KY 40507
(859) 254-5522

Bryant Law Center, PSC
601 Washington St.
Paducah KY 42002
(270) 908-0596
http://www.bryantpsc.com

Miller, Griffen & Marks, PSC
271 West Short St., Ste. 600
Lexington KY 40507
(859) 402-1976
www.kentuckylaw.com

Moore, Malone & Safreed
104 East Fourth St
Owensboro KY 42302
(270) 683-4513
http://www.cemoorelaw.com

Dorsey, King, Gray, Norment & Hopgood
318 Second St

Shari Karney

Henderson KY 42420
(270) 826-3956
http://www.dkgnlaw.com

Neely, Brien & Wilson
238 Seventh St
Mayfield KY 42066
(888) 399-3821
http://www.neelybrien.com

Louisiana

Gregory G. Elias
300 Washinton St., Ste. 100F
Monroe LA 71201
(381) 387-4355
http://www.neelybrien.com

Blue Williams, LLP
1590 W. Causeway Approach, Ste. 1
Mandeville LA 70471
(985) 626-0058
http://bluewilliams.com

Gieger, Laborde & Laperouse, LLC
701 Poydras St.
New Orleans LA 70139
(504) 322-1496
http://www.glllaw.com

Rittenberg, Samuel & Philips, LLC
715 Girod St
New Orleans LA 70130
(504) 524-5555
www.rittenbergsamuelllc.com

Cameron Murray & Associates
401 Hudson Lane
Monroe LA 71201
(318) 362-0057
http://cameronmurraylaw.com

Guste, Barnett, Schlesinger, Henderson & Alpaugh
639 Loyola Ave., Ste 2500
New Orleans LA 70113
(504) 322-1498
http://gbshanola.com

Provosty, Sadler, deLaunay Fiorenza & Sobel, PC
934 Third St., Ste. 800
Alexandria LA 71309
(318) 445-3631
http://www.provosty.com

Lamothe Lea Aertker, LLC
724 East Boston St.
Covinton LA 70433
(888) 532-1937
http://www.llajustice.com

Michael L. Barras, PLC
110 E. Pershing St
New Iberia LA 70560
(337) 465-4391
http://www.barraslaw.com

Veron, Bice, Palemo & Wilson, LLC
721 Kirby St
Lake Charles LA 70601
(337) 310-1600
http://www.veronbice.com

Hailey, McNamara, Hail, Larmann & Paple, LLP
One Galleria Blvd.
Metairie LA 70001
(504) 836-6500
www.haileymcnamara.com

Arthur A. Lemann III & Assoc.
643 Magazine St., Ste. 300
New Orleans LA 70130
(504) 522-8104
http://alemannlaw.com

Smitko & Ory, APC
622 Belanger St.

Houma LA 70361
(985) 746-9346

The Truitt Law Firm
149 N. New Hampshir St
Covington LA 70433
(888) 380-4407
http://www.truittlaw.com

H. Lyn Lawrence, Jr. PLC
3985 Airline Dr
Bossier City LA 71111
(318) 759-0194
http://lynlawrence.com

Davidson, Meaux, Sonnier, McElligott, Fontenot, Gideon & Edwards, LLP
810 S. Buchanan St
Lafayette LA 70502
(337) 205-7242
www.davidsonmeaux.com

Cardone Law Firm
829 Baronne St
New Orleans LA 70113
(504) 322-7909

Weiler & Rees, LLC
909 Poydras St., Ste. 1250
New Orleans LA 70112
(504) 264-9551

Onebane Law Firm, PC
400 Travis St., Ste. 1000
Shreveport LA 71101
(318) 674-9770

Shari Karney

Maine

Gross, Minsky & Mogul, PA
23 Water St., Ste. 400
Bangor ME 04402
(888) 427-5654
http://www.grossminsky.com

Givertz Scheffee & Lavoie, PA
215 Commercial St
Portland ME 04112
(888) 220-8112
http://mainefamilylawyer.com

Robert J. Rubin, PA
480 West Street
Rockport ME 04856
(207) 236-8260
http://www.rjrmelaw.com

Gilbert & Greif, PA
82 Columbia St
Bangor ME 04402

(207) 947-2223
http://www.yourlawpartner.com

Shankman & Associates Legal Center
11 Lisbon St
Lewiston ME 04240
(888) 791-7062
http://www.shankmanlegal.com

Norman, Hanson & De Troy, LLC
415 Congress St
Portland ME 04112

(207) 591-4711
http://www.nhdlaw.com

Lipman, Katz & McKee, PA
227 Water St
Augusta ME 04332
(877) 607-5725
http://www.lipmankatzmckee.com

Hodsdon & Clifford, LLC
56 Portland Rd
Kennebunk ME 04043
(207) 985-6184
http://hodsdonclifford.com

Jensen Baird Gardner & Henry
11 Main St., Ste. 4
Kennebunk ME 04043
(207) 985-4676
http://www.jbgh.com

Perkins Thompson
One Canal Plaza
Portland ME 04112
(888) 339-9034
www.perkinsthompson.com

Ainsworth, Thelin & Raftice, PA
7 Ocean St.
South Portland ME 04106
(888) 342-3061
http://atrlaw.pro

Libby O'Brien Kingsley & Champion, LLC
62 Portland Rd., Ste. 17
Kennebunk ME 04043
(207) 985-1815
http://www.lokllc.com

Drummond & Drummond, LLP
One Monument Way
Portland ME 04101
(866) 605-5927
http://www.ddlaw.com/

Isaacson & Raymond, PA
75 Park Street
Lewiston ME 04243
(207) 795-5000
http://isaacsonraymond.com

Hale & Hamlin, LLC
4 State St.
Ellsworth ME 04605
(888) 795-2690
http://halehamlin.com

Richard, Whitman, Large & Badger, PC
465 Congress St
Portland ME 04101
(207) 774-7474

Bernstein Shur
100 Middle St
Portland ME 04104
(207) 774-1200

Maryland

Cumberland & Erly, LLC
481 Main St
Prince Frederick MD 20678
(443) 295-6264
http://www.celawfirm.com

Mudd, Mudd & Fitzgerald, PA
105 St. Mary's Ave
La Plata MD 20646
(301) 934-9541
http://laplatamdlawfirm.com

Timchula & Smith, PA
181 E. Main St
Westminster MD 21157
(410) 840-7524

Hollman, Maguire Titus & Korzenewski
189 East Main St
Westminster MD 21157
(410) 848-3133
www.carroll-lawyers.com

Grossbart, Portney & Rosenberg, PA
One North Charles St
Baltimore MD 21201
(410) 837-0590

Royston, Mueller, McLean & Reid, LLP
102 West Pennsylvania Ave., Ste. 600
Towson MD 21204
(410) 846-0737
http://www.rmmr.com

Stein, Sperling, Bennett, De Jong, Driscoll
25 West Middle Lane
Rockville MD 20850
(310) 838-3201
www.steinsperling.com

Levin & Gann, PA
502 Washington Ave
Towson MD 21204
(410) 630-4442
http://www.levingann.com

Bell, PA
101 West Jefferson St
Rockville MD 20850
(301) 762-3535
http://johnbelllawfirm.com

Anderson, Coe & King, LLP
201 N. Charles St., Ste. 2000
Baltimore MD 21201
(401) 752-1630
http://www.acklaw.com

Law Office of Thomas E. Pyles
2670 Crain Highway, Ste. 411
Waldorf MD 20601
(301) 710-5265
http://tompyleslaw.com

Law Office of Robert J. Fuoco
105 Padfield Blvd
Glen Burnie MD 21061
(410) 768-6733

Law Offices of Max D. Miller, PA
5 South Hickory Ave
Bel Aire MD 21014

(410) 879-3300
http://www.lawmaxpa.com

Law Office of Joseph H. LaMore, Jr
1415 Madison Park Dr
Glen Burnie MD 21061
(410) 609-4109
http://www.lamorelaw.com

Byron L. Warnken, Esq
300 East Joppa Rd., Ste. 303
Baltimore MD 21286
(443) 275-9891
http://www.warnkenlaw.com

Law Offices of Gary H. Gerstenfield, PC
8720 Georgia Ave., Ste. 301
Silver Spring MD 20910
(888) 499-0616

McNamee, Hosea,Jernigan, Kim, Greenan & Lynch, PA
888 Bestgate Rd., Ste. 304
Annapolis MD 21401
(410) 266-9909
http://www.mhlawyers.com

Ethridge, Quinn, Kemp, McAuliffe, Rowan & Hartinger
33 Wood Lande
Rockville MD 20850
(301) 762-1696
http://www.eqmrh.com

Thomas & Libowitz, PA
100 Light St., Ste. 1100
Baltimore MD 21202
(410) 752-2468
http://www.tandllaw.com

Shari Karney

Barkley & Kennedy Chartered
51 Monroe St., Ste. 1407
Rockville MD 20850
(301) 251-6600
http://barkenlawfirm.com

Cos & Associates, LLC
9303 Philadelphia Rd., Ste. A
Baltimore MD 21237
(410) 780-0328
http://coslawfirm.com

Neuberger, Quinn, Gielen, Rubin & Gibber, PA
One South St. 27th Flr
Baltimore MD 21202
(443)992-4551
http://www.nqgrg.com

Day & Schiszik
326 West Patrick St
Frederick MD 21701
(301) 662-8811
http://www.nqgrg.com

Massachusetts

O'Connell, Plumb & Mackinnon, PC
75 Market Place
Springfield MA 011013
(413) 306-4963
http://www.ocpllaw.com

Campoli & Monteleone
27 Willis St
Pittsfield MA 01202
(413) 443-6485
http://www.campolilaw.com

Law Office of Lee D. Flournoy, PC
75 North St., Ste 310
Pittsfield MA 01201
(413) 358-4285
www.flournoylaw.com

Karon & Dalimonte, LLP
85 Devonshire St., Ste 1000
Boston MA 02109
(617) 245-0136
http://www.kdlaw.net

Arrowood Peters
Ten Post Office Square
Boston MA 02109
(617) 849-6200
www.arrowoodpeters.com

Sarrouf Law, LLP
2 Oliver St.
Boston MA 02109
(617) 245-0146
http://www.sarrouflaw.com

Michaels, Ward & Rabinovitz, LLP
One Beacon St., Second Flr
Boston MA 02108
(617) 350-4040
www.michaelsward.com

Cohen Kinne Valicenti & Cook, LLP
28 North St., 3rd Flr
Pittsfield MA 01201
(413) 358-4804
www.cohenkinne.com

Crowe & Dunn
141 Tremont St
Boston MA 02111
(617) 245-0218
http://www.crowedunn.com

DelVecchio & Houseman
15 Front St
Salem MA 01970
(617) 800-0852
http://www.altmanllp.com

O'Connor & Ryan, PC
61 Academy St
Fitchburg MA 01420
(978) 345-4166
www.oconnorandryan.com

Deutsch Williams Brooks DeRensis & Holland, PC
One Design Center Pl., Ste. 600
Boston MA 02210
(617) 951-2300
http://www.dwboston.com

Stephen A. Lechter
300 Norrth Main St.

Attleboro MA 02703
(877) 314-5127
http://salechter-law.com

Gallagher & Cavanaugh LLP
100 Foot of John St
Lowell MA 01852
(978) 319-4516
www.gcattorneys.com

Tucker, Heifetz & Saltzman, LLP
100 Franklin St
Boston MA 02110
(617) 557-9696
http://www.ths-law.com

Law Office of Richard C. Bardi
6 Beacon St., Ste. 800
Boston MA 02108
(617) 963-0517
www.richardbardi.com

Craig and Macauley, PC
600 Atlantic Ave
Boston MA 02210
(617) 245-0627
www.craigandmacauley.com

Brodigan and Gardiner, LLP
40 Broad St
Boston MA 02109
(617) 963-0326

Lynch, Brewer, Hoffman & Fink, Llp
75 Federal St., 7th Flr
Boston MA 02110
(617) 431-1349
www.lynchbrewer.com

Michigan

Orton, Tooman, Halle, McKown & Kiel, PC
314 Trowbridge St
Allegan MI 49010
(269) 692-9413
www.ortontoomanlaw.com

Cunningham Dalman, PC
321 Settlers Rd
Holland MI 49422
(616) 392-1821
http://www.holland-law.com

Bruce J. Thorburn, PC
2731 South Adams Rd., Ste. 100
Rochester Hills MI 48309
(248) 844-9677
http://thorburnlawfirm.com

Law Office of Julian J. Poota, PLC
29777 Telegraph Rd., Ste. 2500
Southfield MI 48034
(248) 566-6779
http://www.pootalaw.com

Robert Harrison & Associates, PLC
200 East Long Lake Rd., Ste. 110
Bloomfield Hills MI 48304
(248) 283-1600
www.harrisonlawonline.com

Kotz, Sangster, Wysocki & Berg, PC
12 Longmeadow Village Dr., Ste. 100
Niles MI 49120
(269) 591-6915
http://www.kotzsangster.com

Foley, Baron & Metzger, PLLC
38777 Six Mile Rd., Ste. 300
Livonia MI 48152
(734) 742-1800
http://www.fbmlaw.com

Moran, Raimi, Goethel & Karnani
320 North Main St., Ste. 101
Ann Arbor MI 48104
(734) 274-6981
http://www.annarborpersonalinjury.com/

Jacobs, McDonald & Silc, PC
319 East Aurora St
Ironwood MI 49938
(866) 685-5143
http://www.ironwoodlaw.com

Beals Hubbard, PLC
30665 Northwestern Highway, Ste. 100
Farmington Hills MI 48334
(248) 932-1101
www.bealshubbard.com

Ribitwer & Sabbota, LLP
26862 Woodward Ave., Ste. 200
Royal Oak MI 48067
(248) 543-8000
http://www.ribitwersabbota.com

William D. Enemann, PC
206 S. Eighth St
West Branch MI 48661
(989) 345-5330
http://williamdengemann.com

Mancini Schreuder Kline, PC
28225 Mound Rd

Warren MI 48092
(587) 751-3900
http://www.mancini-law.com

Murphy, Brenton & Spagnuolo, PC
4572 S. Hagadorn Rd., Ste., 1A
East Lansing MI 48823
(517) 351-2020
http://www.mbspclaw.com

Ready, Heller & Ready, PLLC
204 S. Macomb St
Monroe MI 48161
(734) 344-4501
http://readysullivan.com

Morganroth & Morganroth, PLLC
344 N. Old Woodward Ave., Ste. 200
Birmingham MI 48009
(248) 864-4000
http://www.morganrothlaw.com

Hendricks & Watkins, PLC
4981 Cascade Rd.
SE Grand Rapids MI 49546
(616) 431-4037
http://www.morganrothlaw.com

Mumford, Schubel, Norlander, Macfarlene & Barnett, PLLC
68 E. Michigan Ave
Battle Creek MI 49017
(269) 968-6146
http://westmichiganlawyers.com

Minnesota

Kraft, Walser, Hettig, Honsey & Kleiman, PllP
107 North Ninth St
Olivia MN 56277
(320) 523-1322
http://www.kraftwalser.com

McGrann Shea Carnival Straughn & Lamb Chartered
800 Nicollet Mall, Ste. 2600
Minneapolis MN 55402
(612) 338-2525
http://www.mcgrannshea.com

Katz, Manka, Teplinsky, Graves & Sobol, Ltd
225 South Sixth St., Ste. 4150
Minneapolis MN 55402
(612) 284-4335
http://katzmanka.com

Grannis & Hauge, PA
1260 Yankee Doodle Rd
Eagan MN 55121
(651) 456-9000
http://www.grannishauge.com

Vogel & Gorman, PLC
454 West 4th St
Red Wing MN 55066
(651) 388-2833
www.vogelgormanplc.com

Rajkowski Hansmeier Ltd
11 Seventh Ave
St. Cloud MN 56302
(320) 251-1055
http://www.rajhan.com

Shari Karney

Thornton, Reif, Dolan, Bown & Klecker
1017 Broadway
Alexandria MN 56308
(320) 762-2361
www.thorntonlawoffice.com

Henderson, Howard & Pawluk, PA
6200 Shingle Creek Pkwy, Ste. 385
Brooklyn Center MN 55430
(612) 246-3158
http://www.hhandplaw.com

Quinivan & Hughes, PA
400 South First St., Ste. 600
St. Cloud MN 56301
(320) 251-1414
http://www.quinlivan.com

Baquero Law Office
7344 Cedar Ave
Minneapolis MN 55423
(612) 872-6727
http://baquerolaw.com

Swenson Lervick Syverson Trosvig Jacobson Schultz, PA
710 Broadway St
Alexandria MN 56308
(320) 298-4772
www.alexandriamnlaw.com

Charlson & Jorgenson, PA
119 West Second St.
Thief River Falls MN 56701
(866) 557-6533
www.charlsonjorgensonlaw.com

Eckberg, Lammers, Briggs Wolff & Vierling, PLLP
1809 Northwestern Ave

268

Stillwater MN 55082
(651) 439-2878
www.eckberglammers.com

Rolsch Law Offices
423 Third Ave
Rochester MN 55903
(507) 280-1943
http://www.rolschlaw.com

Tentinger Law Firm, PA
1380 Corporate Center Curve, Ste. 318
Eagan MN 55121
(952) 641-7603
www.tentingerlawfirm.com

Wagner, Falconer & Judd, Ltd
80 South Eighth St
Minneapolis MN 55402
(612) 284-3748
http://www.wfjltd.com

Falsani, Balmer, Peterson, Quinn & Beyer
20 Lake St. North, Ste. 302
Forrest Lake MN 55025
(651) 464-1990

Barna, Guzy, Steffen, Ltd
200 Coon Rapids Blvd
Coon Rapids MN 55433
(763) 515-4125
http://www.bgs.com

Mississippi

Gore, Kilpatrick & Dambrino, PLLC
135 First St
Grenada MS 38901
(662) 226-1891

http://gorekilpatrick.com
Freeland Shull, PLLC
405 Galleria Lane, Ste. C
Oxford MS 38655

(662) 234-1711
www.freelandshull.com

Diamond & Blalock, PC
220 Main St
Natchez MS 39120
(888) 397-1532
www.diamondblalock.com

Tollison Law Firm, PA
103 North Lamar
Oxford MS 38655
(662) 234-7070
www.tollisonlaw.com

Young Williams, PA
210 E. Capitol St., Ste. 2000
Jackson MS 39201
(601) 714-2470
www.youngwilliams.com

Taylor, Jones & Taylor
961 Main St
Southaven MS 38671

(662) 342-1300
www.taylor-law-firm.com

Self, Jacob & Kieronski, LLP
1010 19th Ave., Ste 10
Meridian MS 39302
(601) 693-6994
http://sjandk.com

Allen, Allen, Breeland & Allen, PLLC
214 Justice St
Brookhaven MS 39602
(888) 684-0285
http://aabalegal.com

Heidelberg, Steinberger, Colmer & Burrow, PA
711 Delmas Ave
Pascagoula MS 39567

(228) 762-8021
http://hscbpa.com

James L Farrior, Attorney At Law
1912 Pass Road
Biloxi MS 39531
(228) 207-2117
http://jameslfarrior.com

Cumbest, Cumbest, Hunter & McCormick, PA
729 Watts Ave
Pascagoula MS 39567
(228) 205-4346
http://cchmlawyers.com

Boyce Holleman, PA
1720 23rd Ave
Gulfport MS 39501

Shari Karney

(228) 863-3142
www.boyceholleman.com

Lewis Law Firm
2621 W. Oxford Loop, Ste. C
Oxford MS 38655
(662) 550-4130

Bryan Nelson, PA
6524 US Highway 98
Hattiesburg MS 39404
(601) 261-4100
www.bnlawfirm.com

Page, Mannino, Peresich & McDermott, PLLC
460 Briarwood Dr., Ste. 415
Jackson MS 39236
(601) 896-0114

Varner Parker & Sessums, PA
1110 Jackson St
Vicksburg MS 39181
(601) 638-8741

G. David Garner
124 Main St.
Raleigh MS 39153
(601) 782-9090

Page, Kruger & Holland, PA
10 Canebrake Blvd., Ste. 200
Jackson MS 39215
(601) 420-0333

Dukes, Dukes, & Wood
226 West Pine St
Hattiesburg MS 39403
(601) 544-4121

272

Missouri

O'Loughlin, O'Loughlin & Koetting, LC
1736 N. Kingshighway Cape
Girardeau MO 63701
(888) 339-8091
www.oloughlinlawfirm.com

Wasinger, Parham, Morthland, Terrell & Washinger
2801 St. Marys Ave
Hannibal MO 63401
(573) 221-3225
www.wasingerlaw.com

Bertram & Graf, LLC
4717 Grand Ave., Ste. 800
Kansas City MO 64112
(816) 523-2205

Ford, Parshall & Baker, LLC
3210 Bluff Creek Dr
Columbia MO 65201
(573) 355-9267
www.fpb-law.com

Kempton and Russell
114 East 5th St
Sedalia MO 65302
(660) 827-0314
www.kemptonrussell.com

Onder, Shelton, O'Leary & Peterson, LLC
110 East Lockwood Ave, Second Flr
St. Louis MO 63119
(314) 963-9000
http://www.onderlaw.com

Riley & Dunlap, PC
13 East Fifth St
Fulton MO 65251
(877) 487-3060
http://rileydunlap.com

Law Office of Devon F. Sherwood
155 Park Central Square
Springfield MO 65806
(417) 233-0111

McCarthy, Leonard & Kaemmerer, LC
400 S. Woods Mill Rd., Ste 250
Chesterfield MO 63017
(314) 392-5200
www.mlklaw.com

Thurman Law Firm
One Thurman Court
Hillsboro MO 63050
(636) 789-2601
www.thurmanlaw.com

Kirksey Law Firm
711 S. Albany Ave
Bolivar MO 65613
(417) 727-0024
www.kirkseylawfirm.com

Wagstaff & Cartmell, LLP
4740 Grand Ave., Ste. 300
Kansas City MO 64112
(816) 701-1100
www.wagstaffcartmell.com

Hesse Martone, PC
1650 Des Peres Rd., Ste. 200
St. Louis MO 63131

(314) 862-0300
www.bobroffhesse.com

Freedman & Freedman, PC
212 N. Kingshighway Ste. 1021
St. Louis MO 63108
(314) 450-8139
www.fredmanlaw.com

Steward, Cook, Constance & Minton, LLC
501 W. Lexington Ave
Independence MO 64050
(816) 833-1800
http://sccmlaw.com

Kennedy, Kennedy, Robbins & Yarbro, LC
1165 Cherry St
Poplar Bluff MO 63901
(573) 686-2459
www.kkrylawfirm.com

Legal Writes, LLC
601 N. Nifong Blvd., Ste. C
Columbia MO 65203
(573) 355-5242
www.legalwritesllc.com

Montana

Keller, Reynolds, Drake, Johnson & Gillespie, PC
50 South Last Chance Gulch, Third Flr.
Helena MT 59601
(877) 750-6895

Faure Holden Attorneys at Law, PC
615 Second Ave North, Ste. 201
Great Falls MT 59401
(406) 564-1708
www.faureholden.com

Jon M. Hesse, PC
411 East Calander St
Livingston MT 59047
(406) 222-6037
http://jmhesselaw.com

Browning, Kaleczyc, Berry & Hoven, PC
825 Great Northen Blvd.
Helena MT 59601
(406) 443-6820
http://www.bkbh.com

Tipp & Buley, PC
2200 Brooks Ave
Missoula MT 59806
(406) 549-5186

Moriarity, Badaruddin, Brooke, LLC
124 West Pine St., Ste. B
Missoula MT 59802
(406) 552-4251
www.mbblawfirm.com

Doubek & Pyfer, LLC
307 N. Jackson St
Helena MT 59601
(406) 442-7830
http://doubekpyfer.com

Hedman, Hileman & Lacosta
204 Central Ave
Whitefish MT 59937
(406) 862-2528

Woodward Law Firm, PLLC
10 N. 27th St., Ste. 200
Billings MT 59101
(406) 545-0118

Johnson, Berg, McEvoy & Bostock, PLLP
221 First Ave
East Kalispell MT 59903
(406) 755-5535

Schulte Law Firm, PC
2425 Mullan Rd
Missoula MT 59808
(406) 721-6655

Bosch, Kuhr, Dugdale, Martin & Kaze, PLLP
335 Fourth Ave
Havre MT 59501
(888) 380-7319

Holland & Hart, LLP
401 North 31st St.
Billings MT 59103
(406) 252-2166

Nebraska

Sodoro, Daly, & Sodoro, PC
7000 Spring St
Omaha NE 68106
(402) 397-6200
www.sodorolaw.com

Bradford & Coenen, LLC
1620 Dodge St., Ste. 1800
Omaha NE 68102
(402) 575-9271
www.bradfordcoenen.com

Moyer & Moyer
114 West Third St
Madison NE 68748
(402) 454-3321

www.moyermoyer.com
Dalke, Smith & Maurstad Attorneys at Law
609 Elk St
Beatrice NE 68310
(402) 223-5257
http://dalkelaw.com/

Fraser Stryker, PC LLO
409 South 17th St
Omaha NE 68102
(402) 341-6000
www.fraserstryker.com

Strope & Gotschall, PC LLO
125 North 4th St
O'Neill NE 68763
(402) 336-2277
http://stropegotschall.com

Waite, McWha & Schreiber
116 North Dewey St
North Platte NE 69103
(308) 532-2202
www.northplattelaw.com

Shamberg, Wolf, McDermott & Depue
308 North Locust
Grand Island NE 68802
(308) 384-1635
http://giattorneys.com

Bartle, Geier Law Firm
1141 H Street
Lincoln NE 68501
(402) 476-2847

Matzke, Mattoon & Miller, LLC
907 Jackson St
Sidney NE 69162
(866) 426-2173

Jacobsen, Orr, Nelson, Lindstrom & Hollbrook, PC
322 West 39th St
Kearney NE 68848
(308) 234-5579

Sipple, Hansen, Emerson & Schumacher
2503 13th St
Columbus NE 68601
(402) 564-2848

Fitzgerald, Vetter & Temple
1002 Riverside Blvd, Ste. 200
Norfolk NE 68701
(402) 371-7770

Gross & Welch, PC
2120 South 72nd St
Omaha NE 68124
(402) 392-1500

Seiler & Parker, PC
726 East Side Blvd
Hasting NE 68902
(402) 463-3125

Nevada

Piet & Wright
3130 S. Rainbow Blvd., Ste. 304
Las Vegas NV 89146
(702) 566-1212
www.pietwright.com

Dempsey, Roberts & Smith
1130 Wigwarm Parkway
Henderson NV 89074
(702) 388-1216
www.drsltd.com

Marquis & Aurbach, PC
10001 Park Run Dr
Las Vegas NV 89145
(702) 979-2405
http://www.maclaw.com

Fabian & Clendenin, PC
601 South 10th St., Ste. 102
Las Vegas NV 89101
(702) 233-4444
www.fabianlaw.com

Law Offices of Jennifer S. Anderson & William F. Heckman
212 E. Washington St
Carson City NV 89701
(775) 841-5888
www.andersonheckmanlaw.com

Richard Harris Law Firm
801 South Fourth St
Las Vegas NV 89101
(702) 444-4444
www.richardharrislaw.com

Shari Karney

Law Offices of Kenneth E. Lyon, III
150 W. Huffaker Lane, Ste. 101
Reno NV 89511
(775) 823-7700
http://kennethlyon.com

Calvert & Hubach, LLC
435 Court St
Reno NV 89501
(775) 636-9892
http://calvertandhubach.com

Robison, Belaustegui, Sharp & Low
71 Washington St
Reno NV 89503
(775) 636-6809
http://www.rbslattys.com

Law Offices of Richard F. Cornell
150 Ridge St., 2nd Flr
Reno NV 89501
(775) 636-8757
http://rfcornellaw.com

De Castroverde Law Group
1149 South Maryland Pkwy
Las Vegas NV 89104
(702) 997-1468
www.decastroverdelaw.com

Fredrickson, Mazeika & Grant, LLP
333 South Sixth St., Ste. 230
Las Vegas NV 89101
(702) 384-4048
http://www.fmglegal.com

Law Offices of John Springgate
203 S. Arlington Ave

Reno NV 89501
(775) 323-8881
http://springgatelaw.com

Mainor Eglet, LLP
400 South Fourth St., Ste. 600
Las Vegas NV 89101
(702) 997-8649
www.mainorlawyers.com

Huggins Law Office
228 Sourth Fourth St., 2nd Flr
Las Vegas NV 89101
(702) 387-4014
www.hugginslawfirm.com

Chesnoff & Schonfeld, PC
520 South Fourth St
Las Vegas NV 89101
(702) 577-3997

Law Offices of Richard W. Young
327 Marsh Ave
Reno NV 89509
(775) 322-9477

Gary D. Fairman, PC
482 5th St
Ely NV 89315
(775) 289-4422

Tiffany & Bosco, PA
212 S. Jones Blvd
Las Vegas NV 89107
(702) 258-8200

Cooper Levenson April Niedelman & Wagenheim, PA
6060 Elton Ave., Ste. A

Shari Karney

Las Vegas NV 89107
(702) 366-1125

New Hampshire

Backus, Meyer & Branch, LLP
116 Lowell St
Manchester NH 03105
(603) 836-4364
www.backusmeyer.com

Howard Gross
466 Central Ave., Ste. 9
Dover NH 03821
(603) 742-1212
http://howardgross.com

Gottesman and Hollis, PA
39 East Pearl St
Nashua NH 03060
(603) 889-5959
www.nh-lawyers.com

Hoefle, Phoenix, Gormley & Roberts, PA
402 State St
Portsmourth NH 03802
(603) 436-0666
http://www.hpgrlaw.com

Shaheen & Gordon, PA
107 Storrs St
Concord NH 03302
(603) 369-4500
www.shaheengordon.com

Maggiotto & Belobrow, PLLC
58 Pleasant St
Concord NH 03301
(603) 565-0163

Robert Stein & Associates, PLLC
One Barberry Lance
Concord NH 03302
(603) 228-1109

Cooper, Cargill, Chant, PA
2935 White Mountain Highway
North Conway NH 03860
(603) 356-5439

McLane, Graf, Raulerson & Middleton, PA
900 Elm St
Manchester NH 03105
(603) 625-6464

Bernstein Shur
670 North Commercial St
Manchester NH 03101
(603) 623-8700

New Jersey

Mayfield, Turner, O'Mara, Donnelly & McBridge, PC
2201 Route 38, Ste. 300
Cherry Hill NJ 08002
(856) 667-2600
www.mayfieldturner.com

Shivers, Gosnay & Greatrex, LLC
1415 Route 70
East Cherry Hill NJ 08034
(856) 616-8080
www.sgglawfirm.com

Feintuch, Porwich & Feintuch
721 Newark Ave
Jersey City NJ 07306
(201) 656-8600
www.Lawyer-Jersey-City.com

McCusker, Anselmi, Rosen & Carvelli, PC
98 East Water St
Toms River NJ 08753
(732) 914-9114
http://www.marc-law.com

Carluccio, Leone, Dimon, Doyle & Sacks, LLC
9 Robbins St
Toms River NJ 08753
(732) 606-4083
www.cldds.com

Davis, Saperstein, & Salomon, PC
375 Cedar Lane
Teaneck NJ 07666
(201) 820-0324
http://www.dsslaw.com

Blume, Goldfaden, Berkowitz, Donnelly, Fried & Forte, PC
One Main St
Chatham NJ 07928
(973) 309-7969
http://www.njatty.com

Hardin, Kundla, McKeon & Poletto, PA
673 Morris Ave
Springfield NJ 07081

(973) 912-5222
http://hkmpp.com

Hellring Lindeman Goldstein & Siegal
One Gateway Center
Newark NJ 07102
(973) 621-9020
http://hlgslaw.com

Indik & McNamara, PC
1100 Cornwall Rd., Ste. 203
Monmouth Junction NJ 08852
(732) 821-2500
http://www.indik-mcnamara.com

Lomurro, Davison, Eastman & Munoz, PA
100 Willbrook Rd
Freehold NJ 07728
(732) 333-3085

Wisniewski & Associates, LLC
17 Main St
Sayreville NJ 08872
(732) 707-0218

Gelman Gelman Wiskow & McCarthy, LLC
34 East Blackwell St
Dover NJ 07801

(973) 607- 2771
http://www.ggwmlawoffice.com

Grimes & Grimes, LLC
1230 Brace Rd
Cherry Hill NJ 08034
(856) 428-2299
http://grimeslawfirm.com

Avolio & Hanlon, PC
3150 Brunswick Pike, Ste. 120
Lawrenceville NJ 08648
(609) 219-1810
http://www.avoliohanlon.com

Starkey, Kelly, Kenneally, Cunningham & Turnbach
1593 Route 88
West Brick NJ 08724
(732) 451-6928
http://www.skbklaw.com

Ferrara, Turtiz, Harraka & Goldberg, Pc
505 Main St
Hackensack NJ 07601
(201) 489-8787
http://www.fthglaw.com

Cohn Lifland Pearlman Herrmann & Knopf, LLP
250 Pehle Ave., Ste 401
Saddle Brook NJ 07663
(201) 258-3976
http://www.njlawfirm.com

Nagel Rice, LLP
103 Eisenhower Parkway
Roseland NJ 070668
(973) 559-5852
http://www.nagelrice.com

Shari Karney

Szaferman, Lakind, Blumstein & Blader, P.C.
101 Grovers Mill Rd., Ste. 200
Lawrenceville NJ 08648

New Mexico

Clark & Jones, LLC
1322 Paseo de Peralta
Santa Fe NM 87501
(505) 216-2385

Fredlund & Bryan, Attorneys at Law
616 E. Bender Blvd
Hobbs NM 88240
(505) 369-0563
http://fredlundlaw.com

Scheuer, Yost & Patterson, PC
125 Lincoln Ave., Ste. 223
Santa Fe NM 87501
(505) 982-9911

Garrett Law Firm, PA
920 North Main St
Clovis NM 88101
(575) 762-4545
http://garrettlawfirmpa.com

Bryant, Schneider-Cook Law Firm, PA
159 Mescalero Trail, Ste. 8
Ruidoso NM 88345
(877) 535-2483

Briones Law Firm, PA
407 North Auburn St
Farmington Hills NM 87401
(505) 325-0258
http://brionespa.com

Jones, Snead, Wetheim & Wentworth, PA
1800 Old Pecos Trail

Santa Fe NM 87505
(505) 216-2389
www.thejonesfirm.com

Kennedy & han, PC
201 12th St. NW
Albuquerque NM 87102
(505) 715-4840

McCormick, Caraway and Tabor, LLP
112 N. Canyon
Carlsbad NM 88221
(505) 234-1937

Collopy Law Offices
203 East Sanger ST
Hobbs NM 88240
(575) 397-3608

Long, Pound & Komer, PA
2200 Brothers Rd
Santa Fe NM 87505
(505) 982-8405

Davis Miles, PLLC
320 Gold Ave SW, Ste. 1401
Albuquerque NM 87102
(505) 246-0231

New York

Friedman Harfenist Kraut & Perlstein, LLP
2975 Westchester Ave., Ste. 415
Purchase NY 10577
(914) 701-0800
www.fhkplaw.com

Jonathan Marks, PC
220 Fifth Ave, Third Floor
New York NY 10001
(877) 726-6894
http://jonmarks.com

Philip J. Kaplan
350 Saint Marks Pl., Ste. 301
Staten Island NY 10301
(718) 442-6262
www.philipkaplanlaw.com

Gibson, McAskill & Crosby, LLP
69 Delaware Ave., Ste. 900
Buffalo NY 14202
(716) 856-4200
http://www.gmclaw.com

Green & Seifter Attorneys, PLLC
110 West Fayette St, One Lincoln Center, Ste. 900
Syracuse NY 13202
(315) 422-1391
http://www.gslaw.com

Jeffry Samel & Partners
150 Broadway, 20th Flr
New York NY 10038
(212) 587-9690

The Zalkin Law Firm, P.C.
1515 Broadway
11th Floor
New York, NY 10036
Toll Free:
(800) 724-3235
New York:
(212) 889-1300
http://www.zalkin.com/

Cuomo LLC
9 East 38th St
New York NY 10016
(212) 448-9933
http://cuomollc.com

Birzon, Strang & Associates
222 East Main St., Ste. 212
Smithtown NY 11787
(631) 862-5710
http://bsb-lawyers.com

The Orlow Firm
7118 Main St
Flushing NY 11367
(347) 571-9310
www.orlowlaw.com

Callan, Koster, Brady & Brennan, LLP
One Whitehall St., 10th Flr
New York NY 10004
(212) 248-8800
http://www.ckbblaw.com

Brown & Hutchinson
925 Crossroads Building, Ste. 925
Rochester NY 14614

(585) 563-5445
www.brownhutchinson.com

Friedman, Levy, Goldfarb & Green, PC
250 West 57th St., Ste. 1619
New York NY 10107
(212) 863-9178
www.flgpclaw.com

Newman & Greenberg
950 Third Ave., 32nd Fl
New York NY 10022
(212) 308-7900
www.newmangreenberg.com

Tarshis, Catania, Liberth, Mahon & Milligram, PLLC
One Corwin Ct
Newburgh NY 12550
(845) 234-4836
www.tclmm.com

Law Office of E. Diane Brody
44 Wall St., Ste. 1200
New York NY 10005
(646) 736-3563
http://www.edianebrody.com

Ashcraft Franklin Young & Peters, Llp
150 Allens Creek Rd.
Rochester NY 14618
(585) 442-0540
http://afylaw.com

Rosenthal & Mintz, LLP
330 Vanderbilt Motor Pkwy., Ste. 300
Hauppauge NY 11788
(631) 952-3500
http://rosemintzllp.com

Brunstein & Zuckerman
123 Main St., 17th Flr
White Plaines NY 10601
(914) 997-6220

Donohue, McGahan, Catalano & Belitsis
380 North Broadway
Jericho NY 11753
(516) 681-3100
http://dmcblaw.com

Breedlove & Noll, LLP
10 Maxwell Dr., Ste. 105
Clifton Park NY 12065
(518) 289-4829
www.pbnlawyers.com

North Carolina

Ragsdale Liggett PLLC
2840 Plaza Pl
Raleigh NC 27612
(919) 787-5200
www.randlaw.com

Gordon, Hicks and Floyd, PA
609 South Atkinson St
Laurinburg NC 28353
(910) 534-4099
www.gordonhicksandhlaw.com

Guthrie, Davis, Henderson & Staton, PLLC
719 East Blvd.
Charlotte NC 28203
(704) 372-5600
http://www.gdhs.com

Homesley & Wingo Law Group, PLLC
330 South Main St
Mooresville NC 28115
(704) 664-2162
www.lakenormanlaw.com

Blanco Tackabery & Matamoros, PA
110 South Stratford Rd., Ste. 500
Winston-Salem NC 27114
(336) 293-9000

http://www.blancolaw.com
Moser, Garner & Bruner, PA
600 E. South Main St., Ste. E
Laurinburg NC 28353
(910) 534-4096
http://mosergarnerlaw.com

Kennedy & wulfhorst, PA
3758 Highway 16
N. Denver NC 28037
(704) 483-3415
http://www.kandwlaw.com

James, McElroy & Diehl, PA
600 South College St., Ste. 3000
Charlotte NC 28202
(704) 315-2505
http://www.jmdlaw.com

Neaves & Gillespie, PA
124 West Main St
Elkin NC 28621
(336) 835-2522

Bell, Davis & Pitt, PA
227 West Trade St
Charlotte NC 28202
(704) 227-0400
http://www.belldavispitt.com

Cannon Law, PC
370 Main St., Ste. 300
Waynesville NC 28786
(828) 476-4189
www.cannonlawpc.net

Hurman R. Sims
222 New Bridge St
Jacksonville NC 28540
(910) 378-0369
www.hsimsesq.com

Crossley McIntosh Collier Hanley & Edes, PLLC
1430 Commonwealth Dr., Ste. 202

Wilmington NC 28403
(910) 762-9711

Hester, Grady & Hester, PLLC
115 Courthouse Dr
Elizabethtown NC 28337
(910) 862-3191
http://www.hghgp.com

Blanchard, Miller, Lewis & Isley, PA
1117 Hillsborough St
Raleigh NC 27603
(919) 755-3993

Tomblin, Farmer & Morris, PLLC
330 South Lafayette St.
Shelby NC 28150
(828) 286-3866
www.farmermorris.com

Baucom Claytor, Benton, Morgan & Wood, PA
1351 East Morehead St., Ste. 201
Charlotte NC 28235
(704) 376-6527
www.baucomclaytor.com

Cheshire Parker Schneider & Bryan, PLLC
133 Fayetteville Street Mail, Ste. 500
Raleigh NC 27601
(919)833-3114
www.cheshirepark.com

Forman Rossabi Black, PA
3623 North Elm St., Ste. 200
Greensboro NC 27455
(336) 378-1899
http://www.frb-law.com

Beaver Holt Sternlicht & Courie, PA
230 Green St
Fayetteville NC 28301
(888) 876-0175
http://www.beaverholt.com

Seth H. Langson
428 E. 4th St., Ste. 101
Charlotte NC 28202

North Dakota

Kelsch Kelsch Ruff & Kranda
103 Collins Ave
Mandan ND 58554
(704) 214-6113
http://www.kelschlaw.com

Nilles, Ilvedson, Plambeck & Selbo
201 North 5th St
Fargo ND 58108
(701) 205-3626
http://www.nilleslaw.com

Greenwood & Ramsey, PLLP
30 First Ave
East Dickinson ND 58602
(888) 736-2641
http://markgreenwoodlaw.com

Vogel Law Firm
218 NP Ave
Fargo ND 58102
(701) 237-6983
http://www.vogellaw.com

Ohio

Kropf, Wagner, Lutz & VanSickle, LLP
100 N. Vine Street
Orrville OH 44667
(330) 516-1626
www.orrvillelaw.com

The Thomas Law Office
112 North Barron St
Eaton OH 45320
(937) 456-4103
http://jthomaslaw.com

Robey & Robey
14402 Granger Rd
Cleveland OH 44137
(888) 285-3411
www.ohio-criminal-lawyer.com

Gallagher & Yosick, Ltd
216 South Lynn St
Bryan OH 43506
(419) 216-2001
http://www.nwohiolaw.com

Rendigs, Fry, Kiely & Dennis, LLP
1 West Fourth St., Ste. 900
Cincinnati OH 45202
(513) 381-9200
http://www.rendigs.com

Drake, Philips, Kuenzil & Clark
301 S. Main St., Ste. 301
Findlay OH 45840
(419) 299-4465
www.Findlaylaw.com

McCaslin, Imbus & McCaslin, PA
632 Vine St., Ste. 900
Cincinnati OH 45202
(513) 448-1653
www.mimlaw.homestead.com

Matan, Wright & Noble
261 South Front St
Columbus OH 43215
(614) 602-4690
www.mgwlawfirm.com

Dinn, Hochman & Potter, LLC
5910 Landerbrook Dr., Ste. 200
Cleveland OH 44124
(440) 446-1100
http://www.dhplaw.com

Lyden, Liebenthal & Chappell, Ltd
5470 Main St., Ste. 300
Sylvania OH 43560
(419) 867-8900
http://www.lydenlaw.com

Roger Isla, Esq.
2615 Sunset Blvd
Steubenville OH 43952
(866) 935-9708
www.islalawoffices.com

Montgomery, Rennie & Jonson, LPA
36 East Seventh St., Ste. 2100
Cincinnati OH 45202
(513) 824-8187
http://www.mrjlaw.com

Koblentz & Penvose, LLC
55 Public Square Ste. 1170

Shari Karney

Cleveland OH 44113
(216) 592-8383

Mansour, Gavin, Gerlack & Manos Co., LPA
55 Public Square, Ste. 2150
Cleveland OH 44113
(216) 592-8783
http://www.mggmlpa.com

Cooper & Wallinski LPA
900 Adams St
Toledo OH 43604
(419) 241-1200
http://cooperwalinski.com

Bieser, Greer & Landis, LLP
6 North Main St
Dayton OH 45402
(937) 630-4886
www.biesergreer.com

The Law Firm of Richard M. Lewis
295 Pearl St
Jackson OH 45640
(740) 395-0005
www.richard-m-lewis.com

O. Ross Long
125 North Sandusky St
Delaware OH 43015
(740) 513-2952

Thompson and DeVeny, Co. LPA
1340 Woodman Dr
Dayton OH 45432
(937) 684-9347
www.thompsonanddeveny.com

Bonezzi Switzer Murphy Polio & Hupp
1300 East 9th St., Ste. 1950
Cleveland OH 44114
(216) 875-2767
http://www.bsmph.com

Oklahoma

Glendening McKenna & Prescott, PLLC
10108 East 79th St.
Tulsa OK 74133
(918) 494-7037
www.gmpoklaw.com

James R. Gotwals & Associates, PC
525 South Main St., Ste. 1130
Tulsa OK 74103
(918) 289-2721
http://www.jrgotlaw.com

Edwards Law Firm
321 South Third Ste. 1
McAlester OK 74502
(918) 302-3700
www.edwardslawok.com

Tomlinson Rust McKinstry Grable
211 North Robinson Ave., Ste. 450
Oklahoma City OK 73102
(405) 518-4139
www.tomlinsonoconnell.com

Brewster and DeAngelis, PLLC
2617 East 21st St.
Tulsa OK 74114
(918) 347-6783
www.brewsterlaw.com

Rhodes, Hieronymus, Jones, Tucker & Gable, PLLC
100 West 5th St., Ste. 400
Tulsa OK 74103
(918) 925-9186
www.rhodesokla.com

Lenora & Upton
116 West Eighth St
Chandler OK 74834
(405) 258-1334
http://lenoraaandupton.com

Godlove, Mayhall, Dzialo, Dutcher & Erwin, PC
802 C Ave
Lawton OK 73502
(580) 353-6700
http://gmdde.net

Eagleton, Eagleton & Harrison, Inc
320 South Boston Ave., Ste. 1700
Tulsa OK 74103
(918) 584-0462
http://eehlaw.com

Taylor, Burrage, Foster, Mallett, Downs, Ramsey & Russell, PC
400 West Fourth St
Claremore OK 74018
(918) 343-4100
http://www.soonerlaw.com

Atkins & Markoff
9211 Lake Hefner Pkwy., Ste. 104
Oklahoma City OK 73120
(888) 500-1347
www.atkinsandmarkoff.com

Mercer & Belote
510 East Choctaw Ave
McAlester OK 74501
(918) 420-5850
http://www.todmercerlaw.com

Mullins, Hirsch, Edwards, Heath, White & Martinez, PC
100 Park Ave., Ste. 400

Oklahoma City OK 73102
(405) 235-2335
www.oklahomafamilylaw.com

Salem Law Offices
101 E. Gray St., Ste. C
Norman OK 73069
(405) 366-1234

Benson Law Firm
124 North 9th St
Frederick OK 73542
(580) 335-7541

The Barkett Law Firm
1408 South Harvard Ave
Tulsa OK 74112
(918) 856-3197

Gungoll, Jackson, Collins, Box & Devoll, PC
323 West Broadway
Enid OK 73701
(580) 701-4618

Jones, Gotcher & Bogan, PC
3800 First Place Tower
Tulsa OK 74103
(918) 581-8200

Szlichta & Ramsey
8 Main Place
Stillwater OK 74076
(405) 377-3393

Stephen D. Beam
110 South Broadway
Weatherford OK 73096
(580) 772-2900

Oregon

Frohnmayer, Deatherage, Jamieson, Moore, Armosino & McGovern, PC
2592 E. Barnett Rd
Medford OR 97504
(541) 210-5392
http://www.fdfirm.com

Monahan, Grove & Tucker
105 North Main St
Milton-Freewater OR 97862
(590) 593-4371
www.monahangrovetucker.com

Brownstein, Rask, Sweeney, Kerr, Grim, DeSylvia & Hay. LLP
1200 SW Main St
Portland OR 97205
(503) 766-3975
www.brownrask.com

Kivel & Howard, LLP
111 SW Fifth Ave., Ste. 1775
Portland OR 97204
(503) 766-3792
http://www.k-hlaw.com

Corey, Byler, Rew, Lorenzen & Hojem, LLP
222 Southeast Dorion St
Pendelton OR 97801
(541) 276-3331
www.corey-byler.com

Parks & Ratiff, PC
620 Main St.
Klamath Falls OR 97601
(541) 882-6331
http://www.corey-byler.com

Kilmer, Voorhees & laurick, PC
732 NW Nineteenth Ave
Portland OR 97209
(503) 224-0055
http://www.kilmerlaw.com

Barbara J. Garland Law Office
230 Northeast Second Ave, Ste. H
Hillsboro OR 97124
(503) 615-8233
http://garlandfamilylaw.com

Lynch & Vandenberg
620 North First St
Lakeview OR 97630
(541) 947-2196

Pennsylvania

Law Office of Gary M. Gusoff
1617 John F. Kennedy Blvd.
Philadelphia PA 19103
(215) 268-7703
http://gusofflaw.com

Fairlie & Lippy, PC
1501 Lower State Rd., Ste. 304
North Wales PA 19454
(215) 716-1285
http://fairlielaw.net

Appel & Yost LLP
33 North Duke St
Lancaster PA 17602
(717) 207-7436
http://www.appelyost.com

Caroselli, Beachler, McTiernan & Conboy, LLC
20 Stanwix St., 7th Flr
Pittsburgh PA 15222
(412) 391-9860
http://www.cbmclaw.com

Gordon Liebmann
4 Terry Dr., Ste. 4
Newtown PA 18940
(215) 375-7848
www.glfamilylaw.com

Strassburger McKenna Gutnick & Gefsky
444 Liberty Ave
Pittsburgh PA 15222
(412) 253-2584
http://smgglaw.com

Howel, Howell & Krause
109 Ninth St
Honesdale PA 18431
(570) 253-2520

The Perry Law Firm, LLC
305 Linden St
Scranton PA 18503
(570) 344-6323
www.theperrylawfirm.com

3C Law
507 Linden St
Scranton PA 18503
(570) 346-0747
http://www.3claw.com

Eizen Fineburgh & McCarthy, PC
2001 Market St
Philadelphia PA 19103
(215) 352-4136
http://www.efm.net

Reilly, Janiczek & McDevitt, PC
The Widener Building, Ste. 410
Philadelphia PA 19107
(215) 972-5200

Asteak Law Offices
726 Walnut St
Easton PA 18042
(610) 258-2901
http://www.asteak.com

Lenahan & Dempsey, PC
216 North River St., Ste. 410, Court Square Towers
Wilkes-Barre PA 18702

(570) 346-2097
www.lenahandempsey.com

Soloff & Zervanos, PC
1525 Locust St., 8th Flr
Philadelphia PA 19102
(215) 732-2260
www.thephillyinjurylawyers.com

Lamb McErlane PC
24 East Market St
West Chester PA 19381
(484) 881-3207
www.lambmcerlane.com

Baer Romain, LLP
1288 Valley Forge Rd., Ste. 63
Valley Forge PA 19482
(484) 933-4426
http://www.baerlaw.net

Dorian, Goldstein, Wisniewski & Orchinik
2410 Bristol Rd
Bensalem PA 190202
(215) 375-7341
www.doriangoldstein.com

Lavery, Faherty, Young & Patterson, PC
225 Market St., Ste. 304
Harrisburg PA 17101
(717) 233-6633
http://www.laverylaw.com

Anapol, Schwartz, Weiss, Cohan, Feldman & Smalley, PC
1710 Spruce St
Philadelphia PA 19103
(215) 735-1130
http://www.anapolschwartz.com

Shari Karney

Eckell, Sparks, Levy, Auerbach, Monte, Sloane, Matthews & Auslander, PC
344 West Front St.
Media PA 19063
(484) 842-0292
http://eckellsparks.com

Rhode Island

Sullivan Whitehead & DeLuca, LLP
86 Weybosset St., Ste. 400
Providence RI 02903
(401) 861-9900
http://swdlawfirm.com

Moore, Virgadamo & Lynch, Ltd
97 John Clarke Rd
Middletown RI 02842
(401) 367-4926
http://www.mvllaw.com

Revens, Revens & st. Pierre, PC
946 Centerville Rd
Warwick RI 02886
(888) 350-4940
http://www.rrsplaw.com

Ratcliffe Harten Burke & Galamaga LLP
40 Westminister St. 7th Flr., Ste. 700
Providence RI 02903
(401) 331-3400
http://www.rhbglaw.com

Roberts, Carroll, Feldstein & Peirce
10 Weybosset St., 8th Flr
Providence RI 02903
(401) 536-9828
http://www.rcfp.com

William T. Murphy Law Offices, Inc
1 Turks Head Pl., Ste. 312
Providence RI 02940
(401) 354-7218

Edwards Wildman Palmer LLP
1320 Bellevue Ave
Newport RI 02840
(401) 849-7800

Adler Pollock & Sheehan PC
1 Citizens Plaza, 8th Flr
Providence RI 02903
(401) 274-7200

South Carolina

Richardson Plowden & robinson, PA
1900 Barnwell St
Columbia SC 29201
(803) 771-4400
www.richardsonplowden.com

Moore Taylor & Thomas, PA
1700 Sunset Blvd
West Columbia SC 29171
(888) 843-9951

Mooneyham Berry & Karow LLC
1225 South Church St
Greenville SC 29604
(864) 469-4580
www.upstatetriallawyers.com

Uricchio, Howe, Krell, Jacobson, Toporek, Theos & Keith, PA
17 1/2 Broad St
Charleston SC 29401
(843) 723-7491
http://www.uricchio.com

Felder & McGee, LLP
641 NFR Huff Dr.
St. Matthews SC 29135
(866) 679-3481
http://feldermcgee.com

Stoudemire & sprouse, PA
811 By-Pass 123
Seneca SC 29679
(864)973-4608
http://feldermcgee.com

Shari Karney

Thurmond Kirchner Timbes & Yelverton
15 Middle Atlantic Wharf, Ste. 101
Charleston SC 29401
(843) 937-8000
http://tktylawfirm.com

James E. Smith, Jr. PA
1422 Laurel St
Columbia SC 29201
(803) 933-9800
www.jamessmithpa.com

Pope & Hudgens, PA
1508 College St
Newberry SC 29108
(803) 276-2532
www.popeandhudgens.com

Jones, Simpson & Newton, PA
7 Platation Park Dr., Ste. 3
Bluffton SC 29910
(843) 706-6111
http://www.jsplaw.net

The David F. Stoddard Law Firm
320 East River St
Anderson SC 29624
(864) 642-4380
www.stoddardattorney.com

Rogers Townsend & Thomas PC
220 Executive Center Dr
Columbia SC 29210
(803) 771-7900
http://www.rtt-law.com/

Barrett Mackenzie LLC
100 Mills Ave

Greenville SC 29605
(864) 232-6247
www.barrettmackenziellc.com

Ballenger, Barth & Hoefer, LLP
205 North Irby St
Florence SC 29503
(843) 536-4520
http://www.bbhlawfirm.com

Law Offices of Fletcher M Johnson
14 Westburty Park Way Ste. 100
Bluffton SC 29910
(843) 757-6444
www.fletcherjohnsonlaw.com

Howei Law Firm
100 St. Johns St
Darlington SC 29540
(843) 968-4790
http://www.howlelaw.com

Jack B. Swerling
1720 Main St., Ste., 301
Columbia SC 29201
(888) 363- 4981
www.jackswerling.com

Aiken Bridges Elliott Tyler & Saleeby
181 East Evans St., Ste. 409
Florence SC 29506
(843) 669-8787
http://aikenbridgeslaw.com

Baker, Ravenel & Bender, LLP
3710 Landmark Dr., Ste. 400
Columbia SC 29204

Shari Karney

(803) 799-9091
http://www.brblegal.com

Roe Cassidy Coates & Price, PA
1052 North Church St
Greenville SC 29603
(864) 349-2600
http://www.roecassidy.com

South Dakota

Gunderson, Palmer, Nelson & Ashmore
440 Mount Rushmore Rd
Rapid City SD 57709
(605) 342-1078
www.gundersonpalmer.com

Siegel, Barnett & Schutz, LLP
415 South Main St
Aberdeen SD 57402
(605) 225-5420
http://www.sbslaw.net

Thomas Braun Bernard & Burke, LLP
4200 Beach Dr., Ste. 1
Rapid City SD 57702
(605) 348-7516
http://www.tb3law.com

Riter, Rogers, Wattier & Northrup, LLP
319 South Coteau St
Pierre SD 57501
(605) 224-5825
http://www.riterlaw.com

Myers & Billion, LLP
300 North Dakota Ave., Ste. 510
Sioux Falls SD 57101
(605) 610-4926
www.myersbillion.com

May, Adam, Gerdes & Thompson LLP
503 South Pierre St
Pierre SD 57501
(605) 224-8803

Bangs, McCullen, Butler, Foye & Simmons LLP
101 West 69th St., Ste. 200
Sioux Falls SD 57108
(605) 339-6800

Richardson, Wyly, Wise, Sauck & Hieb LLP
One Court St
Aberdeen SD 57402
(605) 225-6310

Zimmer, Duncan and Cole
120 N. Main St
Parker SD 57053
(605) 297-4446

Fritz Law Office
1911 8th Ave NE
Aberdeen SD 57401
(605) 225-5890

Beardsley, Jensen & Von
4200 Beach Dr., Ste. 3
Rapid City SD 57709
(605) 721-2800

Bantz, Gosch & Cremer, LLC
305 Sixth Ave SE
Aberdeen SD 57402
(605) 225-2232

Schmidt, Schroyer, Moreno, Lee & Bachand, PC
124 South Euclidd
Pierre SD 57501
(605) 224-0461

Tennessee

Tune, Entrekin & White PC
315 Deaderick St
Nashville TN 37238
(615) 244-2770
www.tewlawfirm.com

Adrian H. Altshuler Attorney at Law
604 North High St
Columbia TN 38401
(615) 599-1785
http://altshulerlaw.com

Wilkerson Gauldin Hayes & Jenkins
112 West Court St
Dyersburg TN 38025
(731) 286-2402
http://tenn-law.com

Batson, Nolan, Pearson, Miller & Joiner
121 S. 3rd St.
Clarksville TN 37040
(931) 647-1501
www.batsonnolan.com

Jones Hawkins & Farmer, PLC
150 Fourth Ave North, Ste. 1820
Nashville TN 37219
(615) 338-7264

Pryor, Flynn, Priest & Harber
625 Gay St
Knoxville TN 37901
(865) 522-4191
www.pfph-law.com

The Wyatt Law Firm
73 Union Ave
Memphis TN 38103
(901) 522-1813
www.mcwhirter-wyatt.com

Bateman & Bateman, PC
212 Madison St, Second Flr
Clarksville TN 37041
(931) 647-5959
http://batemanlaw.com

William H. Stover Attorney at Law
500 Church St., St. Cloud Corner, Ste. 450
Nashville TN 37219
(615) 338-7894
http://www.wstoverlaw.com

Lynch, Lynch & Lynch
107 First Ave
Winchester TN 37398
(931) 967-2228
http://lynchlawoffices.com

Jenne, Scott & Jenne, PLLC
260 Ocoee St
Cleveland TN 37364
(423) 476-5506

Williams & Schwalb, PLLC
108 Fourth Ave South, Ste. 207
Franklin TN 37064
(615) 794-7100
www.williamsandschwalb.com

The Bosch Law Firm PC
712 South Gay St
Knoxville TN 37902

(865) 637-2142
www.boschlawfirm.com

Mark G. Rothberger
615 Lindsay St., Ste. 150
Chattanooga TN 37403
(423) 933-1506
www.markrothberger.com

Luther-Anderson PLLP
1110 Market St., Ste. 500
Chattanooga TN 37401
(423) 208-9196
www.lutheranderson.com

Evans Petree PC
1000 Ridgeway Loop Rd., Ste. 200
Memphis TN 38120
(901) 525-6781
www.evanspetree.com

Grant, Konvalinka & Harrison PC
633 Chestnut St
Chattanooga TN 37450
(423) 756-8400
http://www.gkhpc.com

Johnson, Scruggs & Barfield
95 White Bridge Road
Nashville TN 37205
(615) 352-8326
http://www.jsblaw.com

Kennedy, Koontz & Farinash
320 North Holtzclaw Ave
Chattanooga TN 37404
(423) 622-4535
http://www.kkflawfirm.com

James McMurtry Gulley
119 S. Main St, Ste. 500
Memphis TN 38103
(901) 300-2506

Texas

Law Offices of Kenneth G. Wincorn & Assoc.
100 North Central Expressway, Ste. 1301
Richardson TX 75080
(214) 630-1221
http://www.wincornlaw.com

The Moore Law Firm, LLP
100 North Main
Paris TX 75460
(903) 784-4393
http://www.moorefirm.com

Stradley, Chernoff & Alford
917 Franklin, Ste. 600
Houston TX 77002
(713) 581-8430
www.houstoncriminallaw.com

Munson, Munson, Cardwell & Tillett, PC
301 West Woodard St
Denison TX 75021
(903) 463-3750
www.munsonlaw.com

Killeen & Stern, PC
1770 St. James Place, Ste. 300
Houston TX 77056
(866) 935-3691
http://www.killeen-law.com

Smith, McDowell & Ginn
315 Gilmer St.
Sulphur Springs TX 75483
(903) 689-4331
www.easttexaslaw.com

Roerig, Oliveira & Fisher, LLP
10225 North Tenth St
McAllen TX 78501
(956) 393-6300

Vogel & Thomas
507 West Central Ave
Ft. Worth TX 76164
(817) 625-8866
http://vtplaw.com

Sims Moore Hill Gannon & Crain, LLP
211 East Franklin St.
Hillsboro TX 76645
(254) 221-0547

Reagan Burrus PLLC
401 Main Plaza, Ste. 200
New Braunfels TX 78130
(830) 387-2205
http://www.reaganburrus.com

Joyce E. Stevens, PC
4381 West Green Oaks Blvd., Ste. 108
Arlington TX 76016
(817) 422-5323

The Law Office of Tim Smith PC
322 West Woodlawn Ave
San Antonio TX 78212
(866) 941-3561
http://timsmithlaw.com

Anderson Legal Group, PC
5209 Heritage Ave., Bldg 2, Ste. 200
Colleyville TX 76034
(817) 778-4529
www.andersonlegalgroup.com

Glasgow, Taylor, Isham & Glasgow PC
505 North Graham St
Stephenville TX 76401
(254) 965-5069
http://gtiglaw.com

Laney Law Firm
600 Ash Street
Plainview TX 79072
(806) 221-2599

Smither, Martin, Henderson & Blazek, PC
1414 11th St
Huntsville TX 77340
(936) 295-2624
www.smithermartin.com

Stubbeman, McRae, Sealy, Laughlin & Browder, Inc
550 W. Texas Ave., Ste. 800
Midland TX 79701
(432) 897-2461

Hill & Woodard, LLP
1300 S. University Dr., Ste. 602
Fort Worth TX 76107
(817) 210-4935
www.hillwoodard.com

The Shapiro Law Firm
701 East 15th St., Ste. 204
Plano TX 75074
(972) 212-5267
http://shapiroattorney.com

Kevin R. Madison
13062 Hwy. 290 West
Austin TX 78737

(512) 708-1650
www.kevinmadison.com

Kris A. Davis-Jones
1004 West Ave
Austin TX 78701
(888) 645-3984
www.krisdavisjones.com

O'Hanlon, McCollom & Demertah
808 West Ave
Austin TX 78701
(877) 494-9949
www.txinjurylawfirm.com

Utah

Smith & Glauser, PC
1218 East 7800 South, Ste. 300
Sandy UT 84094
(801) 562-5555
http://www.smithglauser.com

Larson Law
1218 W. South Jordan Pkwy, Ste. B
South Jordan UT 84095
(888) 826-1384
http://www.bestattorneys.com

Tesch Law Offices, PC
314 Main St., Second Flr
Park City UT 84060
(435) 649-0077
http://www.teschlaw.com

Clyde Snow & Sessions, PC
201 South Main St
Salt Lake City UT 84111
(801) 322-2516
http://www.clydesnow.com

King & Burke, PC
7390 South Creek Rd., Ste. 104
Sandy UT 84093
(801) 532-1700
http://kingburke.com

Hanks & Mortensen, PC
8 East Broadway
Salt Lake City UT 84111
(801) 207-7523
http://www.hmlawslc.com

Shari Karney

Diumenti and Edwards
505 S. Main St
Bountiful UT 84010
(801) 683-0974
www.diumentiandedwards.com

Scalley Reading Bates Hansen & Rasmussen, PC
15 West South Temple, Ste. 600
Salt Lake City UT 84101
(801) 790-0592
www.scalleyreading.com

Snow, Christensen & Martineau, PC
10 Exchange Place, Eleventh Flr
Salt Lake City UT 84145
(801) 521-9000

Bishop & Leigh Attorneys at Law
36 North 300
West Cedar City UT 84720
(435) 586-9483

LaMar J. Winward
150 North 200 East, Ste. 204
St. George UT 84770
(435) 628-1191

Van Cott, Bagley, Corwall & McCarthy, PC
36 South State St., Ste. 1900
Salt Lake City UT 84111
(801) 532-3333

Durham Jones & Pinegar, PC
111 East Broadway, Ste. 900
Salt Lake City UT 84111
(801) 415-3000

Jones, Waldo, Holbrook & McDonough, PC
170 South Main St., Ste. 1500
Salt Lake City UT 84101
(801) 521-3200

Ray Quinney & Nebeker, PC
36 South State St., Ste. 1400
Salt Lake City UT 84145
(801) 532-1500

Vermont

Tepper Dardeck Levins & Gatos, LLP
73 Center St
Rutland VT 05701
(802) 282-4663
http://www.tdlglaw.com

Plante & Hanely, PC
82 Fogg Farm Rd.
White River Junction VT 05001
(603) 276-3099

Kirkpatrick & Goldsborough, PLLC
1233 Shelbourne Rd., Ste. E-1
South Burlington VT 05403
(802) 651-0960
http://www.vtlawfirm.com

Paul Frank & Collins, PC
One Church St
Burlington VT 05402
(802) 658-2311
http://www.pfclaw.com

Birmingham & Moore, PC
71 Main St.
Ludlow VT 05149
(802) 228-4444

Virginia

Grenadier, Anderson, Starace, Duffett & Keisler, PC
649 South Washington St., Ste. 230
Alexandria VA 22314
(703) 683-9000
www.vafamilylaw.com

Ritzert & Leyton, PC
11350 Random Hills Rd., Ste. 400
Fairfax VA 22030
(703) 934-2660
www.ritzert-leyton.com

Sher, Cummings & Ellis
3800 North Fairfax Dr
Arlington VA 22203
(703) 525-1200
www.shercummingsandellis.com

The Creekmore Law Firm PC
318 North Main St
Blacksburg VA 24060
(540) 443-9350
www.creekmorelaw.com

Osterhoudt, Prillaman, Natt, Helscher, Yost, Maxwell & Ferguson, PLC
3140 Chaparral Dr., Ste. 200-C
Roanoke VA 24018
(540) 765-4191
http://opnlaw.com

Breeden & Breeden
265 Steamboat Rd
Irvington VA 22480
(804) 438-9595
www.breedenandbreeden.com

Shari Karney

Weiner & Spivey, PLC
10605 Judicial Dr., Ste. B6
Fairfax VA 22030
(703) 763-0958
www.wrsattorneys.com

Gerald Gray Law Firm, PC
221 Main St
Clintwood VA 24228
(276) 926-4607
www.geraldgraylawfirm.com

Gayheart & Willis, PC
142 East Davis St., Ste. 100
Culpeper VA 22701
(540) 827-4068
www.gayheartandwillis.com

Altizer, Walk and White, PLLC
209 East Main St
Tazewell VA 24651
(866) 497-8142
http://www.awwlaw.com

Gilmer, Sadler, Ingram, Sutherland & Hutton, LLP
65 East Main St
Pulaski VA 24301
(540) 980-1360
www.gsish.com

Wexell-Milman
10480 Armstrong St
Fairfax VA 22030
(703) 349-7529
http://www.fairfaxvalawfirm.com

Martin, Ingles & Hensley, Ltd
6516 Main St

Gloucester VA 23061
(804) 693-2500
http://ingleslaw.com

Wharton Aldhizer & Weaver PLC
15-E N. Randolph St
Lexington VA 24450
(540) 463-3691
http://wawlaw.com/

Gillespie, Hart, Altizer & Whitesell, PC
126 East Main St
Tazewell VA 24651
(276) 988-5525
http://ghawlaw.com

Madigan & Scott
7880 Backlick Rd.
Springfield VA 22150
(703) 455-1800
www.madiganandscott.com

Cravens & Noll, PC
9011 Arboretum Pkwy
Richmond VA 23236
(804) 977-2273
www.cravensnoll.com

Harrell & Chambliss LLP
707 East Main St., Ste. 1000
Richmond VA 23219
(877) 753-4259
http://www.hclawfirm.com

Greenberg, Costle, PC
908 King St., Ste. 350
Alexandria VA 22314

Shari Karney

(703) 448-3007
http://greenbergcostle.com

Washington

Faubion, Reeder, Fraley & Cook, PS
5920 100th St. SW, Ste. 25
Tacoma WA 98499
(253) 617-7420
http://www.fjr-law.com

Armstrong, Klym, Waite, Atwood & Jameson, PS
660 Swift Blvd., Ste. A
Richland WA 99352
(509) 392-4305
http://www.akwalaw.com

Winston & Cashatt, PC
601 W. Riverside Ste. 1900
Spokane WA 99201
(509) 838-6131
www.winstoncashatt.com

Brewe Layman, PS
3525 Colby Ave
Everett WA 98206
(425) 252-5167
http://www.brewelaw.com

Ellis, Li & McKinstry, PLLC
2025 First Ave, Penthouse A
Seatte WA 98121
(206) 682-0565
http://www.elmlaw.com

Witherspoon Kelley
422 West Riverside, Ste. 1100
Spokane WA 99201
(509) 252-0618
http://www.wkdtlaw.com

Skellenger Bender, PC
1301 5th Ave., Ste. 3401
Seattle WA 98101
(206) 462-4574
www.skellengerbender.com

Morgan, Glessner & Roti, PS
15 South Grady Way
Renton WA 98057
(425) 654-4964
http://www.mgrlaw.com

McCarthy, Causseaux & Hurdelbrink, Inc
902 South 10th St
Tacoma WA 98405
(253) 272-2206
http://mchlawoffices.com

Costello & Associates, PLLC
1000 Second Ave., Ste. 1780
Seattle WA 98104
(206) 462-3287

Connaughton Law Office
514 B North 1st St
Yakima WA 98901
(509) 249-0080
http://bconnlaw.com

Van Sicien, Stocks & Firkins
721 45th St NE
Auburn WA 98002
(253) 656-0473
http://www.vansiclen.com

Law Offices of James Newton
428 West Harrison St
Kent WA 98032

(253) 236-3004
www.jimnewtonlaw.com

Phillabaum, Ledlin, Matthews & Sheldon
421 West Riverside Ave
Spokane WA 99201
(509) 838-6055
http://www.spokelaw.com

Carey & Lillevik, PLLC
1809 Seventh Ave., Ste. 1609
Seattle WA 98101
(206) 859-4550
www.careylillevik.com

Brown Lewis Janhuen & Spencer, PC
101 South Main
Montesano WA 98563
(360) 249-4800
http://lawbljs.com

Etter, McMahon, Lamberson, Clary & Oreskovich, PC
618 West Riverside Ave., Ste. 210
Spokane WA 99201
(509) 747-9100
www.ettermcmahon.com

Feltman, Gebhardt, Greer & Zeimantz, PS
421 W. Riverside Ste., 1400
Spokane WA 99201
(509) 838-6800
www.fggzlaw.com

West Virginia

Bailey & Wyant, PLLC
1219 Chapline St
Wheeling WV 26003
(304) 233-3100
www.baileywyant.com

Stroebel & Johnson, PLLC
405 Capitol St, Mezzanine, Ste One
Charleston WV 25301
(304) 520-0189
http://www.sandjlaw.com

Bouchillon, Crossan & Colburn, LC
731 Fifth Ave
Huntington WV 25701
(304) 521-1654

Ferrell, White & Legg PLLC
914 Fifth Ave
Huntington WV 25772
(304) 522-9100
http://www.farrell3.com/

Gibson, Lefler & Associates
1345 Mercer St
Princeton WV 24740
(304) 425-8276
http://gibsonlefler.com

Pritt & Pritt, PLC
300 Capitol St., Ste 1101
Charleston WV 25301
(304) 768-5813
http://www.prittlaw.com

Burton Kilgore & Lazenby, PLLC
1439 Main St., Ste. 2
Princeton WV 24740
(304) 425-2143

Jeffrey S. Bowers
200 South Main St
Franklin WV 26807
(304) 358-333

Dickie, McCamey & Chilcote, LC
1233 Main St., Ste 2002
Wheeling WV 26003
(304) 233-1022

Wisconsin

Spisma, Hahn & Brophy, LLC
701 East Washington Ave., Ste. 201
Madison WI 53703
(608) 243-1230
http://www.shblawyer.com

Johns, Flaherty & Collins, SC
205 Fifth Ave South, Ste. 600
La Crosse WI 54602
(608) 784-5678
www.johnsflaherty.com

Bosshard Parke Ltd.
505 King St., Ste. 334
La Crosse WI 54601
(608) 782-1469
www.bosshardparkelaw.com

Brazeau, Wefel, Kryshak & Nettesheim, LLP
262 West Grand Ave
Winconsin Rapids WI 54495
(715) 423-1400
http://brazeaulaw.com

Philips, Cymerman & Stein
161 W. Wisconsin Ave., Ste. 5000
Milwaukee WI 53203
(888) 368-7590
www.themilwaukeelawyer.com

Lawton & Cates, SC
10 East Doty St., Ste. 400
Madison WI 53703
(608) 807-0723
www.lawtoncates.com

Kravit, Hovel & Krzwczyk, SC
825 North Jefferson St., Ste. 500
Milwaukee WI 53202
(414) 271-7100
www.kravitlaw.com

Godfrey, Braun & Frazier, LLP
735 North Water St., 16th Flr
Milwaukee WI 53202
(414) 209-7037
http://www.gbf-law.com

Consigny Law Firm, SC
303 East Court St
Janesville WI 53545
(608) 755-5050
www.janesvillelaw.com

Hale, Skemp, Hanson, Skemp & Sleik
King on 5th Bldg., Ste. 300
La Crosse WI 54602
(608) 784-3540

Robinson Law Firm
103 East College Ave
Appleton WI 54911
(920) 731-1817

Spears & Carlson
122 West Bayfield St
Washburn WI 54891
(715) 373-2628

Mawicke & Goisman, SC
1509 North Prospect Ave
Milwaukee WI 53202
(414) 224-0600

Shari Karney

Halvorsen Law Offices, SC
2115 South Taylor Dr
Sheboygan WI 53081
(920) 458-0331

Lee, Kikelly, Paulson & Younger, SC
One West Main St
Madison WI 53701
(608) 256-9046

346

Wyoming

Wolf, Tiedeken & Woodard, PC
401 West 19th St
Cheyenne WY 82003
(307) 459-1747
www.wolftiedeken.com

Messenger & Jurovich, PC
116 North 5th St
Thermopolis WY 82443
(866) 654-4923

Lathrop & Rutledge, PC
1920 Thomes Ave
Cheyenne WY 82003

(307) 222-1499

Law Office of Hampton Young, Jr.
254 N. Center St., Ste. 100
Casper WY 82601
(307) 462-0038

MacPherson, Kelly & Thompson
616 West Buffalo
Rawlins WY 82301
(888) 792-7167

The Spence Law Firm, LLC
15 South Jackson St
Jackson WY 83001
(307) 733-7290

Williams, Porter, Day & Neville
159 North Wolcott St., Ste. 400
Casper WY 82602

(307) 265-0700
http://www.wpdn.net

Worral & Greear, PC
1112 Robertson Ave
Worland WY 82401
(307) 347-9801

Elizabeth Greenwood
217 North Tyler
Pinedale WY 82941
(307) 367-614

Schwartz, Bon, Walker & Studer
141 South Center, Ste. 500
Casper WY 82601
(888) 552-6957

Hooper Law Offices, PC
115 North 7th East
Riverton WY 82501
(307) 856-4331

Simpson, Kepler & Edwards, LLC
1135 14th St
Cody WY 82414
(307) 527-7891

Washington D.C.

Geoffrey D. Allen
1730 Rhode Island Ave NW, Ste. 206
Washington DC 20036
(202) 559-1421
http://www.allenlawdc.com

Douglas & Boykin, PLLC
1850 M Street, NW, Ste 640
Washington DC 20036
(866) 664-0544
http://douglasboykin.com

Tobin, O'Connor & Ewing
5335 Wilsconsin Ave., NW Ste 700
Washington DC 20015
(202) 250-3275
http://tobinoconnor.com

Bou & Bou
1001 Connecticut Ave., NW Ste. 204
Washington DC 20036
(202) 559-1453
http://boulaw.com

Law Offices of Roger M. Adelman
1100 Connecticut Ave., NW Ste 730
Washington DC 20036
(202) 559-1439
http://rogeradelmanlaw.com

Mitchell & Hibey, LLP
1146 19th St., NW
Washington DC 20036
(202) 407-9482
http://mitchellhibey.com

Artabane & Belden, PC
818 18th St., NW Ste 410
Washington DC 20006
(202) 861-0070

Liotta, Dranitzke & Engel, LLP
1666 Connecticut Ave., NW Ste. 250
Washington DC 20009
(202) 360-4860

Dickstein Shapiro, LLP
1825 Eye St., NW
Washington DC 20006
(202) 420-2200

Manat, Phelps & Phillips, LLP
700 12th St., NW
Washington DC 20005
(202) 585-6500

Meyer, Suozzi, English & Klein, PC
1300 Connecticut Ave., NW Ste 600
Washington DC 20036
(202) 955-6340

Alston & Bird, LLP
950 F St, NW
Washington DC 20004
(202) 756-3300

Arnold & Porter, LLP
555 Twelfth St., NW
Washington DC 20004
(202) 942-5000

Semmes, Bowen & Semmes, PC
1025 Connecticut Ave., NW Ste. 100

Washington DC 20036
(202) 822-8250

Edwards Wildman Palmer, LLP
1255 23rd St., NW Eighth Flr
Washington DC 20037
(202) 478-7370

Vory, Sater, Seymour and Pease, LLP
1909 K St., NW Ste. 900
Washington DC 20006
(202) 467-8800

LeClairRyan
1101 Connecticut Ave., NW Ste. 600
Washington DC 20036
(202) 659-4140

Support Groups and Organizations

Childhelp National Child Abuse Hotline
15757 N. 78th Street
Suite #B
Scottsdale AZ 85260
(800) 422-4453
www.childhelp.org

WLALA
634 S. Spring St. STE 617
LA CA 90014

(213) 892-8982

Survivors Healing Center (SHC
2301 Mission St., Ste. C-1
Santa Cruz CA 95060
(831) 423-7601
www.survivorshealingcenter.org

California Protective Parents Association
P.O. Box 15284
Sacramento CA 95851
(866) 874-9815
www.protectiveparents.com

Courageous Kids Network
P.O. Box 1903
Davis CA 95617
www.courageouskids.net

Survivorship
3181 Mission St. PMB 139
San Francisco CA 94110
www.survivorship.org

National Coalition Against Domestic Violence
1120 Lincoln St., Ste. 1603
Denver CO 80203
(303) 839-1852
www.ncadv.org

National Crime Victim Bar Assocation (N.C.V.C)
2000 M Street NW, Ste 480
Washington DC 20036
(800) FYI-CALL
www.victimbar.org

RAINN
2000 L Street, NW
Suite 406

Washington DC 202.544.3064
(800) 656-HOPE
www.rainn.org

National Center for Victims of Crime
2000 M Street, NW, Ste. 480
Washington DC 20036
800-211-7996
www.ncvc.org

Survivors Netword of Those Abused by Priests (S.N.A.P)
PO Box 6416
Chicago IL 60680
(877) 762-7432
www.snapnetwork.org

The Family Dialogue Project, The Center for Contexual Change
9239 Gross Point Rd.
Kokie IL 60077
(847) 676-4447
www.centerforcontexualchange.org

Incest Resources Inc.
46 Pleasant St
Cambridge MA 02139
www.incestresourcesinc.org

The Lionheart Foundation
P.O. Box 194, Back Bay
Boston MA 02117
(781) 444-6667
www.lionheart.org

Stop It Now!
351 Pleasant St. Suite 319
Northampton MA 01060
(888) PREVENT
www.stopitnow.org

SMART
P.O. Box 1295
Easthampton MA 01027

BASTA! Boston Associates to Stop Treatment Abuse
528 Franklin St
Cambridge MA 02139
(671) 277-8066
www.advocateweb.org/basta

Sidran Institute
200 East Joppa Rd. Ste. 207
Baltimore MD 21286
410-825-8888
www.sidran.org

Survivors of Incest Anonymous (SIA
P.O. Box 190
Benson MD 21018
410-893-3322
www.siawso.org

The Awareness Center, Inc (Jewish Coalition Against Sexual Abuse/Assult)
P.O. Box 65273
Baltimore MD 21209
(443)857-5560
www.theawarenesscenter.org

Gift From Within
16 Cobb Hill Rd
Camden ME 04843
(207) 236-8858
www.giftfromwithin.org

Mothers Against Sexual Abuse
P.O. Box 371
Huntersville NC 28070
(704) 895-0489
www.againstsexualabuse.org

S.E.S.A.M.E: Stop Educator Sexual Abuse, Misconduct and Exploitation
P.O. Box 94601
Las Vegas NV 89193
(702) 371-1290
www.sesamenet.org

Shalom Task Force, Domestic Abuse Hotline
P.O. Box 137 , Bowling Green Station
NY NY 10274
(888) 883-2323
www.shalomtaskforce.org

The Leadership Council
191 Presidential Blvd., Ste C-132
Bala Cynwyd PA 19004
(610) 664-5007
www.leadershipcouncil.org

National Sexual Violence Resource Center
123 North Enola Dr.

Enola PA 17025
(877) 739-3895
www.nsvrc.org

National Resource Center on Domestic Violence
6400 Flank Dr. Ste 1300
Harrisburg PA 17112
(800) 537-2238
www.nrcdv.org

Survivor Connections Inc
52 Lyndon Rd
Cranston RI 02905-1121
www.survivorconnections.net

Darkness to Light
7 Radcliffe Street, Suite 200
Charleston SC 29403
(866) 367-5444
www.darkness2light.org

Justice for Children
2600 Southwest Freeway, Ste. 806
Houston TX 77098
(800) 733-0059
www.justiceforchildren.org

National Organization for Victim Assistance (NOVA)
510 King Street, Suite 424
Alexandria VA 22314
(800) 879-6682
www.trynova.org

Peaceful Families Project
P.O. Box 771
Great Falls VT 22066
(703) 474-6870
www.peacefulfamilies.org

The Safer Society Foundation, Inc. (SSFI)
P.O. Box 340
Brandon VT 05733
(802) 247-3132
www.safersociety.org

King County Sexual Assault Resource Center
P.O. Box 300
Renton WA 98057
(425) 226-5062
www.kcsarc.org

Faith Trust Institute
2400 N. 45th St. #10
Seattle WA 98103
(206) 634-1903
www.faithtrustinstitute.org

National Suicide Prevention Lifeline
1-800-273-TALK (8255)
www.suicidepreventionlifeline.org

National Domestic Violence Hotline
(800) 799-7233
www.ndvh.org

KIDPOWER TEENPOWER FULLPOWER International
831-426-4407
www.kidpower.org

Bikers Against Child Abuse
(866) – 71-abuse
www.bacausa.com

SOC-UM
www.soc-um.com

Ritual Abuse, Ritual Crime and Healing
www.ra-info.org

Advocate Web: Helping Overcome Prfession Exploitation
http:/advocateweb.org

TELL: Therapy Exploitation Link Line
www.theraphyabuse.org

SASIAN: Sibling Abuse Survivor's Information & Advocacy Network
www.sasian.org

MaleSurvivor: The National Organization on Male Sexual Victimization
(NOMSV)
www.malesurvivor.org
www.martindale.com

Legal Resources for Survivors of Sexual Abuse and Their Lawyers
www.smith-lawfirm.com

Love, support, & courage – Shari

Made in the USA
Lexington, KY
27 September 2014